MW01092675

The Debates of *Liberty*

The Debates of *Liberty*

An Overview of Individualist Anarchism, 1881–1908

Wendy McElroy

LEXINGTON BOOKS
Lanham • Boulder • New York • Oxford

LEXINGTON BOOKS

Published in the United States of America
by Lexington Books
A Member of the Rowman & Littlefield Publishing Group
4720 Boston Way, Lanham, Maryland 20706

PO Box 317
Oxford
OX2 9RU, UK

British Library Cataloguing in Publication Information Available

Library of Congress Control Number: 2002115198

ISBN 0-7391-0473-X (cloth : alk. paper)

Printed in the United States of America

♾™ The paper used in this publication meets the minimum requirements of American
National Standard for Information Sciences—Permanence of Paper for Printed Library
Materials, ANSI/NISO Z39.48–1992.

To N. Stephan Kinsella and Doug Casey . . . two stand-up guys with whom Benjamin R. Tucker would have undoubtedly been on drinking terms. My love and thanks to both of you.

Contents

Acknowledgments

I am deeply indebted to the Earhart Foundation, from which I received a generous grant to complete *The Debates of Liberty*. I wish to thank Leonard Liggio and Andrea Rich (of Laissez Faire Books) in particular. Without you and Earhart, this book would not exist. I also commend Earhart for the confidence they demonstrate in scholars, and for how pleasant the Foundation is to work with. In this regard, I must say "thank you, Ingrid."

The Debates of Liberty is the culmination of twenty years' work on Benjamin Tucker's periodical *Liberty*, an index of which I published in 1982 through Michael E. Coughlin, Publisher. As a young, impoverished radical, Michael cranked out the *Index* in his garage-publishing shop—a true labor of love. I shall forever be indebted to Ken Gregg for suggesting the project and for his moral support throughout the indexing. The Center for Libertarian Studies provided me with a grant that enabled me to divert time into the project, for which I offer special thanks to Murray Rothbard and Joseph Peden.

No one can write about Tucker or nineteenth-century Individualist Anarchism without crediting James J. Martin, whose book *Men Against the State* pioneered scholarship in this area and set a high standard of excellence for those of us who follow.

Ivan R. Dee, the publisher of an anthology I edited—*Liberty for Women*—deserves hearty appreciation. Ivan R. Dee is part of the Rowman & Littlefield family of publishers and, when I passed *The Debates of Liberty* across his desk, Ivan decided, first, it was not right for his label, and second, it was a book that should remain "in-house." Because he took a special interest in the book, *The Debates of Liberty* is being issued by Lexington, another division of Rowman & Littlefield. Special thanks are due to Serena Leigh for her stewardship there.

The last person I thank in every book I write is my husband, Bradford Rodriguez. Last but definitely not least. Thank you, sweetheart. You know for a fact that nothing I do is possible without you.

Chapter 1

Benjamin Tucker, *Liberty*, and Individualist Anarchism

"Liberty, Equality, Fraternity, these three; but the greatest of these is Liberty. Formerly the price of Liberty was eternal vigilance, but now it can be had for fifty cents a year." So wrote Benjamin Ricketson Tucker (1854-1939) on the first page of the first issue of *Liberty*.[1]

The American periodical *Liberty*,[2] edited and published by Tucker from August 1881 to April 1908, is widely considered to be the finest Individualist Anarchist periodical ever issued in the English language. Over its twenty-seven-year life span, during which it appeared first from Boston and then from New York (1892), *Liberty* chronicled the personalities and the shifting controversies of Individualist Anarchism in the United States and abroad.

It also fostered those personalities and controversies. The scroll of contributors to *Liberty* reads like an honor roll of nineteenth-century Individualism: Lysander Spooner, Auberon Herbert, Joshua K. Ingalls, John Henry Mackay, Victor Yarros, and Wordsworth Donisthorpe are only a partial listing. Speaking with a cosmopolitan and avant-garde voice, *Liberty* also published such items as George Bernard Shaw's first original article to appear in the United States,[3] the first American translated excerpts of Friedrich Nietzsche,[4] and reports from economist Vilfredo Pareto on the political conditions in Italy.

Of seminal importance in the history of Individualist ideas, Tucker's periodical also served as the main conduit of Stirnerite egoism, Proudhon's economic theories, and of radical Spencerian thought from Europe to America.[5] As such, *Liberty* was both an innovator in Individualist theory and a mainstay of that tradition.

The periodical was also remarkable for the consistently high quality of its content and for the clarity of its style. The issues debated within its pages have a sophisticated, almost contemporary ring, ranging from radical civil liberties to economic theory, from children's rights to the basis of rent and interest. Con-

1

tributors to *Liberty*, as well as other Individualists who published articles elsewhere, often found themselves on the defense against Tucker's intransigent demand for "plumb line" consistency in all things.

As a professional journalist,[6] Tucker also insisted upon a clear, precise style. He took great pride in raising *Liberty* far above the standards for layout and grammar of most other radical periodicals of the day.

Tucker's Background

Tucker was born on April 17, 1854, in South Dartmouth, Massachusetts.[7] Coming from both a Quaker and a radical Unitarian background, Tucker grew up in an atmosphere of dissent and free inquiry, and attended the Friends Academy in New Bedford, a nearby seaport. At his parents' prompting, he later attended the Massachusetts Institute of Technology in Cambridge for three years.

In Boston, Tucker became politically involved with the 1872 presidential campaign of Horace Greeley, and made the acquaintance of the veteran Individualist Anarchists Josiah Warren and William B. Greene through attending a convention of the New England Labor Reform League in Boston, a veritable hotbed of Individualists.[8] Greene, who served as the chairman, made an immediate and deeply favorable impression upon the young M.I.T. student.[9] The introduction to both Greene and Warren had been facilitated by the abolitionist and labor reformer Ezra Heywood. Tucker would later look back upon these initial encounters as the pivotal point in his career as a radical.[10] At the convention, Tucker purchased Greene's book entitled *Mutual Banking* (1850) and Warren's *True Civilization* (1869), along with some of Heywood's pamphlets.

An ongoing association with Heywood, the publisher of the Princeton labor reform periodical *The Word*, soon followed.[11] From his involvement in the labor reform movement, Tucker became convinced that economic reform must underlie all other steps toward freedom. From a later admiration of the radical abolitionist Spooner,[12] Tucker's voice acquired a radical antipolitical edge as well. To these influences were added the European flavor of Herbert Spencer, Pierre Joseph Proudhon,[13] Max Stirner,[14] and Michael Bakounine.

In editing *Liberty*, Tucker both filtered and integrated the theories of such European thinkers with the uniquely American labor, freethought,[15] and free love[16] movements in order to produce the rigorous system of Individualist Anarchism subsequently identified with him. It became known as "Philosophical Anarchism" or, in a phrase that was often applied derogatorily, "Boston Anarchism."

In 1876, in what may be considered Tucker's debut into radical circles, Heywood published Tucker's English translation of Proudhon's classic work *What Is Property?* Shortly afterward Tucker commenced publication of a freethought publication entitled *Radical Review* (New Bedford, Mass., 1877-1878), which lasted only four issues. A substantial portion of the four issues, however, were devoted to publishing a partial translation of Proudhon's *Systems of Economical Contradictions*, also rendered into English by Tucker.

Although Tucker was a prolific writer, virtually the entire body of his work, other than those titles constituting translations, appeared as articles in *Liberty*; some of these articles were subsequently issued as pamphlets. Tucker's key work, entitled *Instead of a Book, by a Man Too Busy to Write One* (1893), was a selected compilation of articles from *Liberty* with the subtitle, *A Fragmentary Exposition of Philosophical Anarchism*.

The Social Context of *Liberty*

In the late nineteenth century, Tucker and *Liberty* were the vital core around which a radical Individualist movement reconstituted itself in the wake of the Civil War and grew. In a wider social and cultural context, however, *Liberty* was merely one among many radical periodicals published in America around the turn of the nineteenth century.

The post-Civil War decades were a time of social turmoil and erratic economic growth, with many voices calling for reform. The ideologies expressed ranged from State Socialism to Populism, Progressivism, and Anarchism. A jumble of issues fought for space in newsprint: single-tax, temperance, women's suffrage, labor unions, land reform, birth control, and State-funded education. A wide array of movements offered different solutions to societal problems. Few of these movements were Individualistic.

True to the maxim "war is the health of the State," the Civil War had nearly killed the radical Individualist movement in America. The rampant growth of government caused by the war and its aftermath had established an environment increasingly hostile to individual rights. Moreover, the groups and personalities who had constituted the driving core of the Individualist movement—such as William Lloyd Garrison and his abolitionist cadre—had been badly divided by internal conflicts largely about whether or not to support the war.

After the devastation, radical Individualism tended to be expressed not as an integrated movement in its own right but as an extreme faction within other movements, particularly within labor reform, freethought, and free love. Against this broader social and political backdrop, *Liberty* began its career. It became the focus around which a distinctive Individualist movement coalesced and revitalized.

Major Themes

Radical Individualism in nineteenth-century America is commonly called Individualist Anarchism. As part of this continuing ideological tradition, *Liberty* neither emerged from nor operated within an intellectual vacuum. The tradition from which *Liberty* arose revolved around two fundamental themes.

The first was "the Sovereignty of the Individual," sometimes expressed as "self-ownership"—a term popularized by Garrisonian abolitionism. Self-ownership maintains that every human being, simply by being human, has an inalienable moral jurisdiction over his or her own body and over what he or she produces. This universalizable right, or claim, was what Tucker meant whenever he used the Spencerian phrase "the law of equal liberty." As Tucker wrote, "Equal liberty means the largest amount of liberty compatible with equality and mutuality of respect, on the part of individuals living in society, for their respective spheres of action."[17]

The second theme of Individualist Anarchism was economic: in general, the movement espoused a version of the labor theory of value, which it often expressed through the phrase "Cost the Limit of Price."[18] Adherents of the labor theory of value claimed that all wealth is created by labor and usually implied that, therefore, all wealth belongs unquestionably to the laborer. Individualist Anarchism considered this concept to be a direct extension of self-ownership. As Tucker phrased it:

> It will be seen from this definition that Anarchistic property concerns only products. But anything is a product upon which human labor has been expended. It should be stated, however, that in the case of land, or of any other material the supply of which is so limited that all cannot hold it in unlimited quantities, Anarchism undertakes to protect no titles except such as are based on actual occupancy and use.[19]

Liberty Appears

Liberty first issued on August 6, 1881, from Boston with an introduction that was typical of Tucker, then a journalist in the editorial department of the *Boston Globe*.[20] "It may be well to state at the outset," he declared of *Liberty*, "that this journal will be edited to suit its editor, not its readers."[21] Despite this caveat, *Liberty* was a relatively open forum for radical Individualist debate, with many of the early unsigned editorials, often ascribed to Tucker, being actually written by Spooner or Henry Appleton.

Fittingly, the subtitle of *Liberty* was a quotation from Proudhon—"Liberty: not the daughter but the mother of order." The journal's primary commitment was to economic reform. It was broad enough in its interests, however, to feature a portrait of Sophie Perovskaya, a Russian nihilist martyr, in the center of its front page. As in issues thereafter, the first page was entitled "On Picket Duty" and presented a survey of contemporary periodicals, events, and personalities. The remainder of the issue dealt with labor, freethought, rights theory, and other antistatist issues.

Liberty served as a clearinghouse for contemporary Individualist periodicals, with Tucker ever alert to the appearance of a relevant new journal in America or abroad, ever poised to jump on the deviations of an established one.

He reprinted appropriate or egregious articles and often praised or engaged in debate with editors and contributors. Debates were especially common with British Individualists such as J. Greevz Fisher, with whom *Liberty* disputed economic theories of interest and the tangled question of children's rights.[22]

Liberty and Literature

Although *Liberty* focused on politics and social theory, Tucker appreciated the importance of culture and its impact on societal attitudes.

For example, literature played a prominent role in *Liberty*'s emphasis on internationalism. Tucker kept current on the state of art and letters in France, England, and America. When Max Nordau published his antimodernist work *Degeneration (Entartung)*, Tucker was discerning enough to solicit a critique from the one man best able to handle it—George Bernard Shaw. Shaw's subsequent essay, entitled "A Degenerate's View of Nordau," was the first original article by the British literary giant written specifically for an American audience. Among the literary works *Liberty* translated and published were: Claude Tillier's *My Uncle Benjamin*,[23] Emile Zola's *Money*,[24] Octave Mirabeau's *A Chambermaid's Diary*,[25] Felix Pyat's *The Rag Picker of Paris*,[26] and Sophie Kropotkin's *The Wife of Number 4,237*[27]—an account of her experience with her husband Pierre Kropotkin at Clairvaux prison.

This fascination with cosmopolitan literature led Tucker to publish *The Transatlantic* (1889-1890), a biweekly literary magazine. The advertisement for this publication in *Liberty* promised: "Every number has a complete translated novelette, a piece of European Music, a Portrait of a Foreign Celebrity and part of a translated European Serial." *The Transatlantic* was said to consist of the "cream of the European press translated into English. Not only from foreign periodicals, but from books as well."[28] Predictably, much of the literature that interested Tucker had political implications. When Oscar Wilde's plea for penal reform, *The Ballad of Reading Gaol*,[29] was widely criticized, for example, Tucker enthusiastically endorsed the poem, urging all of his subscribers to read it. Tucker, in fact, published an American edition. From its early championing of Walt Whitman's *Leaves of Grass*[30] to a series of short stories by Francis du Bosque in its last issues, *Liberty* was a vehicle of controversial, avant-garde literature.

Liberty Abroad

Tucker and *Liberty* were hybrids. Their roots were embedded both in the uniquely American tradition of Individualist Anarchism and in some distinctively foreign traditions. The cosmopolitan Tucker acknowledged no intellectual boundaries and tolerated no political ones; national boundaries were simply the physical manifestations of government, an institution he adamantly rejected.

Tucker's stress on internationalism was apparent from the first page of the first issue of *Liberty* on which, under the column "About Progressive People," he reported news of foreigners such as Percy Shelley, whose son had died; Patrick Egan, who had just purchased the "Dublin Irishman"; and Lord Kimberley, who had been suddenly converted to the cause of Land Reform. Here, and in subsequent issues, Tucker made particular note of foreign periodicals. For example, he declared to America that "the first number of a weekly journal called 'Victor-Hugo' recently appeared in Paris."[31]

His embrace of international Anarchism was reflected in the many articles *Liberty* reprinted from foreign journals and in the correspondents who reported on the progress of liberty in their native countries. These correspondents included David Andrade (Australia), Pareto (Italy), and Donisthorpe (England), founder of the Liberty and Property Defense League.

Distinctly foreign events and concerns, such as the plights of Russian nihilists or of Irish tenants, often received more attention from *Liberty* than American concerns. Tucker was outraged by the imprisonment of the Italian Amilcare Cipriani, the trial of Louise Michel, and the plight of Russian refugees in Paris. His attempt to establish Individualist Anarchism as an international movement was best exemplified by *Libertas*, a German-language version of *Liberty*, published by Tucker and edited by George and Emma Schumm. "This will be the only thoroughly Anarchistic German journal ever published in the world." Tucker wrote in announcing *Libertas*. "The paper will be of the same shape and size as the English *Liberty*, and the two will alternate in the order of publication—the English appearing one week and the German the next."[32] *Libertas* was short lived.

In terms of contributing articles and engaging in debate, the British Individualists were the most active foreign presence in the pages of *Liberty*.[33] For the most part, they advocated limited government and, like their mentor Herbert Spencer, they shied away from Anarchism. The labor theory of value, so integral to *Liberty*'s philosophy, was not widely accepted among the British Individualists. Nor was Stirnerite egoism. An exception was the bimonthly *The Eagle and the Serpent* from London (1898-1902), edited by John Basil Barnhill under the pseudonym of Erwin McCall.

Auberon Herbert's *Free Life* (1890-1901), quoted nineteen times in *Liberty*, was perhaps the most prominent British Individualist periodical. Its prospectus, as it appeared in *Liberty*, read: "We shall oppose all hereditary privilege, all religious establishments, all artificial regulations tending to monopoly in land; and we shall equally oppose all attacks upon property of every kind."[34] Of *Free Life* and Herbert, Tucker wrote: "In a letter to me, written when he was contemplating the establishment of *Free Life*, Mr. Herbert proposed that, in case of any friendly discussion between his journal and mine, each should reprint all that the other might say. Mr. Herbert will observe that I have been prompt to act upon his suggestion, and I have no doubt that he will reciprocate."[35] The "friendly discussion" referred to involved Anarchism.

Wordsworth Donisthorpe, editor of *Jus: A Weekly Organ of Individualism* (1885-1888), became the British correspondent of *Liberty* and its most frequent British contributor.

During the early years of *Liberty*, however, Tucker's attraction to the Irish No-rent movement prompted close connections with Patrick Ford's *Irish World*. "*Liberty* is not always satisfied with it," Tucker wrote, "but, all things considered, deems it the most potent agency for good now at work on this planet."[36] Two of *Liberty*'s most frequent contributors, Henry Appleton and Sidney H. Morse, wrote columns for *Irish World* under the pseudonyms of Honorius and Phillip, respectively; Joshua K. Ingalls also contributed to the Irish periodical. Some of the early issues of *Liberty* were virtually devoted to the 'no-rent' question.[37]

Given the immense influence of Proudhon, *Liberty* naturally felt strong ties to radical movements in France. These ties manifested themselves largely in two ways: translations and reprints because Tucker, along with several of *Liberty*'s associates, was a bilingual Francophile. Some of these were reprinted within *Liberty* itself; others were offered for sale independently and were advertised within *Liberty*.[38] The shorter translated pieces were generally articles rendered directly from French periodicals. "The State: Its Nature, Object and Destiny" by Proudhon, for example, was translated by Tucker directly from Proudhon's popular periodical *La Voix du Peuple*.

The periodical from which articles were most frequently translated and reprinted in *Liberty* was Henri Rochefort's *L'Intransigeant*.

David Andrade, *Liberty*'s Australian correspondent, contributed several excellent articles on the progress of radical Individualism in Australia. Part of this progress was Andrade's *Honesty* (1887-1889), an Anarchist periodical from Melbourne. *Honesty*'s advertisement proclaimed: "It is sufficient description of *Honesty*'s principles to say that they are substantially the same as those championed by *Liberty* in America."[39] *Honesty* listed Tucker's name and address for subscriptions.

Although Stirner had immense impact upon *Liberty*, German periodicals were not followed with the same interest as British or French ones. Tucker's inability to read German fluently may have accounted for this oversight. Much of his knowledge of Stirner and other matters requiring German translation came from George Schumm.

It is difficult to assess *Liberty*'s connection with Spanish periodicals. *Revista Social* and *La Revolución Social* were mentioned briefly, and *Liberty* contributor Steven Byington—considered one of the three or four brightest Tuckerites—engaged in debate over Individualist Anarchism with the editor of *A Vida*. *A Vida* had printed a Spanish translation of an article which Byington had submitted to Tucker.[40] *A Vida*'s source for the article was a French paper which had translated Byington's piece directly from *Liberty*. Whether other foreign periodicals were in the habit of translating and reprinting *Liberty* is speculation.

Although Tucker exhibited great interest in Russian nihilism and in the assassination of the Czar (1881), few Russian periodicals were mentioned in

Liberty. Victor Yarros who had fled Russia to avoid arrest was probably the only associate of *Liberty* with enough background in that language and culture to appreciate and translate the various periodicals. There is, however, no evidence that he did so. *Liberty* did, nevertheless, follow the career of the Christian Anarchist Leo Tolstoi.[41]

An examination of the complicated network of connections between *Liberty* and virtually every other Individualist periodical issued in English during its publication span would require a book-length treatment.[42]

The Demise of *Liberty*

Liberty came to a sudden, tragic end. In 1907, Tucker rented a ground floor space at 502 Sixth Avenue in New York City, which housed "Benj. R. Tucker's Unique Book Shop." Some blocks away, at 225 Fourth Avenue in a structure known as the Parker Building, Tucker stored the stock of the books he published and the equipment to set print for *Liberty*. On January 10, 1908,[43] the Parker Building was consumed by a fire that he described in what was to be the last issue of *Liberty*.

Tucker, who had been publishing and stockpiling material for thirty years, had pursued a deliberate policy of not holding insurance in order to protest the artificially high premiums propped up by the legal system. To offset the total loss, friends of *Liberty* launched a fund-raising drive, and Tucker continued to sell the stock that had survived by virtue of being at the Sixth Avenue address.

The efforts to salvage *Liberty* were not successful, however, and Tucker announced, "It is my intention to close up my business next summer, and, before January 1, 1909, go to Europe, there to publish *Liberty* (still mainly for America, of course) and such books and pamphlets as my remaining means may enable me to print."[44]

These plans never materialized. The April 1908 issue of *Liberty* was the last. Tucker moved to Europe, living first in France until World War I erupted, then settling in Monaco, where he died at the age of eighty-five on June 22, 1939. Born seven years before the start of the Civil War, he died the same year that World War II began. For the last decades of his life, Tucker's writing efforts were largely limited to correspondence with friends and acquaintances.

In many ways, Tucker exemplified the golden age of radical Individualism, which faltered in the face of growing statism and militarism. Like other Individualists, Tucker watched this growth of the State and became pessimistic. From Europe he wrote, "I hate the age in which I live, but I do not hate myself for living in it."[45]

During the advance of statism, his views began to shift. It was no longer clear to Tucker that economic freedom alone could overcome the problems created by government monopoly. His pessimism increased with time. In a letter to his old friend C. L. Swartz, a despondent Tucker expressed his belief that civilization was in its death throes.

Perhaps it was this despair, coupled with his love of French culture, that led Tucker to support the Allies in World War I. Although he kept informed of affairs in America—for example, he expressed sympathy for the Communists Sacco and Vanzetti who were being persecuted by the American State—Tucker displayed increasingly less interest in his former homeland. Two days after his death, he was buried in Monaco with a private, civil ceremony. He was survived by his wife and daughter.

Other than writing a few articles and conducting a correspondence with the editors of various journals, Tucker's last years were unproductive. From June 1913 to March 1914, his articles appeared in a London periodical entitled *The New Freewoman*, edited by Dora Marsden.[46] In his essay, "The *New Freewoman*: Dora Marsden & Benjamin R. Tucker," S. E. Parker commented: "although he [Tucker] contributed frequently, most of his contributions consisted of translations from the French press, often under the general heading of *Paris Notes* or *Lego and Penso*. From time to time he wrote a short piece of his own—either a comment on a news item or a reply to a critic."[47]

Nevertheless, Tucker retained his radical edge until the moment of death. His daughter Oriole reported: "Father's attitude towards communism never changed one whit, nor about religion. . . . In his last months he called in the French housekeeper. 'I want her,' he said, 'to be a witness that on my death bed I'm not recanting. I do *not* believe in God!'"[48]

Tucker's death, like that of Spencer, marked the end of an era. Individualist Anarchism as an organized movement in America would not appear again for many years.

Liberty: Success or Failure?

When the elder Tucker was asked what he had achieved that was of lasting value to the world, he replied: "'Nothing' is the only truthful answer. I aimed to contribute a stone to the social edifice, a cathedral if one may call it so. . . . I have contributed that stone . . . But I see now that the cathedral will never be finished, and that the portion already built is destined soon to tumble into ruins."[49]

Was *Liberty* or, more generally, nineteenth-century radical Individualism successful? The answer depends on the standard of success being employed. By its own stated goals of changing society toward individual freedom and away from State control, radical Individualism was a failure. But one of Tucker's greatest achievements lies in his many translations of foreign radicals, such as Proudhon, Bakounin, Hugo, Tolstoi, and Chernyshevsky.[50] History, though, is more likely to credit the impact of these works entirely to the authors rather than to the translator.

A more generous approach to *Liberty's* legacy, however, is to assess the movement's externally imposed limitations and to ascertain how much it achieved in spite of them.

The last decades of the nineteenth century were a golden age for radicalism in America. Anarchists issued nearly 500 periodicals in a dozen languages ranging from French to Yiddish. Only a minority of these periodicals were Individualistic, for the dominant radical philosophy of the day was Socialism in its many forms.

In essence, the Civil War had dealt such a severe blow to the Individualist movement that it never recovered. The War ushered in conscription, the suspension of habeas corpus, widespread censorship, military law, political prisoners, legal tender legislation, as well as soaring taxes and tariffs. The status and functions of government inflated as never before.

Equally important, the prevailing view of government changed. With the Declaration of Independence and the cry of "no taxation without representation," government had been deemed to rule through the consent of the people. When the North refused to permit the South to withdraw its consent through secession and when it imposed an unpopular government upon the South, the consensual view of government was severely weakened. Moreover, instead of viewing the relatively autonomous States as forming a loose federal union—as composing "*these* United States"—a new description arose, "*the* United States." And this centralized nation was deemed to be "One Union under God."

In addition, the Civil War had caused extremely divisive schisms within the Individualist movement. Some of the abolitionists had welcomed the conflict almost as a holy war to end slavery. Others had considered it to be an unavoidable evil in pursuit of good and, therefore, supported the North as the least objectionable alternative. Even the staunch pacifist Garrison had supported the North. His support had horrified other abolitionists, such as Heywood and Spooner, who saw the War as a massive violation of life and property, which could not be justified by reference to any goal. By the end of the Civil War, Individualist principles had been so compromised and the State had achieved such prominence that the Individualist Anarchist movement could not be a significant force in American politics.

After 1865, radical Individualism existed as an extreme faction within various other reform movements such as freethought, free love, and the labor movement. Although the basis of a systematic philosophy was present in the writings of such theorists as Warren and Spooner, it lacked cohesion. Not until Tucker's publication of *Liberty* did radical Individualism become a distinct, independent movement functioning in its own name and seeking its own unique goals.

This consolidation was the primary accomplishment of *Liberty*. It discussed and integrated ethics, economics, and politics to build a sophisticated system of philosophy. For three decades it provided a core around which a revitalized movement could flourish. During those years Tucker issued an unremitting flood of pamphlets and books promoting Individualist thought. Even in the last days of *Liberty*, translations such as Paul Eltzbacher's *Anarchism: Exponents of the Anarchist Philosophy* appeared. As with many of the translations offered by *Liberty*, the imprint of the Anarchist translator—in this case, Byington—was keenly felt, not only in the word choices but also in his many added notes and his preface.[51]

Tucker himself was acutely aware of the slow progress of social reform. He wrote, "The fact is that Anarchist society was started thousands of years ago, when the first glimmer of the idea of liberty dawned upon the human mind, and has been advancing ever since—not steadily advancing, to be sure, but fitfully, with an occasional reversal of the current."[52]

Yet radical Individualism hindered itself. The historian David De Leon in *The American as Anarchist* observed: "Nineteenth century anarchism failed primarily because it seemed archaic in the twentieth century."[53] Perhaps most destructively, Individualist Anarchism clung to the labor theory of value and refused to incorporate the economic theories that were rising within other branches of Individualist thought, theories such as marginal utility. The stagnant movement failed to comprehend the logical alternative to the State—a free market laissez-faire capitalist system.

Notes

1. Benjamin R. Tucker, "On Picket Duty," *Liberty* 1 (August 6, 1881): 1. Representative excerpts from *Liberty* are available in Benjamin R. Tucker, *Instead of a Book, by a Man Too Busy to Write One; A Fragmentary Exposition of Philosophical Anarchism* (New York: B. R. Tucker, 1893) and Benjamin R. Tucker, *Individual Liberty*, ed. Clarence Lee Swartz (New York: Vanguard Press, 1926).

2. The periodical began in a four-page newspaper format and went to an eight-page format on May 17, 1884. It returned to a four-page format in July 25, 1891, varied from sometimes twelve to mostly eight pages from February 24, 1894, until the February 1906 issue, in which Tucker announced a format and publication change that would continue until close to *Liberty*'s last issue in April 1908. "*Liberty* expects to greet its readers bimonthly hereafter, in the form given to the present issue—a pamphlet of sixty-four pages." During its run, *Liberty* varied from a weekly to a fortnightly and then finally to a monthly schedule.

3. The article was a critique of Max Nordau's *Degeneration*. Reprints of Shaw's work had appeared earlier. The first such reprint was entitled "What's in a Name?" and it appeared in the April 11, 1885 issue, only a month after it had appeared in Henry Seymour's British periodical *The Anarchist*.

4. These excerpts were translated by George Schumm at Tucker's request. Tucker wrote: "I believe that my friend George Schumm, to whom I am indebted for the little knowledge of Nietzsche that I have, could either write, or translate from other sources, a much truer account of this new influence in the world of thought. Will he not do so, and thus make *Liberty* the means of introducing to America another great Egoist." *Liberty* 9 (October 1, 1892): 3.

5. Nineteenth-century "American" Anarchism tended to run along different ideological lines, depending on whether it was based on native or ideology imported from Europe or Russia. The native tradition ran from the writings of Thomas Jefferson and Thomas Paine, through William Lloyd Garrison, Henry David Thoreau, Josiah Warren,

William Greene, and Lysander Spooner directly to the Individualist Anarchism of Tucker. The Communist and Socialist traditions of Anarchism within America owed much to the influx of immigrants, especially of German and Russian radicals.

6. Tucker was an editorial writer for the *Boston Globe* and later for the *Engineering Magazine* (New York), although he refused to write articles which might compromise his Anarchist principles. He was especially proud of *Liberty*'s typography, on which he expounded at length.

7. Perhaps the best portrait of Tucker, the man, remains "Benjamin Tucker and His Daughter" in Paul Avrich, *Anarchist Portraits* (Princeton: Princeton University Press, 1988), 144-52.

8. "Josiah Warren," Tucker subsequently wrote, "was the first man to expound and formulate the doctrine now known as Anarchism; the first man to clearly state the theory of individual sovereignty and equal liberty." "On Picket Duty," *Liberty* 14 (December 1900): 1. Perhaps the best expression of Warren's political philosophy is Stephen Pearl Andrews' *The Science of Society* (New York: Fowler & Wells, 1852). But Josiah Warren's main influence upon Tucker and *Liberty* may well have been more personal. The dedication in Tucker's first book, *Instead of a Book* (1893), read, "To the memory of my old friend and master, Josiah Warren, whose teachings were my first source of light, I gratefully dedicate this volume."

9. Greene was one of the primary conduits of Proudhon to America, largely through his booklet *Mutual Banking*. Greene translated several of Proudhon's works, including "The State" and the extract from *What Is Property?* in which Proudhon declared himself to be an Anarchist. At Greene's prodding, Tucker translated portions of *What Is Property?*

10. Tucker identified much more with the labor movement than with any other. In November 1872, Tucker wrote to Ezra Heywood. "I hope to do some work for the labor cause," he stated, "but first wish to study the question that I may thoroughly understand it." *The Word* (November 1872): 3. Tucker began publishing in *The Word*, then a labor reform paper. Tucker's association with Lysander Spooner undoubtedly strengthened this commitment to labor. Three of Spooner's economic works—*Our Financiers, The Law of Prices,* and *Gold and Silver as Standards of Value*—first appeared in Tucker's *Radical Review*. Labor reform (under its various manifestations of interest, money, banking, rent, capital, unions, and strikes) was the topic most discussed in *Liberty*. Tucker believed that labor reform led directly to Anarchism.

11. Although *The Word* clearly began as a vehicle for labor reform and fit this profile when Tucker became associated with it, Heywood's personal commitment to promoting birth control resulted in its pages becoming increasingly devoted to free love issues—much to Tucker's dismay.

12. In his essay "Lysander Spooner, Tucker & *Liberty*" in *Benjamin R. Tucker and the Champions of Liberty,* eds. Michael Coughlin, Charles H. Hamilton, and Mark A. Sullivan (St. Paul, Minn.: Michael E. Coughlin, 1986), Charles Shively expressed the extent of Spooner's influence. "After 1881 [*Liberty*'s appearance], all of Spooner's work first appeared serially in *Liberty* before becoming books or pamphlets . . . [L]ess familiar are the many editorials which Spooner wrote for *Liberty*. Some nineteen articles appeared, but only one short obituary notice of abolitionist Elizur Wright was signed 'L.S.'" Other articles, Shively notes, appeared without attribution or with the initial 'O'. Tucker's obituary of Spooner—"Our Nestor Taken From Us," *Liberty* 4 (May 28, 1887): 4-5—ascribed to his "Nestor," the editorials he had written.

13. Tucker considered Proudhon to be the "profoundest political philosopher that has ever lived." "Portraits of Proudhon," (adv.) *Liberty* 1 (January 21, 1882): 4. Indeed, *Liberty* not only popularized Proudhon's work in America, it also issued a previously unpublished work of his entitled *Galileo*. A substantial portion of the *Radical Review* was devoted to an English translation from one of Proudhon's major works *System of Economical Contradictions*. *Liberty*, Tucker frankly stated, is "a journal brought into existence almost as a direct consequence of the teachings of Proudhon." "A Statue to Proudhon," *Liberty* 1 (January 7, 1882): 3. Its subtitle—*Not the Daughter But the Mother of Order*—was a quotation from Proudhon's *Solution du problème social*. Perhaps the most ambitious endeavor that *Liberty* pursued was the "Proudhon Library," a projected series of the entire works of Proudhon, translated and sold by subscription.

14. Stirner's influence upon Tucker and *Liberty* rivals that of Proudhon. The English translation of *The Ego and His Own* was first published by Tucker in 1907. In adopting Stirnerite egoism, Tucker rejected natural rights, which had long been considered the foundation of Individualism.

15. Freethought insisted that all spiritual matters be left to the judgment of those involved, with no State involvement. There was deep intersection between Individualism and freethought. For example, Spooner published *A Deist's Reply* and *The Deist's Immortality*. Freethought was probably the first radical influence in Tucker's life. As a young man Tucker read two important freethought periodicals: the *Boston Investigator* and the *Index* (formerly the *Free Religious Index*). *Liberty* reprinted articles from both. Tucker described the *Radical Review* (1877-1878), his first periodical, "I once published a magazine called the *Radical Review*," he wrote later, "which many competent judges pronounced . . . the handsomest freethought magazine ever published in America." *Liberty* 4 (January 22, 1887): 5.

16. Free Love insisted that all sexual arrangements be left to the consent and consciences of those adults involved, with no control by legislation. Tucker was closely associated with Heywood's *The Word* (1872-1890, 1892-1893), issued first from Princeton and then from Cambridge, Massachusetts. *The Word* began as a labor paper but became a vehicle for free love, much to Tucker's dismay. The young Tucker had championed the notorious free love advocate Victoria Woodhull when authorities tried to prevent her from lecturing on "The Principles of Social Freedom." Later, he was literally seduced by her. The most important free love periodical was *Lucifer, the Light Bearer* (1883-1907) edited by Moses Harman, of which Tucker became openly critical due to its policies rather than its principles. When E. C. Walker resigned as co-editor from *Lucifer*, he founded the weekly *Fair Play*. It is significant that, when *Fair Play* ceased, he transferred the current subscriptions to *Liberty*, not *Lucifer*.

17. Tucker, *Instead of a Book*, 65.

18. This key phrase was the title of the second section of *Science of Society*, Stephen Pearl Andrews' presentation of Warren's philosophy. *Liberty* serialized it, October 30, 1886 to December 31, 1887. Thereafter, it was published by Sarah E. Holmes, an intimate of Tucker's, and it was advertised through *Liberty*.

19. Tucker, *Instead of a Book*, 61.

20. In 1892, *Liberty* moved from Boston to New York as a consequence of Tucker becoming the editor of the New York periodical *Engineering Magazine*.

21. "On Picket Duty," *Liberty* 1 (August 6, 1881): 1. During the span of *Liberty*, it showed the imprint of several hands, not the least of which were A. P. Kelly and Victor Yarros, each of whom were associate editors for a period.

22. To the ears of modern Individualists, the economic theories of the British Individualists sound more Austrian and contemporary.

23. This 312-page novel was translated from the French by Tucker and published in both cloth and paper. It was first advertised in *Liberty* 7 (November 29, 1890): 7.

24. This 435-page novel was translated from the French by Tucker and published in both cloth and paper. It was first advertised in *Liberty* 7 (April 4, 1891): 8.

25. This 460-page novel was translated from the French by Tucker and published in both cloth and paper. It was first advertised in *Liberty* 14 (December 1900): 8.

26. This 325-page novel was translated from the French by Tucker and issued in both paper and cloth. It was first advertised in *Liberty* 7 (July 12, 1890): 8.

27. This material was translated from the French by Sarah E. Holmes at Tucker's request and reprinted in five segments, beginning in March 6, 1886.

28. *The Transatlantic*, subtitled *A Mirror of European Life and Letters*, was first advertised in *Liberty* 6 (October 5, 1889): 8, as being issued on the 1st and 15th of the month.

29. Tucker published both a cloth and paper edition, which were first advertised in *Liberty* 13 (May 1899): 8.

30. First advertised in *Liberty* 1 (July 22, 1882): 4. Tucker appended a challenge to various officials responsible for the suppression of *Leaves of Grass*. He advised them of his intention to sell the work and offered to deliver a copy of it to them at their place of choice to be used in evidence against him. There were no takers.

31. Benjamin R. Tucker, "About Progressive People," *Liberty* 1 (August 6, 1881): 1.

32. Benjamin R. Tucker, "Anarchy in German," *Liberty* 5 (December 31, 1887): 4.

33. In *Anarchist Portraits*, Paul Avrich remarks upon how many of the contributors to *Liberty*—quite apart from those representing British Individualism—were either British or born in Britain. In this list, he includes: William Bailie, James L. Walker, Henry Bool, Miriam Daniell, Helena Born, William A. Whittick, Alfred B. Westrup, and A. H. Simpson.

34. Benjamin R. Tucker, "Prospectus of Auberon Herbert's Paper," *Liberty* 6 (March 8, 1890): 2.

35. Benjamin R. Tucker, "Property Under Anarchism," *Liberty* 7 (July 12, 1890): 5.

36. *Liberty* 1 (August 6, 1881): 3.

37. Perhaps Tucker shared the reservations of other Anarchists who were skeptical of a movement that competed with "no rent"—the Homestead movement, which appealed to government. Some did not consider the government regulation of homesteads to be a blow for freedom. For a more sympathetic treatment of the Land Reform movement, and especially of Evans, see Kenneth R. Gregg, Jr., "George Henry Evans & the Origins of American Individualist-Anarchism" in *Benjamin R. Tucker and the Champions of Liberty*, 106-115.

38. At 225 Fourth Avenue, New York, Tucker had a large, radical bookstore. See *Liberty* 15 (June 1906): 9-10 and "On Picket Duty," *Liberty* 15 (August 1906): 1-2 for an account of the establishment.

39. The first advertisement appeared in *Liberty* 4 (June 18, 1887): 8.

40. Steven T. Byington, "Four Points of Anarchism," *Liberty* 15 (August 1906): 24-34.

41. The Jewish Anarchist community was a strong radical element in America, many of whom had immigrated from Russia. Two of the English language papers favored by the Jewish Anarchists were *Liberty* and Dyer Lum's *The Alarm*.

42. See Appendix 1 for a more detailed account of *Liberty*'s connection with other periodicals.

43. The date of the fire is reported as April 1908 in the usually reliable James J. Martin, *Men Against the State* (Colorado Springs: Ralph Myles, 1970), and as January 10, 1908 in Paul Eltzbacher, "Benjamin R. Tucker," in *Anarchism: Exponents of Anarchist Philosophy*, ed. James J. Martin (Plainview, New York: Books for Libraries Press, 1960). An account of the fire was published in the April 1908 issue of *Liberty* in which Tucker announced ambiguously, "No later than January 10 this composing room, together with the entire stock of my publications and nearly all my plates, was absolutely wiped out by fire." Benjamin R. Tucker, "On Picket Duty," *Liberty* 17 (April 1908): 1.

44. Tucker, "On Picket Duty," *Liberty* 17 (April 1908): 1-3.

45. Letter to Ewing C. Baskette, November 7, 1934. The New York Public Library maintains the Tucker Papers, with letters and documents relating to Benjamin Tucker.

46. *The New Freewoman* was a continuation of *The Freewoman*, which appeared in 1911 and received public censure for daring to discuss such topics as lesbianism. *The Freewoman* ceased publication in October 1912: *The New Freewoman* appeared in June 1913. Later, the periodical evolved into *The Egoist*.

47. S. E. Parker, "The *New Freewoman*: Dora Marsden & Benjamin R. Tucker," in *Benjamin R. Tucker and The Champions of Liberty*, 150.

48. As quoted in Paul Avrich "An Interview with Oriole Tucker," in *Benjamin R. Tucker and the Champions of Liberty*, 26.

49. Irving Levitas, "The Unterrified Jeffersonian: Benjamin R. Tucker" (Ph.D. diss., New York University, 1974), 421.

50. Tucker's influence extended beyond the political sphere. The playwright Eugene O'Neill claimed that Tucker had deeply affected "his inner self" and Whitman exclaimed "I love him: he is plucky to the bone." George Woodcock, *Anarchism: A History of Libertarian Ideas and Movements* (Cleveland: Meridian Books, 1962), 459.

51. For example, in Eltzbacher, *Anarchism: Exponents of Anarchist Philosophy*, in footnote 11 to chapter VIII "Benjamin R. Tucker," Byington comments upon what he considers to be a misinterpretation of Tucker's words "the law of equal liberty."

TRANSLATOR'S NOTE: Eltzbacher does not seem to perceive that Tucker uses this as a ready-made phrase, coined by Herbert Spencer and designating Spencer's well-known formula that in justice "every man has freedom to do all that he wills, provided he infringes not on the equal freedom of any other man."

52. Tucker, "On Picket Duty," *Liberty* 14 (December 1900): 1. As a sad note, Tucker himself seemed to lose faith in the inevitability of liberty. In an interview with Paul Avrich, his daughter Oriole reported, "I was never really an anarchist. I don't think it would ever work. Neither did Father at the end. He was very pessimistic about the world and in his political outlook." Avrich, *Anarchist Portraits*, 152.

53. David de Leon, *The American as Anarchist. Reflections on Indigenous Radicalism* (Baltimore: Johns Hopkins University Press, 1978), 82.

Chapter 2

On the State and Politics

To appreciate the debate that erupted in *Liberty* over the propriety of electoral politics, it is necessary to understand the prevailing view of the State expressed by nineteenth-century Individualist Anarchism.[1] The most fundamental and integrating theme of this tradition was the primacy of individuals, which implied an extreme respect for their sovereignty. Accordingly, Individualist Anarchists wished to eliminate all but defensive force from human interaction. Tucker proposed what he called "a society by contract" to replace the society by force he saw around him.[2]

The Enemy: Unjust Authority

Tucker understood unjust authority as "any coercive force not developed spontaneously and naturally out of the constitution of the individual himself or herself."[3] For Tucker, the dual buttresses of "society by force" were the authority of the Church and the authority of the State, a union he referred to as a "double-headed monster."[4] He sought to eliminate both. In place of the forceful jurisdiction of Church and State, he wished to establish the self-jurisdiction of the individual within a voluntary society.

Tucker carefully distinguished the authority of the Church and the authority of the State, or Government.[5] The former did not necessarily use force, whereas the latter was inherently invasive. Tucker did not denounce the act of joining a Church as a personal choice, or the acceptance of religion as a personal code of morality. Indeed, he admired certain religious sects, such as the Quakers who had contributed heavily to the abolitionist movement, a forerunner of Individualist Anarchism.[6] But Tucker absolutely rejected the authority of the Church: that is, he rejected the incorporation of religious values or of privileges for the Church into law. As he stated, "We intend no disrespect to God as an ideal that

17

an individual may hold dear provided such God assumes no authority over others. . . . It is God the office-seeker and office-holder with whom we take issue, and it is only such a God . . . that makes the politician possible."[7]

Tucker acknowledged that noble intentions might well underlie the Christian principle of loving your neighbor. In fact, if the principle of brotherly love were consistently applied, a crime-free society based on human cooperation might be the result. But to enforce brotherly love by force or law was a contradiction in terms. Tucker argued that to convert the principle into "a 'commandment' is the utter denial . . . and a perversion of the word 'love'."[8]

Tucker was equally clear about what constituted the authority of the State, which an individual could never rightfully join or employ. He explained the primary feature of the State, "The anarchist defines government as invasion nothing more or less."[9] Its secondary feature was territoriality, "the assumption of authority over a given area and all within it, exercised generally for the double purpose of more complete oppression of its subjects and extension of its boundaries."[10] A State claimed a monopoly of force and of jurisdiction over a given territory and over all people within that territory, for example, a monopoly over the right to resolve disputes through a police and a court system in order to protect society against deteriorating into open violence. Tucker considered such protective measures to be, in reality, an outright invasion of person and property.

The State maintained itself primarily through two invasive monopolies—the power to tax and to issue money. Through these monopolies, the State negated individuals' "freedom . . . in their industrial, commercial, social, domestic, and individual lives."[11] The State also invaded personal liberty by establishing monopolies over a wide variety of services, thus denying choice to the individual. As an example of such a State monopoly, Tucker pointed to national defense. He argued,

> Defence is a service, like any other service. It is labor both useful and desired, and therefore an economic commodity subject to the law of supply and demand. In a free market this commodity would be furnished at the cost of production. The production and sale of this commodity are now monopolized by the State. The State, like almost all monopolists, charges exorbitant prices. Like almost all monopolists, it supplies a worthless, or nearly worthless, article.[12]

Moreover, in contrast with a society by contract, the State did not allow members to secede peacefully, but demanded they continuously recognize its authority. Statists have often argued that, by continuing to live in a particular society, an individual agrees to be bound by its rules. Tucker countered, "To indefinitely waive one's right of secession is to make one's self a slave. Now, no man can make himself so much a slave as to forfeit the right to issue his own emancipation proclamation."[13]

Nor could a man forfeit the right to defend himself against aggression. Therefore, a society by contract had no right to take action against a "noncontracting party" who did not attempt to enter its territory. As Tucker wrote,

[I]f, somewhere between these divisions of territory, had lived prior to the formation of the association, some individual on his homestead, who . . . had declined to join in forming the association, the contracting parties would have had no right to evict him, compel him to join, make him pay for any incidental benefits that he might derive from proximity to their association, or restrict him in the exercise of any previously enjoyed right to prevent him from reaping these benefits.[14]

To those who maintained what is currently called a love-it-or-leave-it stance, Tucker replied, "By what right am I thrust into the alternative of recognizing the machinery of the State as the only chance left me in rescuing my life, liberty, and possession from invasion."[15]

Our Primary Enemy: The State

In the wake of events such as the publication of Darwin's *Origin of the Species* and the growing popularity of evolutionary theory, Tucker believed the authority of the Church had been severely shaken. But he also believed that the masses had merely transferred their obedience from the Church to the secular State.[16] Tucker wrote passionately of, "those who have lost their faith in gods only to put it in governments, those who have ceased to be Church-worshipers only to become State-worshipers; those who have abandoned pope for king or czar; and priest for president or parliament;—have indeed changed their battle ground, but none the less are foes of liberty still."[17]

Perhaps it was this belief that led Tucker to shift his focus between the first periodical he edited, the *Radical Review*, and the subsequent *Liberty*. The former publication can be viewed primarily as a freethought periodical—that is, one that advocated the separation of Church from State, leaving all spiritual choices to the individual.[18] *Liberty* focused on discrediting the authority of the State, rather than that of the Church. In doing so, Tucker stressed psychological rather than physical disobedience to the State: that is, he stressed the need for people to withdraw their consent and the loyalty upon which the authority of the State rested. He believed that the very concept of the State—along with, especially, the illusion of its legitimacy—was what commanded obedience from the American citizenry. Destroying any particular manifestation of the State would be folly without first destroying the institution's underlying legitimacy, which lent it the air of just authority.[19] Tucker wrote, "Our purpose is the abolition, not only of all existing States, but the State itself. . . . It is not a thing that can be especially defined. . . . The State is a principle, a philosophical error in social existence."[20] Perhaps because of Tucker's philosophical approach to the State—that is, his rejection of the concept of the State rather than merely of its specific manifestations—his form of Anarchism became known as "Philosophical Anarchism."

Destroying the Concept

To destroy the State as a concept, Tucker believed it was necessary to educate a sufficient number of people in the principles of Anarchy.[21] He argued against the use of force to promote Anarchism because such a strategy strengthened the State, rather than weakened it. As long as the common man did not accept Anarchist principles—that is, as long as the State was viewed as legitimate—any violence on the part of radicals would be seen to justify the inevitable backlash of State tyranny that would follow. In short, violence by Anarchists further legitimized the State.[22]

Tucker also believed voting legitimized the State by allowing politicians to claim they ruled through the will of the people. Thus, the majority of those associated with *Liberty* considered any participation in electoral politics to be a violation of Anarchist principles. They rejected both bullets and ballots as means of reform or revolution.[23] Although the *Liberty* circle rejected voting primarily because it legitimized the State, two other basic reasons had nothing to do with legitimization. One was a matter of principle: the other was a matter of strategy.

As a matter of Anarchist *principle*, electoral politics—the process of electing a person to a position of power over others—was considered inherently invasive because the power would be exercised over people who had not consented to it as well as over those who had consented through their votes. In other words, a politician claimed jurisdiction over those who had not voted, or who had voted against him, as well as over his supporters. Thus, anyone who voted for a successful political candidate was an accomplice to an act of "legal force" committed against unconsenting third parties.

As a matter of *strategy*, electoral politics was rejected because power corrupts, as the British classical liberal Lord Acton famously observed. Even the purest and best-intentioned reformer would be degraded by the process of assuming and exercising unjust power. This outcome was to be expected not merely of the politician but also of the judge, the policeman, and of anyone else involved in making or enforcing unjust laws. One of *Liberty*'s regular columns, sardonically entitled "The Beauty of Government," was devoted to this theme. Because Tucker opposed the concept of the State itself, he did not condemn merely the vicious real-world consequences of electoral politics. He denied that the institution, by its very nature, could ever be just or legitimate.

Attacking Legitimacy

More than any other figure, the veteran abolitionist and Anarchist Lysander Spooner set the antistatist tone for both Tucker and *Liberty*.[24] Tucker's extreme admiration of Spooner led him to publish his mentor's lengthy *A Letter to Grover Cleveland, on His False, Self-Contradictory, and Ridiculous Inaugural Address* in nineteen installments within *Liberty*. He issued the work as a book thereafter.[25] For Spooner, too, a free society was based upon voluntary association, and a legitimate Government required the consent of every person over whom it claimed jurisdiction. Without an individual's explicit consent or delegation of authority, the Government had no rightful claim over that person.

What would such delegation entail? According to Spooner, it would require that the person possess the right being delegated; that the delegation be explicit and not merely assumed; and, that the person be able to withdraw his delegation—otherwise he would have given away not simply the exercise of a particular right, but his entire liberty. In short, only those people who had voted for the Government could be deemed to have delegated their rights to it. Those who had not so voted were free from Government's jurisdiction.[26]

Even those who had voted for a particular politician or party could withdraw their support, much as they could cancel the services offered by a lawyer. Indeed, this capacity reflects the meaning of the term *inalienable rights*: the rights belonged to the individual, to exercise or not, to assign or to reclaim. Spooner explained this limitation: "No man can delegate, or give away his own natural right to liberty . . . or to give to another, any right of arbitrary dominion over himself; for that would be giving himself away as a slave. And this no one can do. Any contract to do so is necessarily an absurd one and has no validity."[27]

Predictably, Spooner offered strenuous objections to anyone holding political office, regardless of who the particular officeholder might be.[28] By what right, Spooner asked, can one person occupy a position of power over the life of another peaceful human being if that other human being has not delegated the power? Spooner could discover no circumstances in which such power would be proper.

The Debate within *Liberty* Begins

Tucker clearly and strongly stated his position on voting and office holding: he denied that either ballots or bullets (politics or violence) could be used to construct liberty.[29] An editorial nicely captured the intransigence of his position:

> If liberty has a weak-kneed friend who is contemplating a violation of his anarchist principles by voting just for once, may these golden words from John Morley's "Compromise" recall him to his better self: "A principle, if it be sound, represents one of the larger expediencies. To abandon that for the sake of some seeming expediency of the hour is to sacrifice the greater good for the less on no more creditable ground than that the less is nearer."[30]

Two years later within the pages of *Liberty*, on April 17, 1886, the American Anarchist Henry Appleton took up the theme of "expediency" in political activity and alliances. Indeed, Appleton's opening the subject had been occasioned by his having attended a lecture entitled "Anarchism and Expediency" delivered by another *Liberty* contributor, Gertrude B. Kelly. Although he complimented "the subtlety of the young lady's intellect" and "her personal loveliness,"

Appleton wished to air a disagreement he had with Kelly's arguments and with those of "Brother Tucker."[31] The disagreement revolved around whether it was proper for an Anarchist to support a popular labor organization of the day, the Knights of Labor, which used political activity to further its goals. Appleton clearly opposed the use of ballot boxes to solve the problems of labor. However, he believed in expediency. Moreover, he had infiltrated the Knights of Labor in an attempt to achieve certain goals through the organization and he was determined to defend his actions. He wrote: "Possibly Brother Tucker has yet to learn that compromise is a true scientific principle under Anarchism, and that in its proper sense it is logically enjoined upon the faithful. I have never found a final settlement of any problem yet, save that of my own ignorance: therefore do I rise for prayers, and ask Sister Kelly and Brother Tucker to keep me from going astray."[32]

Directly beneath Appleton article, Tucker published one of his own entitled "Plumb-Line or Cork-Screw, Which?" He prefaced his lengthy reply with the words, "Compelling this discussion, then, he [Appleton] must take the responsibility of its results. If he finds that it involves the saying of things to him unpleasant, harsh, and severe, the blame will rest with him for forcing me, his friend, to speak of him in public with that frankness."[33]

Tucker disputed the main claim of Appleton's article, which he had used to argue for compromise. Appleton claimed to have converted many Irishmen to Anarchism through a series of letters he had written to the *Irish World* under the pseudonym of "Honorius."[34] In those letters, Appleton had compromised Anarchism by refusing to condemn a certain organization. "Instead of this [expressing condemnation]," he wrote, "I 'compromised,' by quietly fishing out whatever I could find of Anarchistic method in the Irish movement, calling it by some other name than Anarchism."[35] Tucker questioned the effectiveness of that strategy, "And after all how many staunch Anarchists, with a deep-rooted comprehension of Anarchism did the 'Honorius' letters ever make?" Answering his own question, Tucker reckoned probably not over a half a dozen. He also wondered whether the letters were truly the cause of the conversions in anything more than a proximate sense.

Appleton had claimed Gertrude Kelly as one among the ranks of those converted by his writings in *Irish World.* Tucker countered, "She became an Anarchist principally because she had brains in her head and was bound to become in very short order." He denied that Appleton had provided anyone with even an "adequate idea of the meaning of liberty."[36] Instead, Tucker attributed the conversions to another Anarchist writer, "H," or "Phillip," both pseudonyms of Sidney H. Morse, whose articles appeared in the *Irish World* at the same time as Appleton's letters.[37]

The next issue of *Liberty* contained an article entitled "Liberty and Compromise," by a more restrained Appleton. Again Tucker responded, in a more muted fashion; but the flurry over the issue of compromise as a strategy continued, even though the bitterness of Tucker's initial response could not have encouraged other contributors to openly support such "compromises" as voting or aligning with organizations that used the ballot.

In his last contribution and goodbye to *Liberty*, Appleton himself confessed to having been intimidated by Tucker.[38] Appleton explained why he was "sneaking out of the ranks." He declared himself to be more of a "builder" than a "fighter." By this Appleton meant that he wished to construct a system to re-place the State rather than merely rail against the existing order, as he implied Tucker was doing. Like several subsequent contributors, Appleton had been driven away not so much by disagreement as by the vicious manner in which the disagreement had been conducted.[39]

The Debate Resumes

Nearly ten years later, the young Russian Anarchist and associate editor of *Liberty*, Victor Yarros, published an article entitled "Anarchists in Politics." It be-gan, "No question seems to be simpler at first blush than that of the proper atti-tude of Anarchists toward political struggles. Absolute non-participation is obviously the clear deduction, the inevitable corollary from the general Anar-chistic philosophy. Yet . . ."[40] Following his provocative "yet," Yarros asked whether, if some immediate and practical good could be achieved by casting a vote, an Anarchist could legitimately do so. Was it not possible that the immedi-ate and practical good could be so beneficial as to outweigh the possibility of a vague far-off harm such as legitimizing the State? Yarros concluded, "Answer this question in the negative, and all reasons for boycotting politics vanish."[41]

According to Yarros, although Leo Tolstoi's Christian Anarchism eschewed violence, scientific Anarchism should adopt a more "situational" ethics, namely, the position "that the ethical propriety of men's acts must be determined by the requirements and possibilities of the situation." Part of the situation was that people still adhered "to governmentalism," and hence Government would have to be abolished gradually. Given the context of gradualism, Yarros did not con-sider it "inconsistent to use government to abolish government" so long as the gains to Anarchism outweighed the damage done. In this case, voting would be a matter of personal preference, not of principle. "I think I should vote in the case supposed, but I am not at all sure that Mr. Tucker would . . . [T]he behav-ior of any individual Anarchist would depend on the vividness of his imagina-tion, the intensity of his feelings, the bent of his mind. Some would unhesitat-ingly make an exception to their general rule, while others would adhere to the rule."[42]

In the same issue, in an article titled "Principle, Policy, and Politics," Tucker replied. He admitted that there were circumstances in which he would use a ballot to further his goals. They were the same circumstances in which he was willing to use dynamite and risk injury to innocent parties. He cautioned Yarros: "Anarchists should be careful to make it plain that to them the use of the ballot is something more and worse than a trivial act of inutility. Mr. Yarros, to be sure, declares parenthetically that use of the ballot is aggression, but certainly the tendency of his article as a whole is to make light of it in its aggressive aspect."[43]

In the following issue, Yarros defused the charge of making light of aggression by stating that to "argue in *Liberty* that majority rule is aggression is to burst in an open door. I passed over the question as too well settled for argumentation." Yet, while admitting the aggressive nature of majority rule, Yarros denied that voting was necessarily an act of force. He offered the example of voting in favor of free trade by voting down a proposed measure that would enforce protectionism. What if one vote alone would ensure free trade. How would casting that one vote violate anyone's rights? [44] "If no one's rights are violated," Yarros concluded, "those who vote for free trade are not guilty of any offence . . . What I did was to vote for freedom, for the absence of restrictions. I injured nobody and hence have not transgressed the limits of equal liberty."[45] Yarros declared such noninvasive voting to be an exception to the general rule that ballots and bullets were inherently aggressive. Instead, he maintained that casting a referendum ballot was an act of self-defense because "the majority has a perfect right, under equal freedom, to prevent the minority from imposing restrictions,—that is, from committing aggression."[46] Yarros freely acknowledged one of Tucker's points, perhaps because it was a point he himself had made in the initial article. The sight of Anarchists voting in *any* fashion could "confuse the public mind" as to what constituted Anarchism and, thus, dilute Anarchism as a force in the larger political life. This objection, however, was a strategic one, not a principled one.

Again, Tucker's response preceded Yarros's article—a tactic the editor often employed, whether for layout reasons or for strategic ones we do not know. In an article titled "Aggression and the Ballot," Tucker accused Yarros of shifting the ground of argument in several ways. One was by tacitly premising "such a transformation of politics that invasion is eliminated." For example, a voting system not financed by taxation: this condition in no way resembled the current state of affairs and, therefore, "has not the slightest bearing on the question whether it is possible for Anarchists to non-aggressively participate in the invasive thing that politics are to-day."[47] Then Tucker hit directly on what he considered the key flaw in Yarros's argument: Yarros conflated electoral voting with voting on referendums, but each produced a distinctly different result. "Voting for a law maker" (electoral voting) involved placing someone in a position of unjust power through which he could impose invasive measures. Tucker added, "If he [Yarros] votes for a man who favors a particular libertarian measure, this man will vote in the legislature . . . not alone for the one libertarian measure, but for a thousand invasive measures. Any man who would not do so could not be elected, for the majority are in favor of invasion in most matters."[48] Moreover, even if Yarros's candidate voted for nothing but "libertarian measures," he would still be paid a salary gathered by compulsory taxation. The costs of the election—for example, counting the ballots—would also be paid by taxation.

The next and last exchange between the two men showed an erosion of goodwill, with Yarros accusing Tucker of taking advantage of what had been "a slip of the pen" by which the former had misstated himself. Again Tucker's reply preceded Yarros's article. Tucker claimed to be pleased by the "manifest weakness" of Yarros's arguments, which relieved him from the task of answering them point by point. The debate on the propriety of Anarchistic voting was over; again more because of ill will than because the issue had been resolved.

Power Corrupts: Furor over Henry George

Another basis for *Liberty*'s rejection of the political process was the belief that power corrupts. Even well-meaning, principled candidates would become corrupt once they were elected. The corruption was an inevitable consequence of holding a position of unjust power: the accommodation with injustice would change anyone for the worse. In the very first issue of *Liberty*, Tucker had firmly condemned Anarchists who ran for political office. "The most lamentable spectacle today is the short sighted reformer attempting to secure greater liberty by advocating the method of greater authority, more intervention, more government."[49] Tucker's contempt for reformers who swelled the ranks of lawmakers never lessened.

Indeed, in the same issue in which the debate between Yarros and Tucker erupted, sandwiched between Yarros's article on voting and Tucker's response, was another article titled "Henry George, Traitor" from the pen of *Liberty*'s editor. Remarking upon the impressive showing George had made as an independent mayoral candidate for New York City (receiving 68,000 votes), Tucker excoriated the reformer for not using his ensuing prominence to call for clemency for the Haymarket martyrs.[50] After the Illinois Supreme Court upheld the stiff sentence imposed upon the so-called Chicago Anarchists, Tucker accused George's newspaper, the *Standard*, of being the only labor paper that did not protest the verdict. Appeals had poured in to George, urging him to speak out against the opinion of the Supreme Court. Tucker declared that George had been placed in an "embarrassing dilemma." "Should he spring to the side of those innocent victims, upon whose fate turned the question of free speech in America, and thereby absolutely ruin the prospect of his immediate political advancement, or should he continue in his mad struggle to attain the goal of his ambition, and leave the innocent to die?"[51] Tucker explained George's silence: the man was campaigning for political office. Tucker further observed,

"In January 1887, he [George] had started his weekly paper, the 'Standard,' and by this and other means he was bending all his energies to the creation of a new political issue in the Single Tax with himself as a standard-bearer of a new political party. He claimed that he would poll 250,000 votes for secretary of State, and that with hard work he could be elected."

When the public pressure for George to take a stand became too great, the Single Taxer made a public declaration on page one of the *Standard* of October

8, 1887. According to Tucker, George declared that he now believed the Chicago Anarchists to be guilty of murder simply because the Illinois Supreme
Court had not overthrown the verdict.

Tucker expressed outrage. Under the heading "The Demagogue and the
Sophist," *Liberty* printed a letter from W. T. Doty that had been rejected by the
Standard, presumably because it criticized George's stand on the Haymarket
defendants. Doty wrote, "Said a gentleman today, after reading yesterday's
'Standard': 'Can it be that Henry George, after all, has become a mere ward
politician, a panderer to the mob?'"[52]

It was a turn of events Tucker had predicted a year before when he had
wished George success in true Tuckerian fashion:

"I hope Henry George will be elected. . . . The laboring men who vote for
him will then have a chance to see how little difference it makes to their welfare.
. . . The only difference that I have ever detected between labor politicians and
the politicians of the other parties is the usual readiness of the former to sell
themselves at a lower price than the latter insist upon."[53]

In the person of George, Tucker believed the maxim "power corrupts" could
be made visible to the laboring man who still harbored a belief in the power of
politics to achieve good.

Conclusion

If Individualist Anarchists of the late nineteenth century had a united strategic
vision with which they approached social problems, it was their opposition to
political solutions.[54] In place of voting, they looked to social reform movements
and grassroots organizations, they sought to repeal laws through education and
nonviolent agitation. They championed strikes, boycotts, peaceful labor unions,
and other means of economic restructuring. They experimented with alternative
education systems, such as the Modern School Movement, and alternative social
arrangements, such as the New Harmony or Utopia communities. In response to
the criticism that Tucker offered no positive structure or program with which to
replace the State, the editor wrote: "we have something very tangible to offer,—
something very rational, practical, and easy of application. We offer cooperation. We offer non-compulsive organization. We offer associative combination.
We offer every possible method of voluntary social union by which men and
women may act together for the furtherance of well-being."[55]

Notes

1. For a more general treatment of the Individualist Anarchist tradition, see James J. Martin, *Men Against the State: The Expositors of Individualist Anarchism in America, 1827-1908* (Colorado Springs: Ralph Myles Publisher, 1970).
2. Tucker was careful to defend the right of self-defense. He wrote: "he who resists another's attempt to control is not an aggressor, an invader, a governor, but simply a defender, a protector"—Benjamin R. Tucker, *Instead of a Book, by a Man Too Busy to Write One; A Fragmentary Exposition of Philosophical Anarchism* (New York: B. R. Tucker, 1893), 23. "Anarchism justifies the application of force to invasive men" (Tucker, *Instead of a Book*, 81). Moreover, he defended the use of collective defensive force, believing that if a victim "has a right to use force himself for such a purpose [reclaiming of property], he has a right to secure such co-operative force from others as they are willing to extend" (Tucker, *Instead of a Book*, 157). Tucker also declared, "there is nothing sacred in the life of an invader" in *Liberty* 7 (August 30, 1890): 4.
3. As quoted in William O. Reichert, "Benjamin R. Tucker on Free Thought and Good Citizenship" in *Benjamin R. Tucker and the Champions of Liberty*, ed. Michael E. Coughlin, Charles H. Hamilton, and Mark A. Sullivan (St. Paul, Minn.: Michael E. Coughlin, 1986), 169.
4. See *Liberty* 1 (August 20, 1881): 2-3, for more on Tucker's theory of the double-headed monster.
5. Tucker tended to use the words "State" and "Government" as synonyms. At one point, after defining the State as "aggression" he wrote, "Aggression, invasion, government, are interconvertible terms" (Tucker, *Instead of a Book*, 23). Elsewhere, however, he distinguished the State and the Government. The State consisted of two factors: aggression and territoriality. Government referred only to aggression. Government was the enforcement arm of the State, and its most visible aspect. Adding to the confusion is the fact that Tucker, like many Anarchists, also used "government" in the sense of the "self-government" of the individual or of a voluntary community. At one point he declared, "The State is not government, since it denies Liberty." *Liberty* 1 (April 15, 1882): 2-3.
6. Abolitionists also tended to view government and religion as joining hands in support of human slavery. It could be argued that the first American Individualist Anarchist was William Lloyd Garrison, the main figure within abolitionism.
7. Benjamin R. Tucker, "The Unholy Root of Despotism," *Liberty* 1 (August 19, 1881): 3.
8. As quoted in Reichert, "Benjamin R. Tucker on Free Thought and Good Citizenship," 167.
9. Tucker, *Instead of a Book*, 22.
10. Tucker, *Instead of a Book*, 22.
11. Tucker, *Instead of a Book*, 57.
12. Tucker, *Instead of a Book*, 32.
13. Tucker, *Instead of a Book*, 48.
14. Tucker, *Instead of a Book*, 44-45.
15. Benjamin R.Tucker, "Anarchism and Consent," *Liberty* 2 (December 9, 1882): 2.
16. The idea that the masses transferred their obedience from the Church to the State was common in nineteenth- and twentieth-century Anarchism. In his essay "Anarchism

and Anarcho-Syndicalism," the twentieth-century Anarchist Rudolf Rocker wrote, "And just as the 'will of God' was used to justify the will of privileged castes, so today there hides behind the will of the state only the selfish interests of those who feel called upon to interpret this will in their own sense and to force it upon the people." Paul Eltzbacher, *Anarchism: Exponents of Anarchist Philosophy*, trans. Steven T. Byington, ed. James J. Martin (Plainview, New York: Books for Libraries Press, 1960), 230.

17. Benjamin R. Tucker, "Our Purpose," *Liberty* 1 (August 6, 1881): 2.

18. To say that *The Radical Review*'s primary focus was freethought does not diminish the importance of its other political and cultural discussions. For example, Tucker's translation of Pierre Joseph Proudhon's *Systems of Economical Contradictions* occupied a great deal of space within the four issues, as did the review of recently published literary works.

19. Etienne de la Boetie is recognized as the first political philosopher to focus upon the strategy of withdrawing legitimacy from the State. In the sixteenth century, he wrote: "Obviously there is no need of fighting to overcome the tyrant, for he is automatically defeated if the country refuses to consent to its own enslavement: it is not necessary to deprive him of anything, but simply to give him nothing." Etienne de la Boetie, *The Politics of Obedience: The Discourse of Voluntary Servitude* (original ca. 1550; reprint, New York: Life Editions, 1975), 50.

20. Benjamin R.Tucker, "What We Mean," *Liberty* 1 (April 15, 1882): 2. One of the most ambitious attempts to define Liberty's "Philosophical Anarchism" was William Bailie's nineteen-part series entitled "Problems of Anarchism," which ran in the first eight months of 1893.

21. When discussing tax resistance, Tucker offered the figure of one-fifth of the population. He asked the reader to imagine "the enormous and utterly irresistible power of a large and intellectual minority, comprising say one-fifth of the population in any given locality, refusing to pay taxes" (Tucker, *Instead of a Book*, 412). He believed the State would have to do more, in both money and oppressive measures, to collect the withheld taxes than the other four-fifths of the people would be willing to support.

22. For more on Tucker's rejection of force as a strategy, see chapter 3, "On Violence."

23. For more on this theme, see Carl Watner, George H. Smith, and Wendy McElroy, *Neither Bullets Nor Ballots: Essays on Voluntaryism* (Orange, Calif.: Pine Tree Press, 1983), or back issues of *The Voluntaryist*, http://users.aol.com/vlntryst/toc.html [16 April 2002].

24. This is not to say that Tucker and Spooner held identical views on electoral politics. Spooner rejected the idea that, by voting, you offer sanction to the State. In *No Treason*, he argued that voting could be a means of self-defense, but it is not clear that Spooner actually advocated voting defensively. Whatever strategy he personally advocated, Spooner clearly rejected the results of electoral politics: that is, politicians in office.

25. The full title is telling: *A Letter to Grover Cleveland, on His False Inaugural Address, the Usurpations and Crimes of Lawmakers and Judges, and the Consequent Poverty, Ignorance and Servitude of the People*. Equally interesting for the legitimacy question are the titles of two earlier works by Spooner: *A Letter to Thomas F. Bayard: Challenging His Right and the Right of All Other So-Called Senators and Representatives in Congress—to Exercise any Legislative Power Whatever over the People of the United States*, and *Natural Law; or the Science of Justice; a Treatise on Natural Law, Natural*

Justice, Natural Rights, Natural Liberty, and Natural Society, Showing that All Legislation Whatsoever Is an Absurdity, a Usurpation and a Crime.

26. Moreover, Spooner doubted whether even those who voted for the government, as constructed by the Constitution, could be said to render consent. He believed that a secret ballot created a secret government, to which no one owed allegiance and for which no one took responsibility. For more on Spooner's theories of "legitimate" government, see "No Treason" No. I, No. II, and No. VI, in *The Lysander Spooner Reader* (San Francisco: Fox & Wilkes, 1992). Originally intended as a six-part series, only three segments appeared.

27. Lysander Spooner, "A Letter to Thomas F. Bayard," *Liberty* 1 (May 27, 1882): 2.

28. *Liberty* presented this particular argument of Spooner's in two parts. The first was entitled "A Letter to Thomas F. Bayard," *Liberty* 1 (May 27, 1882): 2-3. The second part was entitled "A Second Letter to Thomas F. Bayard," *Liberty* 2 (May 17, 1884): 6-7.

29. The phrase "neither bullets nor ballots" became a popular one within nineteenth-century Individualist Anarchism. Tucker explained its meaning, "What is the ballot? It is neither more nor less than a paper representative of the bayonet, the billy, and the bullet. It is a labor-saving device for ascertaining on which side force lies and bowing to the inevitable. The voice of the majority saves bloodshed, but it is no less the arbitrament of force than is the decree of the most absolute of despots backed by the most powerful of armies" (Tucker, *Instead of a Book*, 426-27).

30. Benjamin R.Tucker, "Labor's New Fetich," *Liberty* 2 (August 23, 1884): 4.

31. It is not likely that Appleton was engaging in sarcasm, because he had a high opinion of Kelly. Moreover, the casualness of the address, "Brother Tucker," probably expressed a feeling of comfort and equality with Tucker. Appleton was also a newspaperman (Providence, R.I.), a former contributor to Tucker's first periodical *The Radical Review*, and one of the most frequent contributors to the early issues of *Liberty*, usually signing "X" and sometimes "Honorius." In other words, he probably felt free to take liberties with peers.

32. "X" [Henry Appleton], "Anarchism and Expediency," *Liberty* 4 (April 17, 1886): 4.

33. Benjamin R. Tucker, "Plumb-Line Or Cork-Screw, Which?" *Liberty* 4 (April 17, 1886): 4.

34. *Irish World* was a radical Irish "no-rent" periodical, edited by Patrick Ford, in whose pages various contributors to *Liberty* appeared. For example, J. K. Ingalls and Sidney Morse contributed. Tucker thought well enough of the periodical to declare, "*Liberty* is not always satisfied with it . . . but, all things considered, deems it the most potent agency for good now at work on this planet." *Liberty* 1 (August 6, 1881): 3.

35. Appleton, "Anarchism and Expediency," 4.

36. Tucker, "Plumb-Line," 4.

37. In the same issue as this exchange, there appeared a letter to the editor praising a lecture Appleton had recently delivered to the Knights of Labor. It was from Victor Yarros, with whom Tucker would later lock horns over the issue of voting.

38. By this point, however, Appleton himself had proven willing to sling intellectual mud. He wrote, "in Tucker's eyes I may be a cork-screw, and he in my eyes an intellectual pollywog," *Liberty* 4 (July 17, 1886): 5.

39. Martin (1970) inaccurately ascribes Appleton's departure to the viciousness of another debate, namely, the subsequent natural rights vs. egoism debate.

Chapter 2

40. Victor Yarros, "Anarchists in Politics," *Liberty* 12 (November 1896): 2.

41. Yarros, "Anarchists in Politics," 3.

42. Yarros, "Anarchists in Politics," 3.

43. Benjamin R. Tucker, "Principle, Policy, and Politics," *Liberty* 12 (November 1896): 5.

44. Yarros was pointing out a distinction between voting to elect someone to political office—that is, to a position of unjust power over the lives of unconsenting others—and voting in a referendum—that is, to decide a specific issue with no necessary electoral implications.

45. Victor Yarros, "Principle and Method," *Liberty* 12 (December 1896): 5.

46. Yarros, "Principle and Method," 5.

47. Benjamin R. Tucker, "Henry George, Traitor," *Liberty* 12 (November 1896): 4.

48. Benjamin R. Tucker, "Aggression and the Ballot," *Liberty* 12 (December 1896): 4.

49. Benjamin R. Tucker, "The Anatomy of Liberty," *Liberty* 1 (August 6, 1881): 2.

50. The Haymarket incident of May 4, 1886, at which labor protesters and the police clashed in the streets of Chicago during a meeting organized by largely by Communist Anarchists, caused fatalities on both sides. Although the eight men who were arrested and tried were demonstrably innocent, the incident cemented the connection between Anarchism and violence in the mind of the public. See Henry David, *History of the Haymarket Affair* (New York: Russell & Russell, 1936) and Paul Avrich, *The Haymarket Tragedy* (Princeton: Princeton University Press, 1984).

51. Tucker, "Henry George, Traitor," 4. The article "Henry George, Traitor" was reprinted as a pamphlet and issued separately by Tucker's press.

52. W. T. Doty, "The Demagogue and the Sophist," *Liberty* 5 (December 17, 1887): 4.

53. Benjamin R. Tucker, "On Picket Duty," *Liberty* 4 (September 18, 1886): 1.

54. Since the 1880s, there has been a marked tendency to identify Anarchist strategy with violence, largely stemming from the much-publicized class-violence strategy of Communist Anarchists in Russia: it was called "propaganda by deed." Yet violence was embraced only by one faction of the Anarchist movement, and certainly never incorporated into most other factions, such as Tolstoi's Christian Anarchism (in America, Garrisonian Anarchism) or Individualist Anarchism. See chapter 3, "On Violence."

55. Benjamin R. Tucker, "Liberty the Mother of Order," *Liberty* 2 (October 14, 1882): 2.

Chapter 3

On Violence

Individualist Anarchism repudiated the use of violence as a strategy to achieve any political or personal end other than self-defense.[1] Indeed, in the mid-nineteenth century, the ideology was criticized as being so peaceful that its communities would be defenseless against aggressors. By the late 1800s, however, the public image of Anarchism had changed drastically. In the decades preceding the Russian Revolution, several Communist Anarchist groups repeatedly committed acts of brutal and almost random violence as a strategy to topple capitalism. These acts, called "propaganda by deed," were directed against people who belonged to the capitalist class and included throwing bombs into crowded restaurants on the assumption that only capitalists could afford to eat there.

Violence erupted in America as well. On May 4, 1886, labor protesters and the police clashed in the streets of Chicago during a meeting whose organizers included Communist Anarchists. The event, known to history as the Haymarket affair or incident, left dead bodies on both sides. Although the eight radicals who were arrested and tried thereafter were demonstrably innocent, the Haymarket affair cemented the connection between Anarchism and violence in the mind of the American public. Anarchists became the enemies of society and of civilization. During the Haymarket proceedings, the prosecutor declared: "Law is on trial. Anarchy is on trial. These men have been selected . . . because they are leaders. . . . [C]onvict these men . . . save our institutions, our society."[2]

The radical community reacted with outrage. Yet throughout the arrest and the trial of the Chicago martyrs, and even upon the execution of four defendants and the suicide of one, Benjamin Tucker was reserved in his support of the accused. Tucker wrote: "It is because peaceful agitation and passive resistance are weapons more deadly to tyranny than any others that I uphold them. . . . [B]rute force strengthens tyranny. . . . War and authority are companions; peace and liberty are companions. . . . The Chicago Communists I look upon as brave and earnest men and women. That does not prevent them from being equally mistaken."[3]

The Haymarket incident was the proximate cause of a deep schism that occurred in America between Individualist Anarchists and Communist Anarchists with whom they had formerly aligned, but it was actually the last of a series of events. The schism was rooted in ideology, specifically in the question of whether force could be employed as a political strategy.

Liberty and Violence as a Strategy

To judge from the first page of the first issue of *Liberty* on August 6, 1881, Tucker celebrated both violence as a strategy and the people who employed it for political ends. At the head of the middle column, and dominating the text, was a handsome engraving of the Russian nihilist Sophie Perovskaya—"Liberty's Martyred Heroine"—who was proclaimed to have been "Hanged April 15, 1881, For Helping to Rid the World of a Tyrant [Czar Alexander II]." Tucker declared the engraving to be "the first authentic likeness published in America of the most famous and heroic of the little Russian band . . . Sophie Perovskaya."[4] A memorial poem by Joaquin Miller followed.

Three issues later, Tucker continued to praise the Russian nihilists for their violent resistance to tyranny "which the Nihilists alone are prepared to tear out by the roots and bury out of sight forever. Success to the Nihilists!"[5] Nevertheless, on the same page, an article by Tucker entitled "Liberty's Weapons" began, "Our methods are the methods of peace. Liberty is not the advocate of force."[6]

Realizing that such a jarring juxtaposition of articles might confuse his readers, or lead them to accuse him of inconsistency, Tucker voiced what he imagined to be their reaction, "And yet Liberty finds words of approval for the . . . tyrant-slayers who in secrecy plot the revenges of fate. Why? Because Liberty is forced to choose between one class that slays to oppress and another that slays to free." To those who still expressed confusion, he urged patience in their "great hurry for a full and systematic explanation of Liberty's philosophy and purposes. . . . Patience, good friends, patience!"[7]

Almost thirty issues later and still without the promised "systematic explanation," Tucker commented upon the assassination of the French politician Leon Gambetta with the words, "It is a fitting ending to the life of one of the most dangerous characters of Europe, over whose disappearance Liberty, not in a spirit of triumphant revenge, but simply voicing a sincere desire for the public welfare, can only rejoice."[8]

Yet, whenever acts of violence against politicians occurred within the United States, *Liberty* reacted in a markedly different manner than it did toward similar attacks in Europe. For example, when President Garfield was assassinated by Charles Guiteau in 1881, Tucker declared, "As to the act committed by Guiteau all sensible men agree. Nothing but its insanity saved it from being dastardly, bloodthirsty, and thoroughly devilish, without reason, proper motive, or excuse."[9] Tucker's criticism of the American assassin Guiteau occurred two issues after his idolization of the Russian assassin Sophie Perovskaya. Some two dozen issues thereafter, Tucker expressed joy at the death of the French politician Gambetta, thus eliminating the possibility he had changed his attitude toward violence as a political strategy in the brief interval between praising Perovskaya and repudiating Guiteau.

The explanation of this apparent inconsistency lay in Tucker's view of violence as a last resort strategy that could be justified only when freedom of speech and freedom of the press had been destroyed, as they had been in Perovskaya's Russia. As long as radicals in America could speak out and publish, however, they could educate the public toward "the Anarchistic idea" and inspire rebellion.

Although Tucker was acutely aware of the restrictions on freedom of speech and freedom of the press within the United States, he insisted that newspapers, "if not allowed to say everything they would like to, are able to say all that is absolutely necessary to say in order to finally achieve their end, the triumph of liberty."[10] Then, and only then, with the solid foundation of an educated citizenry could an Anarchist society succeed. Until that foundation had been laid, Tucker counseled radicals in America to eschew violence against the State and to prefer peaceful means of agitation.[11]

Liberty's rejection of tactical violence in the United States was part of a systematic view of strategy.[12] The reasons for this rejection were well expressed in an article entitled "Violence Breeds Violence," written by Florence Finch Kelly under the initials "F. F. K." Kelly flatly stated that no "permanent good" could be achieved through the use of violence. She asked every radical to "stop and study well" the effect of State brutality upon his own heart. She argued: the violence had not convinced him to accept the State or to embrace it as legitimate. The violence had only hardened his beliefs and angered him to respond in kind. So, too, would a strategy of violence affect the American people: the bomb-throwing revolutionary could only "terrify them, and in their terror they can only strike back and hug their beliefs all the closer." The use of violence would result in "nothing but a brute battle for physical supremacy with a rabid determination on each side to exterminate the other. And it happens that the probabilities of extermination are all on the wrong side."[13]

By insisting upon peaceful agitation within the United States, the Individualist Anarchists placed themselves at odds with the Communist Anarchists, some of whom, as immigrants, had imported political strategies of violence with them from Russia and Germany. For example, the Communist Anarchist leader Johann Most arrived in New York from Germany in 1882, where he began publication of the German-language paper *Die Freiheit*, in which he openly called for workers to commit acts of violence against the State.[14] *Liberty* offered a sense of the urgency with which Most called for insurrection through a translated excerpt from *Die Freiheit*. Most cried out, "The existing system will be quickest and most radically overthrown by the annihilation of its exponents. Therefore, massacres of the enemies of the people must be set in motion."[15] Because of his preferred method of explosive "resistance," the editor of *Die Frei-heit* was nicknamed Dynamost.

With such profound theoretical differences between the traditions of Individualist and Communist Anarchism, it was inevitable that a bitter schism would eventually separate them. Nevertheless, Tucker's strong links to European Anarchist periodicals and personalities, as well as his championing of Proudhonian economics, had forged a bond that resisted severing. For example, on July 16, 1881, when the moribund International Working People's Association revived in London, Tucker had been ecstatic. In an article entitled "Vive l'Association Internationale," Tucker enthused, "To this momentous event, which marks an epoch in the progress of the great labor movement. . . . Liberty, in the present issue, devotes a large portion of her space."[16]

As the historian Margaret S. Marsh observed in her book *Anarchist Women*, there had initially been good will and cooperation between the Individualist and Communist Anarchists. "Their conflict . . . came after a brief period of harmony. Tucker and the Individualists had wanted initially to cooperate with the European Anarchist movement. In 1881 the editor of *Liberty* hailed the creation of the anarchist 'Black International,' proposing that his paper serve as its English-language organ."[17]

For a while, *Liberty* served this function. The November 12, 1881, issue carried a report by J. H. Swain who, as a representative of Individualist Anarchism, had attended a follow-up conference in Chicago, where he was extremely well received even though the majority of attendees were Socialists. A year later, the two factions of Anarchism became bitter enemies.

The schism was sped along not only by theoretical differences but also by three specific events: the second Congress of the International held in 1883; *Liberty*'s exposé of the "New York firebugs"; and, the Haymarket incident.

Second Congress of the International

After welcoming Most to America, *Liberty* soon became a vocal critic of the Communist Anarchist leader. Henry Appleton, writing under the pseudonym "X," led the assault on Most, whom he labeled a "State Socialist" rather than an "Anarchist." Appleton pressed Most to answer one question: under the social system he proposed, what would become of a peaceful individual who did not agree to live by his economic theories? Appleton demanded to know "whether Communistic Anarchists propose to let me severely alone, provided I decline to take any part in their schemes, but choose to paddle my own canoe, at my own cost?"

It seemed clear to Appleton that if he withdrew from Most's society and happened "to be personally occupying, cultivating, and using forty acres of land, upon which I have built a home, a barn, and bought tools, domestic animals" that it would be only a matter of time before he was "torn from my bed and cleaned out to make room for one of Herr Most's elect." All he had built and cultivated would be "declared the property of the Commune." For this reason, Appleton concluded, "these Communists are not Anarchists, but, when crowded back upon their basic resources, are at war with Liberty, whose very incarnation true Anarchy is."[18]

In 1883, Chicago Anarchists—many of whom were Communists—organized a conference to be held in Pittsburgh. Its purpose: to establish a platform on which radical agitators of all ideologies, from Marxism to Individualism, could agree. Dominated by Most, the planned conference managed to alienate both the Marxists who refused to attend and the Individualists who broke off all official cooperation with the conference.

On October 6, 1883, on the first page of *Liberty*, Tucker denounced the scheme to promote a latitudinarian platform for radicals, which was to be introduced at the October 14th conference. The scheme itself was embodied in a document prepared by the Communist Anarchist Burnette J. Haskell, editor of the San Francisco *Truth*. Tucker flatly declared the document to be a failure. Moreover, he considered it to be "specious and implausible," calling it "perhaps the most foolishly inconsistent piece of work that ever came to our notice."[19]

In the same issue, Tucker published an open letter to Haskell, upbraiding the *Truth* for being inconsistent and for losing the passion of its first issues. On a more personal note—and, perhaps, the more important one—Tucker professed surprise at reading of Haskell's intention to serialize an English translation of Bakounine's book *God and the State* in the *Truth*. Tucker was curious because he had been the first person to "introduce Bakounine to America in any marked way." He had already announced his own intention to translate and publish an English edition of the referenced work.

In a proprietary tone, Tucker asserted, "I was deeply adverse to having this author first introduced in English handicapped by misleading associates."[20] In short, Tucker did not want the first English translation of *God and the State* to issue from Haskell. Instead, he "hurried to completion" his own translation, "placed it in the hands" of printers, and dispatched an advertisement of the work to the *Truth*. The ad was rejected, purportedly because it included the words, "monstrous schemes of Karl Marx and Lassalle." Haskell explained that he was attempting to reconcile all the forms of Socialism, and to form "common ground for unity between Socialists and Anarchists." The wording of Tucker's advertisement ran counter to this goal.[21]

Tucker responded with characteristic bluntness, "In addition to the eyes of Beelzebub, have you acquired the smooth tongue of Mephistopheles? . . . How gauzy your excuse! Frankly, now, was not the real reason for the rejection of my advertisement a desire to prevent your readers from knowing that I was before you in the publication of 'God and the State'?"[22] As for Haskell's attempt to unify Socialism and Anarchism, Tucker expressed the deepest of skepticism.

Predictably, Haskell answered within the pages of his own paper, thus prompting Tucker to pen yet another open letter to him in *Liberty*. Although the second letter added no substance to the former, clearly the relationship between the two editors had deteriorated into bitterness and ad hominem attacks. When

Haskell wrote privately to Tucker years later asking him for a favor, Tucker declined to accommodate him in a letter published within *Liberty*. He prefaced the public rejection with the observation that "[Haskell] once called frantically and in vain for a Brutus to plunge his dagger into the Anarchist Caesar who sits on the editorial throne of Liberty."[23]

Where Tucker had expressed good will toward both Most and Haskell, the opposite sentiment now existed in perpetuity.

The New York Fire Bugs

In the March 27, 1886, issue of *Liberty*, in an article entitled "The Beast of Communism," Tucker took the remarkable step of publicly airing a "movement" scandal. He named names, and one of them was John Most.[24] Tucker began by condemning Most and the "New York Germans" for converting the word "Anarchist" in the public mind into a term synonymous with criminal activity, violence, and destruction. He wrote, "the word has been usurped, in the face of all logic and consistency, by a party of Communists who believe in a tyranny worse than any that now exists."[25] Tucker labeled this hard core of Communism as "a gang of criminals whose deeds for the past two years rival in 'pure cussedness' any to be found in the history of crime."[26]

Liberty usually reserved such strong language for politicians and other agents of the State. Tucker proceeded to explain why he now directed this language toward fellow radicals. He declared that "a large number of the most active members of the German Group of the International Working People's Association in New York City, and of the Social Revolutionary Club" were setting fire to their own property in order to collect on insurance policies, even though those properties were sometimes tenements with hundreds of occupants.[27] In one such fire, a mother and a newborn baby had burned to death. In another, a mother and two children lost their lives. Tucker listed fire after fire, death after death.

Moreover, Tucker expanded his accusations to include "well-meaning editors of leading journals of so-called Communistic Anarchism." These editors knew of the death of innocents, but they held their silence out of "mistaken party fealty." Tucker pointed his finger specifically at Most, who he said was shielding the criminals from detection. "[A]fter he was made aware of these acts," Tucker continued, "he not only refused to repudiate them, but persisted in retaining as his right-hand men some of the worst of the gang."[28]

After consulting with some of the most prominent Anarchists in the country, Tucker felt impelled to expose the murderous crimes that were being committed in the name of class justice. One event spurred him on. While he had been debating the matter, a mother and her baby had perished in another fire. Tucker bitterly reproached himself: had he published his exposé earlier, the fire would not have been set, and the mother and child would still be alive. Berating himself, Tucker made an overt show of remorse in the pages of *Liberty*.

Then, in a move considered treasonous by many fellow radicals, he called upon "every honorable newspaper in America to lay these facts before its readers, placing the blame where it belongs and distinguishing the innocent from the guilty. And especially do I address the Anarchist press. Every Anarchistic journal ought to copy this exposure and send it forth with the stamp of its approval."[29] Many papers acceded to his request: the respectable mainstream ones did so with glee.

A furor broke out in radical circles, exacerbated by the fact that many "honorable" papers grabbed onto the scandal as a means of discrediting Anarchism. The radical *Der Arme Teufel*—a German weekly published from Detroit by Robert Reitzel—lamented "these charges are published by the capitalistic press with great gusto and satisfaction."[30] Forced by publicity to respond, Most denied any knowledge of the insurance fires, and denounced Tucker's motives in exposing the alleged crimes.

Tucker refused to back down. In an article entitled "Time Will Tell," he reiterated the charges and declared, "I have done what I could to save the lives and possessions of unoffending people and to save Anarchy from being smirched by association, even in name, with crime and criminals."[31] He printed two letters which tended to support his original charges: one from Reitzel, the other from Justus H. Schwab, a prominent member of the International Working People's Association whom Tucker had mentioned favorably for having registered a protest against the fires. Meanwhile, in *Die Freiheit* Most promised to clear up the matter in future issues. Unfortunately for him, subsequent investigations substantiated most of the charges Tucker had brought against the Communist Anarchists.[32]

The turbulence caused by Tucker's exposé had barely subsided before the most significant event to rock nineteenth-century Anarchism occurred: the Haymarket incident. Again, Tucker found himself at odds with the Communist Anarchists.

The Haymarket Incident

The city of Chicago seemed to act as a magnet for immigrant radicals, most of whom were Communist or Socialist, and many of whom were deeply committed to the labor movement. The most popular labor organization, the International Working People's Association, published five papers out of Chicago alone, three of which were in German. Indeed, Chicago sent more delegates than any other city to the Second Congress that Tucker had denounced earlier.[33] The large and vocal population of radicals seemed to inspire extreme brutality within the Chicago police force, who made a point of violently breaking up even peaceful labor assemblies.

Perhaps in response to police brutality, the Chicago Anarchists openly embraced violence as a political strategy. August Spies, the editor of *Die Arbeiter Zeitung*—and one of the Haymarket defendants who was executed—penned a resolution that was passed by the Central Labor Union in that city. It read in part, "We urgently call upon the wage-class to arm itself in order to be able to put forth against their exploiters such an argument which alone can be effective—*Violence!*"[34]

The native American Albert Parsons, editor of the *Alarm*, was no less passionate in his call for armed resistance. He wrote, "The Communist and anarchist urges the people to study their schoolbooks on chemistry and read the dictionaries on the composition and construction of all kinds of explosives and make themselves too strong to be opposed with deadly weapons."[35]

With the emergence of the Eight-Hour Movement in spring of 1886, 65,000 workers in Chicago either went on strike or were locked out by their employers. As May Day drew near, violent encounters between laborers and the police increased. On May 3rd, the police fired upon a crowd of laborers, killing several people. The next day, on May 4th, a protest meeting was held in the Haymarket Square. As the crowd began to break up peacefully due to rain, the police interrupted a speech being delivered by Samuel Fielden, a leader of the demonstration. From the sidelines, someone threw a bomb toward the police, who opened fire. The shots were returned.[36] In the final count, seven policemen died: the death toll of the crowd has never been established, but it has been estimated to be in excess of twenty people.

The city of Chicago was gripped by hysteria. Businesses closed their doors. Respectable society demanded blood for blood. Anarchists were rounded up with no concern displayed for whether or not they had been actually involved in the incident. Thirty-one people were indicted for murder, sixty-nine for lesser crimes. Eventually, eight men remained accused and were tried for murder in a court case that was a travesty of justice and of just procedures. For example, the jury was not chosen in the normal manner: a bailiff was instructed to go out into the street and select whomever he wished to serve.[37] The Haymarket incident and the backlash it inspired in the consciousness of the American public was the beginning of an ongoing prejudice against and hatred of Anarchism. The impact of the incident on radicalism can hardly be overstated, and may be best understood by considering two personal examples.

The Individualist Anarchist and feminist Voltairine de Cleyre, upon reading a newspaper headline announcing that Anarchists had thrown a bomb into a crowd, had exclaimed, "They ought to be hanged!" She regretted the words instantly. Her regret became more bitter as she learned, shortly thereafter, the true circumstances surrounding the Haymarket affair. Fourteen years later de Cleyre was still haunted by her imprudent words, "For that ignorant, outrageous, bloodthirsty sentence I shall never forgive myself."[38] Much of de Cleyre's Anarchistic activity in the ensuing years can be seen as an attempt to expiate her sin, and her most passionate addresses were the ones she delivered at the yearly memorials held for the Haymarket martyrs.

The Communist Anarchist and feminist Emma Goldman described her reaction in her autobiographical *Living My Life*. After becoming hysterical, Goldman fell into a deep sleep. Upon awakening, she discovered something new and wonderful within her soul. It was "a great ideal, a burning faith, a determination to dedicate myself to the memory of my martyred comrades, to make their cause my own."[39] Goldman abandoned her newly wed husband and proceeded to New York to prepare herself for the radicalism that would consume the rest of her life.

Against this backdrop of passionate and profound reaction, Tucker became the main voice for prudence within the radical community.[40] Indeed, his initial response annoyed some associates by its reserved tone. Some of his subdued attitude may have been due to the timing of *Liberty*: the first issue in which Tucker could comment on the Haymarket affair appeared on May 22nd, almost two weeks after the event had occurred. By then, Tucker had undoubtedly read and reflected upon the call-to-arms emanating from other sources. He believed that only the utter suppression of free speech could justify an armed revolution, and this condition did not yet exist, nor had it been present on May 4th in the Haymarket Square.

Tucker clearly denounced the brutality of the Chicago police and of everyone else involved in savaging the arrested men: "The conduct during the last fortnight of the police, the courts, the pulpit, and the press, including many of the labor organs themselves, has been shameful in the extreme." But he also criticized Communist Anarchists in general and the arrested men in particular for having advocated the use of force to achieve political ends. In their meetings, for example, Communist speakers often and consciously incited their listeners to violence. *Liberty* asked rhetorically,

> Have they not been preaching for years that the laborers need no other provo-
> cation than their steady oppression by capital to warrant them in wholesale de-
> struction of life and property? Was not this very meeting [the Haymarket
> meeting] held for the purpose of advising the laborers to pursue such a policy?
> . . . This event at Chicago opens the whole question of the advisability of armed
> revolution.[41]

Nevertheless, Tucker concluded with a backhanded defense of Most, who had been arrested as well for his incendiary views, even though he had been in New York during the bombing. Tucker wrote, "[A]mong the victims of these author-ity-ridden maniacs is John Most. Toward him as a social reformer *Liberty*'s at-titude has been and will be hostile in the extreme, but toward him as a human being deprived of his fundamental rights it can be nothing but sympathetic."[42]

On the next page of *Liberty*, an article by Appleton entitled "The Boston Anarchists" spelled out the peaceful principles and policies of Individualist An-archism, which stood in stark contrast to those of Communist Anarchism. Appleton followed up in the next issue with a piece entitled "Authority-blinded." While not forgiving Most for "the late assaults upon person and prop-erty," Appleton decried the vicious treatment of the arrested man at the hands of the police and in court.[43]

In the same issue and on the opposing page, the Communist Anarchist Dyer D. Lum complained that "the grave situation in which the Chicago 'Communists' (if you will) are placed demands . . . more than dissertations or well-rounded and careful distinctions by 'X' [Appleton] between 'Boston Anarchists' and the 'savage Communists of Chicago'."[44]

Tucker—whom Lum also called to task—replied, "I have denounced the treatment of the Chicago Communists in the strongest terms that I could think of. I could have done nothing more except subscribe for their defense and ask Liberty's constituency to do likewise."[45] Then he expanded on his belief that the use of force in resisting the State merely lent the air of justification to the State's subsequent repression. Recalling the example of Anthony Comstock's persecution of many free speech radicals in the 1870s, Tucker argued that, if the victims of Comstock had responded by shooting their persecutor, the cause of censorship would have been strengthened by the public's outrage.

In one of his first major appearances in the pages of *Liberty*, the Russian immigrant Victor Yarros stirred up controversy by doing something few other contributors dared: he took Tucker publicly to task. Yarros warned that the "Philosophical Anarchists" were in imminent danger of becoming both "respectable" and spoken well of by "a sort of people whose friendship would be the greatest misfortune and disgrace to any serious movement. These are friends that Liberty must be saved from." Yarros was referring to the general press—which lauded both Tucker's condemnation of the New York firebugs and his stated reservations regarding the Haymarket defendants. Yarros declared, "No wonder many of our best friends are disgusted."[46]

Speaking as a Philosophical Anarchist himself, Yarros stated clearly, "I do not wish to be mistaken as opposing the position Liberty has taken on the question of force," but he wished to vigorously protest against Tucker's representation of Anarchism as "pacific" and nonviolent. He expressed contempt for "Christian meekness and all-forgiving love in a radical." As a ringing conclusion, Yarros cried out, "Anarchism means war. . . . We have a right to use force and resist by all means the invasion of the self-constituted rulers."[47]

In an uncharacteristically muted manner, Tucker responded, "While giving hearty assent to what I take to be Mr. Yarros's general meaning . . . I desire to be a little more explicit." He explained that the terms "'philosophical' and 'pacific' do not trouble me, no matter who applies them."

In response to Yarros's declaration of war against the State, Tucker observed that war measures "are almost always violations of rights." Then, he drew an important distinction between the New York Communists who had caused the death of innocents in insurance fires and the Chicago Communists who had been rash and reckless in resisting the State. "The New York firebugs are contemptible villains; the Chicago Communists I look upon as brave and earnest men and women. That does not prevent them from being equally mistaken."[48] Their mistake, however, was not one of principle but of strategic vision.[49]

As the day of execution drew near for the convicted men, Tucker expressed deep sorrow, but he did not change his evaluation of the situation one whit. He wrote, "the day approaches on which the brutal State proposes to execute upon these rash but noble men a base and far more rash revenge." He concluded that the lesson to be gleaned from the upcoming tragedy was this: the State is a monster "that cannot be reformed; *it must be killed*. But how? Not by dynamite; that will not harm it. How, then? By light. It thrives in the darkness of its victims' ignorance; it and they must be flooded with the light of liberty. If the seven must die, such must be the lesson of their death."[50]

On November 11, the executions occurred. The first page of the November 19th issue of *Liberty* was entirely devoted to a poem in memory of and in tribute to the Haymarket martyrs. On page 4, Tucker ran a memorial column. However, he also reprinted a lecture he had delivered before the Anarchists' Club, a few days prior to executions. There, again, Tucker expressed a dual response: he was outraged and sorrowful at the prospect of the State murdering innocent men, but he was determined to distinguish Individualist Anarchism from Chicago "Anarchism."

By now, Tucker was sufficiently sensitive to the reaction of his peers that he had felt it necessary to interrupt the speech to insert a side note of explanation. He had interjected, "And inasmuch as my subject compels me to say something in criticism of these men's opinion, and inasmuch also as five days hence they are to die upon the gallows . . . you will excuse me, I am sure, if I interrupt my argument . . . long enough to qualify my criticism in advance by a word of tribute and a declaration of fellowship."[51] After the brief tribute, a lengthy criticism ensued.

Tucker became so committed to distinguishing Individualist Anarchism from Communist Anarchism that he announced a new German-language periodical entitled *Libertas*, to be edited by his close friends George and Emma Schumm, in order to enunciate Individualist Anarchism to those German-speaking State Socialists and radicals who might be disillusioned in the wake of the executions.

The Wake of the Haymarket

The Socialist historian Morris Hillquit has observed with some justice, "The Chicago incident was practically the closing chapter in the history of the Anarchist movement in this country." Many radicals who had considered themselves to be Communist Anarchists now shifted their energies and allegiances over to the more moderate Socialist cause. Labor organizations, such as the International Working-Men's Association, which had aligned with Anarchists on certain issues, now eschewed anything and anyone Anarchistic.[52] Events of the late nineteenth century cemented rather than dissipated this prejudice.

For example, in July 1892, the Communist Anarchist Alexander Berkman attempted unsuccessfully to assassinate the Carnegie steel magnate Henry C.

Frick. About this debacle, Tucker wrote, "During the conflict now on between capital and labor, seldom a day passes without the shedding of blood. . . . I freely confess that I am more desirous of being saved from friends like Berkman, to whom my heart goes out, than from enemies like Frick, from whom my heart withdraws." Subsequent discussion within *Liberty* of the scandal revolved around Most's public assertion that the Communistic Berkman was actually a devotee of Tucker's Individualist Anarchism and Tucker's denial of the claim.[53]

From a point of early cooperation, Individualist and Communist Anarchists now deemed each other's label to be a damning insult to be publicly hurled and publicly denied.

Conclusion

The primary conflict between Individualist and Communist Anarchists, both in terms of theory and strategy, centered on the issue of violence: what was its definition? and, could it be used as a tactic to achieve social change?

Communist Anarchists defined violence in socioeconomic terms and, by their analysis, a state of war already existed between the laboring and the capitalist classes. As a logical extension, self-defense was defined in such a manner as to allow Communists to attack anyone belonging to the capitalist class on the basis of their class affiliation alone. Since they considered open warfare to already exist, the use of violence to achieve their ends was not only strategic but also necessary.

Individualist Anarchists used either natural rights or Stirnerite egoism as the ideological framework within which to examine the issue of violence. Both approaches considered the individual to be primary and defined violence on an individual rather than on a class basis—that is, individuals were responsible on a personal level for any aggression they committed. Even those members of the oppressing class, politicians, were held individually responsible for the specific acts they committed or facilitated, and *Liberty* commonly referred to them by name. Thus, violence against anyone but an individual who had aggressed could not be justified.

Moreover, the true source and bulwark of political oppression lay not in the actions of politicians but in the sanction, or obedience, rendered to the political system by society. The State could not be destroyed by eliminating a class of people because the State was, in essence, an idea embraced by society. The idea itself had to be eliminated. As Tucker wrote, "Our purpose is the abolition, not only of all existing States, but the State itself. . . . It is not a thing that can be especially defined. . . . The State is a principle, a philosophical error in social existence."[54] The solution: eliminate any sense of legitimacy that the State could claim.

During the twenty-seven-year span of *Liberty*, many strategies were advanced to eliminate the philosophical error that was "the State." In the broadest of terms, the strategies fell into four categories: education, civil disobedience, passive resistance, and the creation of parallel institutions.

An example of *Liberty*'s attempts to educate was the Anarchist Letter-Writing Corps. On March 24, 1894, the egoistic Steven T. Byington announced a strategy of organized letter writing—usually letters to the editor at daily newspapers—aimed at educating the general public, as well as influential individuals, toward the ideas of Individualist Anarchism. Byington wrote, "Those who are at all familiar with the Single Tax movement know that it has been much helped by the 'Single Tax Writing Corps.' . . . A number of persons have pledged themselves to write at least one letter a week, in advocacy of the single tax, to such addresses as may be given by the secretary. . . . With each name is usually a statement of the position taken by the man or paper, or a pertinent quotation from some recent public utterance made by him or it."[55]

As a result of the Single Tax Letter-Writing Corps, Byington declared that the issue had been brought before the eyes of the public and important editors on a weekly basis. The same strategy was successfully employed in the service of Anarchism.

Civil disobedience was another strategy advocated by the *Liberty* circle, but Tucker advised great caution in employing it. For example, an Anarchist should refuse to pay taxes only when he "feels exceptionally strong and independent, when his conduct can impair no serious personal obligations, when on the whole he would a little rather go to jail than not, and when his property is in such shape that he can successfully conceal it."[56]

Tucker's advice was based on personal experience. In August 1875, he had been imprisoned for his Thoreau-like refusal to pay a poll tax, but his protest ended quietly when a friend unilaterally decided to pay the fine. However, Tucker came to believe that civil disobedience was a poor strategy, except when it had an overriding educational value.

A later encounter between Tucker and a poll tax collector on May 17, 1888, illustrates his drift on this particular strategy. The editor paid the tax "under protest" and made an attempt to educate the taxman collecting the fee. Then, Tucker published an account of the exchange in *Liberty*. For example, when offered a receipt for the $1.00 payment, Tucker refused, saying "I never take a receipt for money that is stolen from me."[57]

Tucker registered his protest, while behaving in a manner that acknowledged the superiority of the force being leveled against him. The reason for his compliance: until and unless a general foundation of Anarchistic education had been laid, acts of individual rebellion against unjust law were acts of martyrdom that drained the vitality of a movement and created a backlash of State violence against it. Instead, Anarchists should strive vigorously to create "a public sentiment" that would make unjust laws into dead-letter ones because they would meet too much popular resistance to be enforced.

Passive resistance, as opposed to civil disobedience, involved the passive refusal to obey unjust law rather than the direct confrontation with such laws. A prime example of such passive resistance occurred over the issue of trial by jury.

When a jury selection law passed in New York State to which the *Liberty* offices had moved, Tucker was disheartened and commented, "We are confronted now with a condition, not a theory." He urged readers to adopt the passive resistance strategy employed by the Irish rebel Charles Parnell against the occupying British: that is, "the policy of loud and steady protest, the policy of embarrassment, hindrance, blockade, and obstruction." Then, he went on to explain the specific behavior that constituted such resistance in terms of trial by jury. "If each and every one of you, on being placed in the jury box and before each trial begins, will rise in his place and say to the court: 'I most earnestly protest against having to serve on this jury. . . . I serve here only on compulsion and in a spirit of indignant discontent,'" then—Tucker believed—a powerful contribution to Anarchistic propaganda could be made.[58]

The strategy of parallel institutions was *Liberty*'s attempt to answer a much-asked question: what would happen to the structure of society if Government did not provide essential functions such as courts and defense? Anarchists needed to demonstrate how such essential services could evolve in a voluntary system, and what they might look like. For example, Tucker advocated starting a parallel banking system and forming private defense organizations.

In Eltzbacher's *Anarchism*, the translator Byington commented on the defensive associations: "The defensive associations receive especially frequent mention because of the need of incessantly answering the objection 'If we lose the State, who will protect us against ruffians?' but Tucker certainly expects that the defensive association will from the start fill a much smaller sphere in every respect than the present police."[59]

Tucker speculated that more than one defensive association would exist side by side:

> There are many more than five or six insurance companies in England, and it is by no means uncommon for members of the same family to insure their lives and goods against accident or fire in different companies. Why should there not be a considerable number of defensive associations in England in which people, even members of the same family, might insure their lives and goods against murderers or thieves? Defense is a service, like any other service.[60]

Under such a competitive system, the best agency might well reap the majority of business, but it would do so on the quality of its service, not because it enforced a monopoly.

The rejection of violence as a political strategy led the nineteenth-century Individualist movement into complex and productive lines of reasoning about the alternative strategies through which societal change could be achieved. Given that the oppressive nature of the State has not fundamentally altered since *Liberty*'s voice was stilled, the strategies it advocated are an aspect of the periodical that may sound fresh to modern ears.

Notes

1. For more on the native American tradition, see James J. Martin, *Men Against the State: The Expositors of Individualist Anarchism in America, 1827-1908* (Colorado Springs, Colo.: Ralph Myles Publisher, 1970), Eunice Minette Schuster, *Native American Anarchism: A Study of Left-Wing American Individualism* (New York: AMS Press, 1970), and William Gary Kline, *The Individualist Anarchists: A Critique of Liberalism.* (New York: University Press of America, 1987).

2. As quoted in Philip Foner, *The Haymarket Autobiographies* (New York: Humanities Press, 1969), 8.

3. Appended to Benjamin R. Tucker, "The 'Philosophical Anarchists,'" *Liberty* 4 (July 31, 1886): 1.

4. *Liberty* 1 (August 6, 1881): 1. The likeness of the nihilistic assassin had been reproduced from one privately forwarded to him after the London revolutionary congress had distributed a handful in England.

5. Benjamin R. Tucker, "The Doctrine of Assent," *Liberty* 1 (September 17, 1881): 2.

6. Benjamin R. Tucker, "Liberty's Weapons," *Liberty* 1 (September 17, 1881): 2.

7. Tucker, "Liberty's Weapons," 2-3.

8. Benjamin R. Tucker, "Another Tyrant Fallen," *Liberty* 2 (January 20, 1883): 2. In its eleventh year of publication, *Liberty* was more reserved about rejoicing at the violent death of another French politician, President Carnot. In an article entitled "Violence Breeding Violence," Victor Yarros wrote, "What wonder is there that the revolutionists have taken Carnot's life? The revolutionists are not treated with mercy, why should they be merciful?" Yet, Yarros followed up this sympathetic statement with the balancing observation, "The act is to be regretted; it may have serious consequences." Violence Breeding Violence," *Liberty* 10 (June 30, 1894): 2.

9. Benjamin R. Tucker, "Pity, but Not Praise," *Liberty* 1 (September 3, 1881): 3.

10. Benjamin R. Tucker, "Herr Most on Libertas," *Liberty* 5 (April 14, 1888): 4.

11. For more on this theme, see Morgan Edwards, "Neither Bombs Nor Ballots: Liberty & The Strategy of Anarchism," in *Benjamin R. Tucker and the Champions of Liberty,* ed. Michael E. Coughlin, Charles H. Hamilton, and Mark A. Sullivan (St. Paul, Minn.: Michael E. Coughlin, 1986), 65.

12. The American tradition of Individualist Anarchism had deep roots in nonresistance, dating back to the abolitionist movement of William Lloyd Garrison (1830s), which was largely composed of Quakers. See Lewis Perry, *Radical Abolitionism: Anarchy and the Government of God in Antislavery Thought* (Ithaca, N.Y.: Cornell University Press, 1973).

13. Florence Finch Kelly, "Violence Breeds Violence," *Liberty* 5 (December 3, 1887): 4.

14. The two other most significant voices for such violence were *The Alarm* (Chicago: A. R. Parsons) and *Truth* (San Francisco: Burnette J. Haskell).

15. As quoted by Henry Appleton in "Individualist Visionaries," *Liberty* 3 (June 20, 1885): 4.

16. Benjamin R. Tucker, "Vive l'Association Internationale," *Liberty* 1 (August 20, 1881): 2.

17. Margaret S. Marsh, *Anarchist Women 1870-1920* (Philadelphia: Temple University Press, 1981), 12.

18. Appleton, "Individualist Visionaries," 4.

19. Benjamin R. Tucker, "On Picket Duty," *Liberty* 2 (October 6, 1883): 1.

20. James J. Martin points out that "Tucker had berated Haskell's policy of printing long excerpts from the works of Marx, Proudhon, Bakunin and other socialists and Anarchists without any attempt at discrimination of interpretation, in the hope of creating the impression of their essential sameness" (*Men Against the State*, 223). This is probably what Tucker meant by the words "misleading associates."

21. Benjamin R. Tucker, "Has 'Truth' Become a Liar?" *Liberty* 2 (October 6, 1883): 2.

22. Tucker, "Has 'Truth' Become a Liar?" 3.

23. Benjamin R. Tucker, *Liberty* 3 (March 27, 1886): 5.

24. Tucker consistently anglicized the German "Johann."

25. Benjamin R. Tucker, "The Beast of Communism," *Liberty* 3 (March 27, 1886): 1.

26. Tucker, "The Beast of Communism," 1. For an in-depth discussion of "propaganda by deed," see James Joll, *The Anarchists* (Cambridge, Mass.: Harvard University Press, 1980), chapter V "Terrorism and Propaganda by the Deed."

27. Interestingly, the International Working People's Association had been created at the Second Congress in 1883, of which Tucker was so critical.

28. Tucker, "The Beast of Communism," 1. Most seemed particularly enamored with the idea of revolutionary violence and had written a pamphlet entitled *Revolutionare Kriegswissenschaft* (The Science of Revolutionary Warfare), which outlined how to build and use bombs, as well as how to employ arson to further "the cause." *Die Freiheit* ran articles on the virtues of dynamite and the ways to produce nitroglycerine.

29. Tucker, "The Beast of Communism," 8.

30. *Liberty* 4 (April 17, 1886): 1. The next several issues of *Liberty* reprinted articles on this subject and Anarchism in general, as well as responses to the general press from Tucker. When Tucker did not champion the Haymarket defendants, Yarros wrote, "Clergymen, capitalistic editors and labor reformers begin to smile on 'philosophical anarchism' and pronounce it a very sweet and charming thing." Yarros suggested that *Liberty* needed to be saved from such friends. Victor Yarros, "The 'Philosophical Anarchists,'" *Liberty* 4 (July 31, 1886): 1.

31. Benjamin R. Tucker, "Time Will Tell," *Liberty* 4 (April 17, 1886): 4.

32. Benjamin R. Tucker, "The Facts Coming to Light," *Liberty* 4 (May 22, 1886): 8. Tucker reprinted an article from the *New York Sun* that reflected weeks of research by an independent journalist and which—in Tucker's words—should "convince every fair-minded person that I told the truth." Most was reduced to claiming he did not know the people mentioned in the article, although many of them had been identified repeatedly as "comrades" in earlier issues of *Die Freiheit*.

33. George Woodcock estimates "The actual number of anarchists in the Chicago groups was probably about 3,000, out of the International's total American membership of 6,000" *Anarchism: A History of Libertarian Ideas and Movements* (Cleveland, Ohio: Meridian Books, 1962), 462.

34. Emphasis in original. As quoted in Woodcock, *Anarchism*, 462.

35. As quoted in William Reichart, *Partisans of Freedom* (Bowling Green, Ohio: Bowling Green University Popular Press, 1976), 222.

36. The identity of the bomb thrower remains a mystery to history. Some claim that the responsible party was a police provocateur—namely the so-called anarchist agitator Schnaubelt who was sought by the police, but not found. One thing is evident, however; the eight men tried and convicted of the crime were innocent of the act, though perhaps guilty of contributing to it through their incendiary literature and words.

37. The best sources on the Haymarket incident and subsequent trial are Henry David, *History of the Haymarket Affair* (New York: Russell & Russell, 1936), and Paul Avrich, *The Haymarket Tragedy* (Princeton, N.J.: Princeton University Press, 1984).

38. As reported in Paul Avrich, *An American Anarchist: The Life of Voltairine de Cleyre* (Princeton, N.J.: Princeton University Press, 1978), 49-50.

39. Emma Goldman, *Living My Life*, vol. 1 (New York: Dover, 1970), 10.

40. Tucker believed that Most and most of the other men subsequently arrested in the wake of the Haymarket incident were not Anarchists, but rather State Socialists. Victor Yarros picked up this theme in his critique of an article entitled the "Chicago Anarchists" written by Dyer D. Lum and published in the third issue of the *Alarm*. Lum had protested, "I am pained to see many have used the phrase 'so-called Anarchists' or 'Communists' when referring to them." Arguing persuasively that the men were State Socialists, Yarros labeled Lum's article as "absurdly false and dishonestly misleading." Lum accused his accuser of "being a Yarros." In concluding, Yarros replied, "Not knowing what you mean, I must leave this, together with many other brilliant remarks of a similar character, without an answer." "Neither Fish Nor Flesh," *Liberty* 5 (January 14, 1888): 6.

William Reichert explains that Parsons and many of the other Chicago "Anarchists" adopted that label "more as a matter of convenience than ideological commitment" because the popular press hurled that term at them repeatedly (*Partisans of Freedom*, 216).

41. Benjamin R. Tucker, "Liberty and Violence," *Liberty* 4 (May 22, 1886): 4. James J. Martin observed, "Tucker was, in fact, far more interested in the psychological problem which the actions of the Chicago revolutionaries and of Most presented the radical cause as a whole . . . he was absolutely convinced that the desired social revolution would be possible only through the utility of peaceful propaganda and passive resistance, for to use violence was merely to mark time, historically. Hence the lack of vigor in defending the Haymarket group" (*Men Against the State*, 225).

42. Martin, *Men Against the State*, 225.

43. "X" [Henry Appleton], "Authority-blinded," *Liberty* 4 (June 19, 1886): 4.

44. Dyer D. Lum, "Letter to Editor," *Liberty* 4 (June 19, 1886): 5. Lum's attitude reflected a common response of radicals and Anarchists outside of the Boston Anarchist community.

45. Benjamin R. Tucker, "Mr. Lum Finds Liberty Wanting," *Liberty* 4 (June 19, 1886): 5. In a later issue, Tucker called for readers to "let ample funds flow in, in order that all that can be done may be done, regardless of cost." Benjamin R. Tucker, "The Lesson of the Hour," *Liberty* 5 (September 24, 1887): 4.

46. Among those friends was Charles T. Fowler, who publicly complained in the pages of the *Truth Seeker* that *Liberty* was not protesting the treatment of the Chicago defendants. In *Lucifer, the Light Bearer*, Fowler published an article defending the martyrs. Meanwhile, other radical periodicals denounced the Tuckerites as "sham anarchists." Despite such criticisms, however, it is clear that the Haymarket defendants themselves were somewhat influenced by *Liberty*'s stand. Tucker reports on Parsons's speech

before the court, in which he incorporated material from one of *Liberty*'s articles on the controversy. See Benjamin R. Tucker, "On Picket Duty," *Liberty* 4 (October 30, 1886): 1.

47. Yarros, "The 'Philosophical Anarchists,'" 1. As on many issues, Yarros seemed to change considerably over the years. In an exchange with Auberon Herbert some eight years later, an older and more restrained Yarros wrote that force should be employed only when the choice is either "force" or "entire inactivity." At that point, "force may and should be used for the purposes of acquiring the liberty of using the other and better weapons." Victor Yarros, "Auberon Herbert on Dynamite," *Liberty* 10 (July 14, 1894): 3-4.

48. Benjamin R. Tucker, reply to "The 'Philosophical Anarchists,'" *Liberty* 4 (July 31, 1886): 1.

49. James J. Martin commented that Tucker's actions belied his words. "[F]ew radical periodicals devot[ed] as much space to the defense of the accused men as did *Liberty*. Copious references to the case continued to appear for over ten years thereafter, and he never discarded his conviction that the men were innocent. His only reproach was on the grounds of the incendiary language of their literature and journals, which was a direct invitation to the state to retaliate." (*Men Against the State*, 226). As late as November 1896, Tucker reviewed the Haymarket case at length in the pages of *Liberty*.

50. Benjamin R. Tucker, "The Lesson of the Hour," *Liberty* 5 (September 24, 1887): 4.

51. Benjamin R. Tucker, "General Walker and the Anarchists," *Liberty* 5 (November 19, 1887): 5. In the end, on November 11, 1887, only four of the men were executed: August Spies, Albert Parsons, Adolph Fischer, and George Engel. Louis Lingg had committed suicide in his cell the day before. Samuel Fielden, Oscar Neebe, and Michael Schwab were pardoned a few years later by Gov. Altgeld, who investigated the charges against them and found no evidence of guilt. Tucker lavished praise upon Altgeld for this act of political courage, and contrasted it with Henry George's act of political cowardice in refusing to protest the original Haymarket verdict.

52. Morris Hillquit, *History of Socialism in the United States* (New York: Funk & Wagnalls, 1903): 252. Hillquit chronicles the growth of Socialism in the wake of the Haymarket incident, along with the speed with which organized labor withdrew its support from anything Anarchistic.

53. Berkman himself later abandoned "propaganda by deed" and declared, "It is the means that shape your ends. The means are the seed which bud into flower and come to fruition. The fruit will always be of the nature of the seed you planted. You can't grow a rose from a cactus seed." Alexander Berkman, *Now and After: The ABC of Communist Anarchism* (New York: Vanguard, 1929), 168. Berkman's sentence is remarkably similar to one Gandhi used, "The means are the ends in progress."

54. Benjamin R. Tucker, "What We Mean," *Liberty* 1 (April 15, 1882): 2-3. Perhaps because of Tucker's philosophical approach to the State—that is, his rejection of the *fundamental* State rather than merely one manifestation of it—his form of Anarchism became known as "Philosophical Anarchism." One of the most ambitious attempts to define *Liberty*'s approach to Anarchism was a nineteen-installment series of articles entitled "Problems of Anarchism" by Wm. Bailie, which ran in the first eight months of 1893.

55. Steven T. Byington, "An Anarchist Letter-Writing Corps," *Liberty* 9 (March 24, 1894): 3. Note that Byington also spelled his name "Stephen."

56. Benjamin R. Tucker, *Instead of a Book, by a Man Too Busy to Write One; A Fragmentary Exposition of Philosophical Anarchism* (New York: B. R. Tucker, 1893), 412.

57. Benjamin R. Tucker, "A Seed Planted," *Liberty* 5 (May 26, 1888): 4.

58. Benjamin R. Tucker, "A Blow at Trial by Jury," *Liberty* 13 (August, 1897): 5.

59. Paul Eltzbacher, *Anarchism: Exponents of Anarchist Philosophy*, trans. Steven T. Byington, ed. James J. Martin (Plainview, New York: Books for Libraries Press, 1960): 134.

60. Tucker, *Instead of a Book,* 32.

Chapter 4

Egoism v. Natural Rights

Throughout most of its history, the radical Individualist tradition has embraced a theory of natural rights, by which it referred to a theory of the enforceable claims that one person has in regard to others in society—claims that are based upon the nature of human beings (man). The substance of these claims is generally stated as a right to the protection of person, property, and peaceful actions. Each right is accompanied by a corresponding duty: each right that an individual claims involves a duty to recognize the same right as belonging to others.

Natural rights theory has generally been based on some version of the principle that every human being merely by being human has a moral jurisdiction over his own body. The seventeenth-century English philosopher John Locke, in whom much of the classical liberal tradition is rooted, spoke of having property in one's own person. The early Individualist Anarchists who coalesced around William Lloyd Garrison and abolitionism in the 1830s used the term "self-ownership." Post-Civil War Individualist Anarchists usually preferred the phrase made popular by the pioneering social theorist Josiah Warren: "Sovereignty of the Individual."

As employed by Individualist Anarchists, the tradition of Natural Law rested upon the belief that human values should be grounded in, or based upon, facts that could be discovered through a process of reasoning. It assumed that, as human beings interacted, some concept of right and wrong would naturally evolve. In its simplest statement, then, the Natural Law theory embraced by the Individualist Anarchists was an attempt to ground human values in the facts of reality and of human nature.

The natural rights advocates associated with *Liberty*—Lysander Spooner, John F. Kelly, Gertrude Kelly, Sidney H. Morse, J. Wm. Lloyd, Henry Appleton—claimed that there was an objective right and wrong to human behavior which was based on the nature of man and of reality. More than this, they believed the recognition of such rights was the lifeblood of Anarchism, and absolutely necessary to a free society. For one thing, only by having an objective standard of right and wrong could people have a framework against which to judge whether any specific government law or procedure was just.

For example, the May 27, 1882, issue of *Liberty* ran an original piece by Lysander Spooner, entitled "A Letter to Thomas F. Bayard," in which he critiqued not merely a specific law, but the justice of government legislation in general. In addressing the Senator from Delaware, Spooner contrasted the man-made laws created by Senators and Representatives of Congress with the laws of nature: "[Y]ou hold it to be at least possible that some four hundred men should, by some process or other become invested with the right *to make laws of their own*—that is, *laws wholly of their own device*, and therefore necessarily distinct from the law of nature, or the principles of natural justice."[1]

If the authority of government was not grounded in natural law—if they "had no natural right to impose it, as law, upon a single human being . . . [then] it is your imperative duty to . . . call upon them to burn all the existing statute books of the United States, and then to go home and content themselves with the exercise of only such rights and power as nature has given to them in common with the rest of mankind."[2]

Much of Anarchist policy depended on the yardstick of natural rights against which the justice of different social theories and conditions—including the institution of government itself—could be measured.

Wherein Does Wrongness Lie?

Any theory of natural rights implies that there are natural wrongs. Benjamin Tucker cared passionately about what was wrong. Indeed, one of Tucker's overriding concerns throughout *Liberty* was to discover and to express a clear answer to the question, "what is wrong?"

On the second page of the first issue of *Liberty*, Tucker published an article entitled "The Anatomy of Liberty," which he began with the words, "Nine-tenths of life is spent in complaining of wrongs and trying to abolish them." Yet he concluded that not one in a hundred reformers were able to define what "wrong" essentially was. Without a definition of the essential nature of "wrongness," even well-intentioned reformers were likely to become muddled and harm liberty instead of furthering it. Otherwise stated, if the goal of reform was to construct social structures that promoted the well-being of human beings, then it was necessary to have a precise understanding of what constituted such well-being.

Tucker stated the usual sense in which the word "wrong" had been used politically, "The average standard of condemning a thing as wrong is that it works injustice to some class of individuals." He rejected this definition as scientifically without basis because, "[f]or the class that is injured perhaps a much larger class is benefited by the social practice complained of." Without a clear answer to the question "what is wrong?" the bulk of reforms were doomed to be nothing more than expressions of class warfare—that is, one class within society enriching itself at the expense of another. Analyzing society through a strictly Individualist lens, Tucker rejected the possibility of class benefits. He contended that all wrongs were committed against individuals, not against abstract categories of people:

> There are no class rights or class wrongs. A thing is right, now and forever, because it accords with the immutable law of our being. It is wrong, now and forever, because it is opposed to that law. *What is that law as it pertains to human relations?* is the problem of *Liberty*. . . . The law of liberty is spontaneous association by natural selection. The first condition of its normal operation is that the basic factor of social existence, the individual, shall be let entirely and absolutely free to regulate his life as experimental contact with other equally free individuals may seem to direct.[3]

Tucker's statement of right being based on "the immutable law" of human nature that should be equally applied to all human beings placed him solidly within the Natural Law tradition. When asked his position on law and order, Tucker answered:

> Law! yes: but what law? The law of nature as developed out of a rational analysis of social force and based upon the sovereignty of the individual, or some law manufactured for designing ends before we were born and without our consent? . . . As brave old Lysander Spooner says, it is absurd to talk about "making" laws. Laws *are*, and the only right of a human being is to search after them and obey them for himself, leaving others to do the same, or contrarywise, at their own cost.[4]

Tucker's commitment to Natural Law and to the fundamental question, "what is wrong," was reiterated in an article entitled "The Philosophy of Right and Wrong." Here Tucker wrote, "the very first step in all reasoning looking to human well-being is to fix upon a correct scientific basis of *right* and *wrong*." Although he declared himself to "very positive" of the natural rights basis of right and wrong, Tucker added a comment that presaged what would become *Liberty*'s most explosive and destructive debate. He declared, "but we are fallible, and, if the history of human opinions teaches anything, it is that nothing in this world is a finality."[5]

From June 30, 1885 to May 1, 1886, *Liberty* introduced in serial form a classic work of natural rights literature, "A Letter to Grover Cleveland: On His False, Absurd, Self-Contradictory, and Inaugural Address," by Spooner. During this period, regular contributors, such as Lloyd, felt free to proclaim without fear of contradiction, "Only to natural law is the free man responsible, and in his obedience to that law does his liberty consist."[6]

By late 1886, Tucker had abandoned Natural Law for an ideology called "philosophical egoism," which considered natural rights to be "myths," "ghosts" in the mind: it defined "right" as might. Tucker seemed to take easily to philosophical egoism, perhaps because it fit neatly into at least one aspect of the Sovereignty of the Individual principle espoused by his mentor Warren—that is, the appeal to enlightened self-interest. Although Warren had maintained a Natural Law perspective, he had rejected altruism as a realistic basis for human action. Egoism must have sounded familiar to Tucker.

The debate that publicly ushered in his conversion was sparked by Max Stirner's pivotal work on law, property, and the State, which was entitled *The Ego and His Own* (in German, *Der Einzige und Sein Eigentum*).[7] Stirner, whose real name was Johann Kaspar Schmidt, had published *Der Einzige* in German in 1845 to a widespread but short-lived acclaim.[8] Although every aspect of "Stirnerite egoism" stirred argument in radical circles, the claim that "right was might" became the most controversial. Whatever a man had the might to do, Stirner claimed he also had the right to do.

As for traditional concepts of good and evil, the enlightened egoist realized that these were merely words with no reality behind them. Stirner wrote: "The divine is God's concern; the human, man's. My concern is neither the divine nor the human, not the true, good, just, free, etc., solely what is *mine*, and it is not a general one, but is—unique, as I am unique. Nothing is more to me than myself!"[9]

Philosophical Anarchism proclaimed that the acting individual and no one else should be the beneficiary of his own actions. A man's own welfare should be his highest value, and the only "law" he respected. All other laws devolved to nothing more than orders issued by those who were in a position of might—artificial orders that had no authority to bind the self-enlightened individual. Such an individual had no responsibility but self-enjoyment.

Applying his theory directly to the concept of natural rights, Stirner observed: "Who can ask about 'right' if he is not occupying the religious standpoint just like other people? Is not 'right' a religious concept, i.e. something sacred . . . When Revolution stamped liberty as a 'right' it took refuge in the religious sphere, in the region of the sacred."[10]

Thus, with Stirnerite egoism came the rejection of right and wrong—indeed, the rejection of any obligation whatsoever—except as the individual voluntarily assumed it by subordinating his will to a contract. Even then, the egoist respected a contract only because establishing reciprocity with fellow human beings was in his enlightened self-interest. The act of contracting became the pivotal point in the egoistic social theory: through contract human beings voluntarily relinquished might (or their will) in favor of obligations to others. Society by rights was replaced with "society by contract"—a phrase favored by Tucker.

In the late 1880s, interest in Stirner among American intellectuals had been stirred by the translations and popularization of his works that had offered by *Liberty* contributors the newspaperman James L. Walker, the egoistic Anarchist Steven T. Byington,[11] and John Beverly Robinson, a publisher of the land reform periodical *The Free Soiler*. Walker had independently worked out the principles of egoism for himself some years before reading Stirner and, then, he was amazed to discover the remarkable similarities. Walker published the first twelve chapters of his pioneering work, *Philosophy of Egoism*, in the May 1890 to September 1891 issues of *Egoism*.[12] Even before this series appeared, however, *Liberty* had introduced egoism through a number of articles by Walker and George Schumm, a close associate of Tucker. The American interest in Stirner constituted a rebirth for his philosophy. As Tucker explained in the Publisher's Preface of the 1907 edition of *The Ego and His Own*:

> The memory of Max Stirner had been virtually extinct for an entire generation. But in the last two decades there has been a remarkable revival of interest both in the book and in its author. It began in this country with a discussion in the pages of the Anarchist periodical, *Liberty* in which Stirner's thought was clearly expounded and vigorously championed by Dr. James L. Walker, who adopted for this discussion the pseudonym Tak Kak.[13]

Egoism v. Natural Rights: The Debate Almost Opens

The egoism versus natural rights debate within *Liberty* had a slow start. The March 6, 1886, issue of *Liberty* printed an article by Tak Kak entitled "What Is Justice?" The first sentence to follow this question was, "It is an idea presupposing a power that lays down a rule or law to which the individual owes respect and obedience. God is presented as the supreme egoist. . . . Those who believe in God fear and obey,—not I. Then comes society's justice. . . . Shall I waste my life in setting up and obeying an idea that I must treat all men alike?" Tak Kak went on to conclude, "[I]f there is to be any use for the word justice, it must mean the rules of a union of egoists with benefits to at least balance duties; and these duties are simply matter of contract [sic]."[14]

Immediately following Tak Kak's controversial but abstract discussion of justice was another article from his pen, provocatively entitled "Killing Chinese." The content seemed equally designed to provoke, especially one person in particular. Tak Kak pointedly addressed a former *Liberty* article by the natural rights advocate Gertrude B. Kelly. Kelly—in the belief that all men were "brothers"—had cried out against recent acts of brutality committed by white American workers against the Chinese who had been "imported" to exploit their cheap labor. "Tak Kak" replied contentiously, "The Chinaman is a sort of man more fitted by nature and heredity to remain a slave than the Caucasian. . . . This shocks Gertrude B. Kelly, who is a victim of the fixed idea that all men are brothers,—a poetical fragment dissociated from surviving the idea of the fatherhood of God."

As to the actual murder of Chinese workers, Tak Kak refused to condemn the practice. His brief article concluded with the statement, "I shall not pretend to tell anybody what he ought to do, at least not until I am in some sort of association with him under a mutual agreement."[15]

A commentary by Tucker followed on the heels of Tak Kak's two pieces. Still not publicly stating a hard line on egoism v. natural rights, Tucker defended Kelly's seemingly sentimental use of the word "brother," alleging that she had meant merely to refer to individuals who live in daily contact with each other and who are dependent upon each other's good will. A tacit agreement existed among such "brothers," he argued, "not to trespass upon each other's individuality, the motive of this agreement being the purely egoistic desire of each for the peaceful preservation of his own individuality."

Dismissing altruism as a basis for human conduct, Tucker also rejected obligations and duties of all manner, excepting only those that derived from contract. But, he admitted, if there were no rights to restrain men in society, then the specter of using brute force against those with whom you had not contracted was always present. Tucker—at least at the debate's onset—seemed reluctant to openly embrace this harsh possibility. He concluded his commentary on Tak Kak's article with a statement that seemed to straddle the line between natural rights and egoism. "So as many 'dead white men,' or dead yellow men, as you please, Tak Kak, provided they have been trespassers; and neither Miss Kelly nor myself will shed any tears over their graves."[16]

The controversy Tak Kak clearly hoped to provoke did not come from the pen of "Miss Kelly," although she did publish a subsequent article that Tucker chose to entitle "Justice or Force, Which?" In the piece, Kelly argued that once you abandoned considerations of justice you entered the "domain of force" in which the only standard used to judge an issue was "brute force." Although Kelly's title appeared to be in response to Tak Kak's earlier article entitled "What Is Justice?" her article made no reference to him. Instead, it addressed specific labor questions that had been raised earlier by John Swinton and Appleton.[17] It is interesting to speculate on Tucker's motives for juxtaposing the wording of Kelly's title with that of Tak Kak's earlier piece.

Tak Kak's challenge may have been ignored, but this did not prevent him from responding to Kelly's article on the next page of the same issue of *Liberty*. Nor did Tucker shy from printing it. Again, Tak Kak addressed Kelly by name. In an article entitled "Selfhood Terminates Blind Man's Buff [sic]," Tak Kak wrote of the egoist's relationship to principles such as natural rights, "The individual who finally becomes conscious of himself is, just as he is, a universe,—humanity itself. . . . The process of thought that brings him to recognize himself can nevermore be continued as a process in which himself would be only a factor, for he is a greater fact than his ideas. Henceforth ideas are simply his possession."[18] No debate ensued.

Tak Kak upped the stakes in the subsequent issue through an article entitled "Egoism in Sexual Relations." Tak Kak virtually taunted Kelly by declaring, "A proverb says: 'All is fair in love and war.' This is a recognition of the superior force of egoism in sexual relations."[19] Kelly was not only an outspoken feminist, but also a medical doctor who worked with starving and disease-ridden tenant women. She was keenly aware that differences in the wages offered to men and to women lay at the root of the killing poverty engulfing her patients, and forcing many into prostitution. Tak Kak's cavalier defense of the inequity between the genders must have particularly rankled her. But no response ensued.

Meanwhile, Tak Kak pushed his campaign on a separate front. He offered an egoistic, but polite, interpretation of an article on Henry George written by John F. Kelly—Gertrude's brother—who also advocated natural rights. The egoist's article concluded with these words: "As Mr. Kelly speaks of a tendency to 'disrupt society,' I will note that Stirner has used the word society in such a way that the dissolution of society by individuals becoming independent has no more terrors, when understood, than Proudhon's dissolution of property."[20]

Although Tak Kak's direct challenging of other contributors must have been sanctioned by Tucker, who chose to run the articles, the editor himself assumed an unusually conciliatory tone toward Gertrude Kelly, whom he admired. In response to a criticism of him from her pen, Tucker replied, "So far as this gentle and finely tempered criticism falls upon me, I am disposed to accept it with much thankfulness and some humility. There is vital truth and force in it."[21] Although Kelly continued to publish articles in *Liberty*, she maintained a silence with regard to Tak Kak.

The Debate Opens

Finally, in an article entitled "Morality and Its Origin," John F. Kelly responded to the intellectual gauntlet that had been thrown down repeatedly. Addressing himself "To the Editor of Liberty," Kelly spoke to and of Tak Kak in the third person. Giving a somewhat utilitarian defense of morality, Kelly explained the evolution of and the need for ethics within society, "Morals are, in the primitive sense, the manners and customs of a people, and hence, in the secondary, derivative sense, good manners and customs,—that is, such as tend to perpetuate the social life. Now the manners that best serve towards perpetuating society . . . owe their power to their being in accordance with the inherent laws of the social organism."

Kelly advanced the idea that men became human beings when they felt a spark of regret at having injured another. He considered this regret to be akin to an instinct within men; in words, it was a natural impulse. To Tak Kak's rejection of the "feeling that one should so act as not to injure others" on the grounds that this feeling was "a superstition . . . without rational explanation," Kelly replied that no one could rationally explain an instinct.

As to the central tenet of egoism—the assertion that human beings all act to attain pleasure (including relief from pain)—Kelly noted a circularity in Tak Kak's position. "The only proof that can be given that any action is pleasurable rather than painful is to show that it is performed," Kelly observed. "[T]hat is, we have to fall back upon the general principle that actions are performed because they are pleasurable, the very thing requiring demonstration." Moreover, if all actions were egoistic, it made no sense to speak of the superiority of egoism—as Tak Kak was wont to do—because it was necessary to have non-egoistic actions against which to rate the egoistic ones.

Comparing Tak Kak's position to that of the British philosopher Thomas Hobbes, who believed that natural man existed in a state of nature or a "war of all against all," Kelly declared the Hobbesian position to be "more logical." After all, Hobbes was willing to follow his argument through to a justification of government. As Kelly phrased it, "he argued that force must be lodged with some person or persons to determine the nature of, and enforce this contract [a social contract]. That is, from the necessity of preserving social relationships and the non-existence of natural morality he deduces despotism." Was the Anarchistic Tak Kak willing to do the same?[22]

As a concluding criticism, Kelly observed that Tak Kak had quoted the Shakespearean lines beginning with "To thine own self be true," and made "of them a profession of faith."[23] Yet, as Tak Kak openly declared, truth had no value. People should not be slaves to ideas—to "fixed ideas," as he phrased it—and abiding by principle should never rule anyone's life. Indeed, Tak Kak had claimed, "A declaration of rights is often the pitiful expression of a lack of power. . . . The devotee of a fixed idea is mad. He either runs amuck, or cowers as mesmerized by the idea."[24] When viewed through such an ideological filter, what did the phrase "to thine own self be true" mean?

Engaged in battle after months of attempting to provoke one, Tak Kak responded with his lengthiest article to date, entitled simply "Egoism." To counter Kelly's claim that egoism would justify despotism, he argued that egoism was precisely the social force preventing violence. "The man who wrings from another the fruit of his labor excites me to hostility by this wringing, or wrong, because I will not suffer it if I can help it; but my suffering is not a contest between a moral principle and my own self, but the result of an offence to myself, an obstacle to the realization of my desire."[25] In violence against an innocent third party, the egoist reasonably perceived a threat of violence toward himself and reacted against the aggressor in the spirit of pure self-protection.

Indeed, "the fixed idea" of morality—or of God or the State—to which men "succumb" might well cause violence by acting as a barrier to unleashing man's egoistical goodness. Tak Kak argued:

"Let us suppose all men are Egoists. How would the pope persuade people to support him? How would Bismarck persuade Germans that they have an individual interest in holding the Alsace? . . . How would Grover Cleveland persuade us to support him and coerce the Mormons?" Although egoists would not respond to calls of duty or morality by authority, "[y]et natural sympathy would give all the aid required by any Mormon woman who wanted to leave her husband."

What Kelly would have considered to be moral behavior—that is, the "feeling that one should so act as not to injure others"—would spring naturally from egoism, or it would not be a genuine human emotion at all. "If murder is the tendency of a mind unawed, the social sanction will want an ecclesiastical despotism."[26]

Morality, not egoism, led to tyranny.

As to Kelly's accusation that he (Tak Kak) rejected the "feeling that one should so act as not to injure others," Tak Kak flatly denied it. He merely rejected basing such a sentiment on morality, rather than upon the spontaneity of personal sympathy. As long as it was within human nature to be compassionate, then the egoist who sought to express his own nature would naturally express compassion. Tak Kak suggested that Kelly was, perhaps, crediting morality with inducing good behavior when he should be paying tribute to the inherent egoism of man.

In this argument, Tak Kak echoed the words of Stirner himself, who believed egoism established good will between men. For example, Stirner had written in response to his virulent critic Moses Hess:

> Perhaps at this moment children are running together under his window for a comradeship of play; let him look at them, and he will espy merry egoistic unions. . . . Perhaps he meets a few pleasant acquaintances on the street and is invited to accompany them into a wine-shop; does he go with them in order to do an act of kindness to them, or does he 'unite' with them because he promises himself self-enjoyment from it?[27]

Two issues later, Kelly responded in rather peevish tone. His article opened with the words, "Tak Kak says that language is algebraic . . . but I cannot help entertaining the suspicion that his algebra was learned in the school of that celebrated mathematician who demonstrated that the moon is made of green cheese. Anyway the method of demonstration is the same,—that of using one symbol in two or more senses in the same argument."

With more substance, Kelly fastened on a somewhat vague distinction Tak Kak had drawn between egotism and egoism, and asked for clarification on the terms. It was egotism, as the term was popularly used, against which Kelly rebelled. As for egoism, "I have never pretended that altruism was other than a special form of egoism, taking the latter in its broad sense; I have certainly not advocated the suppression of personality."

Then, in a clever passage that began by apparently conceding Tak Kak's argument, Kelly actually reversed its logic.

> That a man under any given condition will act as to obtain the greatest possible amount of pleasure is almost self-evident, but part of one's pleasure is always due to the good opinion of one's fellows. It is therefore within our power to add to or subtract from the amount of pleasure experienced by anyone. I think that even Tak Kak would not deny that I should be acting normally in disapproving of any action which tends toward producing general unhappiness, even though I myself be sheltered from the consequences of such action. But the moment I begin to approve or disapprove of actions apart from their influence on me, the foundation of a moral code is laid.[28]

Thus, from the starting point of acknowledging the self-evident truth of egoism, Kelly derived the necessity of a moral code which would "add or subtract" from the pleasure anyone might experience from any given act.

As for the argument that egoism was a barrier to despotism, Kelly declared himself unconvinced. For one thing, the egoists fell back upon contracts as the social mechanism through which something akin to "rights" would come about. Yet, at the same moment, the egoists also wished to remove any binding force to the exchange of promises. Without a binding force adhering to the spoken or written word, how could contracts obligate anyone?

Kelly's article ended by returning to his central point:

> In conclusion, I would ask Tak Kak, if egotistically allowable, to complete the two equations following according to his algebra:
>   Egoism =
>   Egotism = [29]

Immediately after these lines, Tucker provided a paragraph of commentary in response to Kelly's repeated appeal for the editor to come forth with a clearly stated position on egoism. The editor had been uncharacteristically silent on this point. Tucker declared himself unwilling to interrupt the flow of a debate of such unusually high caliber by inserting himself. Instead, he wished the exchange to run its natural course. "If, however, Mr. Kelly wishes me to announce my position, I am entirely willing to do so. I believe that egoism is the sole motive of conduct . . . that intelligent egoism is another name for liberty, and that consequently it is the mother of order."[30]

Predictably, Tak Kak swiftly responded to Kelly's demand for clarification. He did so by observing that he had already fully defined egoism some six issues prior in the extensive article entitled "Egoism," and it was not reasonable to demand greater clarity. With regard to Kelly's continuing skepticism as to how contracts would be honored if promises had no moral force, Tak Kak countered with an intriguing passage. He suggested that freeing contracts from morality would make them "become mutually beneficial with appreciable continuity, and by beneficial I mean as well gratifying to the sentiments as to what are popularly appreciated as the material interests of the contracting parties."

The passage is fascinating because, in it, Tak Kak fleetingly hints at one of the core principles that defined much of twentieth-century Individualism and distinguished it from its nineteenth-century roots: that is, the economic principle of subjective value theory. This theory states that individuals value things differently according to their own subjective preferences: that is to say, things have subjective, and not objective, value. When two people willingly exchange goods or services—that is, when they contract—it is because each party subjectively benefits from trade. They get something they want at a price they are willing to pay.

A third party might not consider the trade to be a fair one. For example, he or she might believe ten thousand dollars is far too much to pay for a particular painting. But to the purchaser, the painting is worth ten thousand dollars. The proof of this lies in the fact that he willingly paid that price. Neither evaluation is right or wrong, because each is merely an expression of subjective preferences.

In hinting that egoistic contracts would have to benefit "the sentiments" as well as meet some material criteria, Tak Kak went against the prevailing and almost unquestioned economic theory of the *Liberty* circle. The nineteenth-century Individualist movement in America overwhelmingly accepted an objective theory of value, often expressed as the Warrenite principle "Cost is the Limit of Price." This was a form of the labor theory of value.

Thus, since value had an objective reality, it could be argued that contracts do *not* necessarily benefit each party. Indeed, Tucker believed many of society's contracts fell in the category of theft, for example, contracts involving the payment of interest, which he considered to be usury. After all, according to the labor theory of value, when a man paid a just price for an item, it should be his. Interest charges, which were no part of the labor involved in making the item, were a form of extortion on the same level as taxation.

Nevertheless, Tucker did not advocate prohibiting such contracts, since he believed every man must be free to make a foolish deal. He would have merely denied that a fair contract had occurred because the values exchanged were not objectively equal. Thus, Tak Kak's suggestion that egoistic contracts would appeal to sentiment, or subjective benefits, was a tantalizing glimpse at the ideology of twentieth-century Individualism.

Another such glimpse occurred in the same exchange between Tak Kak and Kelly. It concerned the twentieth-century approach to society perfected by the Austrian economists Friedrich A. Hayek and Ludwig von Mises: namely, methodological individualism. This approach to society—or other collective concepts, such as "government"—was well expressed by Mises in his book *Human Action*: "First we must realize that all actions are performed by individuals. . . . If we scrutinize the meaning of the various actions performed by individuals we must necessarily learn everything about the actions of the collective whole. For a social collective has no existence and reality outside of the individual members' actions."[31]

The egoists surrounding Tucker also insisted that all institutions, including society, were composed of and could be reduced to the interaction of individuals. By contrast, the natural rights advocates appealed to the Spencerian notion of society as an organism whose principles were different from, and perhaps superior to, those that governed individuals. For example, in responding to Tak Kak's claim that the individual was God, Kelly stated, "the evolutionary school . . . into which I hope to have the pleasure of welcoming Tak Kak, holds, and thinks itself able to demonstrate, that society is an organism; that consequently, like all other organisms, it must have special methods of functional activity."[32]

A Schism within *Liberty*

Unfortunately, the possible themes of methodological individualism and subjective value were not developed through counterargument. In his next article, entitled "A Final Statement," Kelly drew the curtain across the exchange of theory by writing, "I suppose I owe the readers of *Liberty* an apology for continuing to occupy space in discussing a subject in regard to which I am told 'everybody' thinks me in the wrong. Well, 'everybody' will soon have a chance to read something else, as, whatever may be the result of the present letter, it will be my last."

After offering Tak Kak mock congratulations on his "ingenuity" in arguing, Kelly made the most telling critique of egoistic contracts to date. "What I contend," he declared as a parting shot, "is that it is impossible to base a society upon contract unless we consider a contract as having some binding effect, and that the binding effect of a contract cannot be the contract itself." In short, rights must predate the concept of contract in order for that concept—an exchange of what is properly mine for what is properly yours—to even make sense.

Much of the remainder of Kelly's article consisted of reprinted excerpts from "De la Justice," a work in which Proudhon—a political thinker much admired by Tucker and Tak Kak—vigorously attacked Stirner. This done, Kelly declared, "I will now step aside, Mr. Editor, and await the glorious results promised as the result of the crusade against morality,—the outburst of enthusiasm and generosity to spring from the preaching of the gospel of selfishness. (By the way, why not use the plain term selfishness instead of egoism?)"[33]

Except for a brief letter to the editor in which Kelly informed Tucker that he would no longer be a distributor of *Liberty*, as in the past, he never again contributed to the periodical.

Tak Kak's rather muted response, entitled "On Mr. Kelly's Final Statement," consisted largely of counterquotations from Proudhon. Perhaps his tone was influenced by "A Letter of Protest" from Gertrude Kelly, which appeared in the same issue. (Tucker seemed to routinely circulate such articles before publication so that contributors could answer each other without a lapse in time occurring.) Her protest ended with the impassioned plea, "My friends, my friends, have you completely lost your heads? Cannot you see that without morality, without the recognition of others' rights, Anarchy, in any other than the vulgar sense, could not last a single day?"[34]

Although Gertrude Kelly did not announce her departure from *Liberty* as her brother had done, she did accuse Tak Kak of dishonesty for writing under a pen name. She accused Tucker of cowardice in allowing Tak Kak to speak in his stead and of unfairness in suppressing material from her brother. Kelly expressed special concern over the conversion to egoism of fellow contributor Victor Yarros, whom she considered "young and enthusiastic." Kelly warned Yarros that he had taken a dangerous and downward path.

The responses she received could not have endeared *Liberty* to the protesting Kelly. Among the comments Tucker appended to her "Letter of Protest" was,

> I conceive that the tone of Miss Kelly's article, when placed in contrast with the dignity and evident self-command which she has shown in almost everything else she has written, is sufficient indication of the weakness of her present position. . . . So far as I know Tak Kak has published nothing over his own name. Where Miss Kelly finds her warrant for the patronizing tone in which she discusses Mr. Yarros is not made plain. . . . Is it possible that her confident assumption of superiority is found solely upon the fact that she is Mr. Yarros's elder—by one year?[35]

In an article on the same page entitled "Miss Kelly,—the Young and the Old," Yarros's reply was more blunt. "My egoism does not prevent me from either feeling or giving expression to deep and sincere regret at the lamentable signs of intellectual feebleness and decline transpiring in Miss Kelly's curious letter."[36] The next issue included two articles by Yarros in support of egoism, one of which criticized John F. Kelly by name.

Other contributors were quick to react to the divisive controversy. Declaring himself to be "afraid" to enter the discussion in earnest, the natural rights theorist J. Wm. Lloyd admitted to having never read Stirner. Thus Lloyd took no solid position, but the conciliatory tone of his piece conveyed the message—let us reason together rather than part ways. On the next page of the same issue, a nonconciliatory letter from Rudolf Weyler disingenuously accused Gertrude Kelly herself of being hired by the enemy, and John Kelly of hiding behind a woman's tears.

Like her brother, Gertrude Kelly ceased to write for *Liberty*: the only further contribution she made was a reprint of a paper, entitled "State Aid to Science," which she had delivered at an earlier date to Women's Medical College of the New York Infirmary. For other reasons, Appleton also soon disappeared from the pages of *Liberty*.[37] With these losses and the defection of Yarros, the natural rights position had a severely weakened representation in future issues of *Liberty*. In particular, the Spencerian influence sharply declined, because both of the Kellys had been major conduits, as well as constructive critics, of Spencer.[38] Not until Victor Yarros—who often functioned as an associate editor of *Liberty* and, next to Tucker, was its most powerful voice—rejected egoism did natural rights become prominent once more.[39]

In the interim, J. M. L. Babcock made an effort to pick up the discussion. He enjoined Yarros in a manner so polite and so flowery in its prose that little theoretical ground was broken. Good will did become strained between them, however, and Babcock retired from the arena, perhaps because Yarros' last reply to him had been entitled simply "Not to Be Continued."

Meanwhile, what would become arguably the most convincing voice for egoism within *Liberty* had entered the fray.[40] John Beverly Robinson wrote a letter to the editor that began,

> It is with fear and trembling that I have resolved to confess myself an Egoist. I trust that my moralist friends will not forthwith cut my acquaintance, but I am afraid that they will. . . . But the strangest thing of all is that, with our totally varying tastes, as it would seem, my moral friends and I lead very much the same kind of lives. I grieve that it should distress them so much to live as I live with a good deal of pleasure, but I honor them for their efforts to imitate what I do solely as a matter of self-indulgence. Perhaps some day they will learn to like it too.[41]

Tucker, who had vowed to stay on the sidelines as long as exchanges of high quality continued, now readily and repeatedly expressed himself. He wrote, "Before contract is the right of might. Contract is the voluntary suspension of the right of might, the power secured by such suspension we may call the right of contract. These two rights—the right of might and the right of contract—are the only rights that ever have been or ever can be. So-called moral rights have no existence."[42]

Although the dispute over egoism erupted in small and relatively mild bursts thereafter, the real debate was over. When Yarros reconverted to Spencerianism (1891), Tucker wrote a column lamenting the fact, but stated adamantly: "This question of rights and obligations was thoroughly threshed out in *Liberty* in the year 1887. . . . I am convinced that nearly everything of value that can be said on the subject was said then, and it is not my intention to renew the controversy in these to any large extent."[43]

As a fire, the debate on egoism v. natural rights had produced more heat than light. It only served to alienate some of the finest minds in the *Liberty* circle from one another and from the periodical. Yarros' return to the Spencerian fold returned a powerful voice for natural rights theory to the pages of *Liberty*. But, on balance, the periodical remained decidedly egoistic.

Perhaps the most frustrating consequence of the natural rights advocates' defection from *Liberty* was the absence of their perspective from ensuing debates. One debate in particular—that on children's rights and how to deal with human beings who could not contract—virtually cried out for a strong natural rights presence.

Postscript

The first English translation of Max Stirner's *Der Einzige und Sein Eigentum* (*The Ego and His Own*) was published by Tucker in 1907. Tucker gave such priority to the work that he decided not to publish the February issue of *Liberty* in order to free more of his time. "Thanks to Mr. Byington, the translator," Tucker wrote, "it is superior to any translation that has appeared in any other language and even to the German original." Tucker's commitment to egoism may be judged by his statement: "I have been engaged for more than 30 years in the propaganda of Anarchism, and have achieved some things of which I am proud; but I feel that I have done nothing for the cause that compares in value with my publication of this illuminating document."[44]

Notes

1. Lysander Spooner, "A Letter to Thomas F. Bayard," *Liberty* 1 (May 27, 1882): 2.

2. Spooner, "A Letter to Thomas F. Bayard," 3.

3. Benjamin R. Tucker, "The Anatomy of Liberty," *Liberty* 1 (August 6, 1881): 2. Emphasis in original.

4. Benjamin R. Tucker, "Liberty the Mother of Order," *Liberty* 1 (October 14, 1882): 2.

5. Benjamin R. Tucker, "The Philosophy of Right and Wrong," *Liberty* 1 (October 29, 1881): 2.

6. J. Wm. Lloyd, "Anarchy and Reform," *Liberty* 3 (September 12, 1885): 7.

7. *The Ego and His Own* was published, in an English translation by Steven T. Byington, in 1907. Before then, much of American egoism was based on the secondary material produced by radicals who read German.

8. Not all readers praised Stirner, of course. Among his critics were Ludwig Feuerback, Moses Hess, Karl Marx, and Friedrich Engels. Marx considered the Stirnerite "self"—a supreme and fundamental selfhood existing independently—to be an absurdity. Marx, who dubbed Stirner "St. Max," believed the "self" existed only as an abstraction derived from the complex interrelationship of "selves" known as society. Marx's critique of Stirner first appeared in *The German Ideology*, Part II, coauthored with Engels.

9. As quoted in Peter Marshall, *Demanding the Impossible: A History of Anarchism,* (London: Harper Collins, 1992), 227.

10. As quoted in Paul Eltzbacher, *Anarchism: Exponents of Anarchist Philosophy,* trans. Steven T. Byington, ed. James J. Martin (Plainview, N.Y.: Books for Libraries Press, 1960), 65.

11. Some ambiguity exists about the spelling of Byington's name. It sometimes appears within *Liberty* as "Steven," and certain secondary sources favor this spelling, but, at other times, *Liberty* lists him as "Stephen." For example, the article "Marriage and Kindred Contracts," *Liberty* 14 (December, 1900): 2-3.

12. *Egoism* (1890-1897), edited by Georgia and Henry Replogle from California, was also a significant vehicle of Stirnerite philosophy. *Egoism* had considerable influence upon Tucker. When Tucker agreed with the natural rights position of J. Greevz Fisher on children, its editor, Henry Replogle (under the pseudonym of "H") rushed to correct him. "'H' very properly takes me to task," Tucker commented in "A Sound Criticism," *Liberty* 11 (June 29, 1895): 3. Tucker changed his position to conform to this criticism. The *Philosophy of Egoism* was eventually published in 1905.

13. Max Stirner, *The Ego and His Own,* trans. Steven Byington (New York: n.p., 1907).

14. Tak Kak, "What Is Justice?" *Liberty* 4 (March 6, 1886): 8.

15. Tak Kak, "Killing Chinese," *Liberty* 4 (March 6, 1886): 8.

16. Tak Kak, "Killing Chinese," 8.

17. Gertrude B. Kelly, "Justice or Force, Which?" *Liberty* 4 (July 3, 1886): 7.

18. Tak Kak, "Selfhood Terminates Blind Man's Buff [sic]," *Liberty* 4 (July 3, 1886): 8.

19. Tak Kak, "Egoism in Sexual Relations," *Liberty* 4 (July 17, 1886): 5.

20. Tak Kak, "The Rational Utilitarian Philosophy," *Liberty* 4 (January 22, 1887): 8.

21. Benjamin R. Tucker, commentary upon "Association as a Means of Reform," *Liberty* 4 (November 20, 1886): 5.

22. In this suggestion, Kelly was clearly wrong. The Stirnerite egoists were no less antigovernment than their natural rights counterparts. They merely constructed Anarchism along different lines. They rejected the State because it sought to chain the individual to the general will. This argument was not a rejection of society, or of its value, which Stirner called "union by advantage." Society provided true and invaluable benefits to the individual, benefits that the State disrupted.

23. John F. Kelly, "Morality and Its Origin," *Liberty* 4 (February 26, 1887): 7.

24. Tak Kak, "Egoism," *Liberty* 4 (April 9, 1887): 5.

25. Tak Kak, "Egoism," 5.

26. Tak Kak, "Egoism," 6.

27. Eltzbacher, *Anarchism,* 70.

28. John F. Kelly, "Intelligent Egotism Anti-Social," *Liberty* 4 (May 7, 1887): 7-8.

29. Kelly, "Intelligent Egotism Anti-Social," 7-8. Kelly's point was well taken. Tak Kak used the word "egoism" alternately to mean "egotism," "enlightened self-interest," and simply acting in pursuit of pleasure (non-pain).

30. Kelly, "Intelligent Egotism Anti-Social," 8. The subtitle of *Liberty* was "Not the Daughter, but the Mother of Order."

31. Ludwig Von Mises, *Human Action* (New Haven, Conn.: Yale University Press, 1949), 42.

32. For Tak Kak's subsequent attacks on the "organism nature of society," see "Must the Ego Count Himself Out?" *Liberty* 8 (November 28, 1891): 4, and "Egoism or Self-Sacrifice?" *Liberty* 8 (February 13, 1892): 2-3.

33. John F. Kelly, "A Final Statement," *Liberty* 4 (July 30, 1887): 7.

34. Gertrude B. Kelly, "A Letter of Protest," *Liberty* 5 (August 13, 1887): 7.

35. Benjamin R. Tucker, comment on "A Letter of Protest," *Liberty* 5 (August 13, 1887): 7.

36. Victor Yarros, "Miss Kelly—the Young and the Old," *Liberty* 5 (August 13, 1887): 7.

37. James J. Martin observes, "Appleton later wrote for the *Alarm,* while the Kellys and Lazarus went over to a short-lived Anarchist journal, *Nemesis,* later joining Appleton." *Men Against the State: The Expositors of Individualist Anarchism in America, 1827-1908* (Colorado Springs, Colo.: Ralph Myles, 1970), 252.

38. Tucker's active dislike for Spencer dated from one event. The editor had greatly admired "The Right to Ignore the State," a chapter in Spencer's classic work on society *Social Statics.* When Spencer deleted that chapter from subsequent revised editions of his work, Tucker reprinted it as a pamphlet (1892), complete with a preface unflattering to the author.

39. Yarros came to view egoism as "monstrously absurd and miserably nonsensical." For Tucker's response see "Obligation? To Whom? To What?"*Liberty* 8 (September 26, 1891): 2-3.

40. John Beverly Robinson provided what is arguably the best statement of philosophical egoism as it related to Anarchism in "The Limits of Governmental Interference," *Liberty* 8 (August 15, 1891): 3-4.

41. John Beverly Robinson, "A Villain Unmasks," *Liberty* 5 (October 8, 1887): 6.

42. *Liberty* 9 (March 4, 1893): 3.

43. Tucker, "Obligation? To Whom? To What?": 2. Although Tucker claimed "my purpose is not to reproach Mr. Yarros" or "to disturb his peace of mind with unpleasant recollections," he reprinted an article entitled "The Reasons Why?" in which Yarros had flamboyantly announced his conversion to egoism years before. Directly following this article was another piece by Yarros—a defense of Spencer and rights. Thus, Tucker arranged the articles so that Yarros seemed to be refuting himself.

44. Benjamin R. Tucker, "On Picket Duty," *Liberty* 16 (April 1907): 1.

Chapter 5

Children's Rights

The debate within *Liberty* over the proper treatment of children under Anarchism was virtually a continuation of its prior discussion of philosophical egoism.

The key question around which issues of children's "rights" and parental responsibility revolved was "What obligation, if any, does a parent (or a third party) have toward an infant who is too young to form contracts?" After all, according to philosophical egoism, rights and obligations arose only from the act of contracting. In the absence of contracts, no one had a rightful claim against anyone else in society, not even the claim to be left unmolested by others. What legal status would such an Anarchist society assign to infants who were unable to contract?

Liberty's Background on Children

Nineteenth-century social reformers often viewed the status of children as "a woman's question." The circle of radicals surrounding *Liberty* seemed to be less influenced by "women's questions" than were many other Individualists of their day. For example, Moses Harman's periodical, *Lucifer, the Light Bearer*—arguably the most prominent vehicle of the free love movement—discussed the treatment and status of children as a natural and necessary extension of its concern for women's questions, such as motherhood and birth control.

By contrast, *Liberty*'s primary focus remained firmly upon economic and labor reform, and it displayed only secondary interest in "sexual issues" such as what constituted "proper" marital or family relations. Indeed, over the years Tucker grew increasingly critical of those who championed controversial sexual issues. He believed such advocacy might hinder progress in the far more important areas of labor and monetary reform.

At the beginning of *Liberty*'s career (1881), Tucker's stand on becoming involved in sexual controversy had been less rigid. In 1882, Tucker had taunted the Boston post office by offering Walt Whitman's book of poetry entitled *Leaves of Grass* for sale through the mail, even though part of it had been declared obscene and, thus, unmailable by the Boston postal authority.[1] The main offending passage was a poem on prostitution. Nevertheless, the younger Tucker felt compelled to enter the fray rather than remain on the sidelines.

By 1890, however, Tucker refused to support the publisher of *Lucifer, the Light Bearer* in the blatant legal persecution that followed Harman's publication of "the O'Neill letter." Written by a medical doctor, the O'Neill letter described an incident of marital rape and passionately called for society to cease tolerating such legal assault under the guise of "a husband's conjugal right." Tucker presented a counter argument, not to the substance of O'Neill's letter, but to the strategic wisdom of adopting a sexually explosive issue as a cause:[2]

> Economic liberty is the only road to that sexual liberty, sexual health, and healthy sexuality which Harman claims to be striving after for society.
>
> As much freedom of discussion as we now enjoy is necessary to the achievement of economic liberty.
>
> This freedom is likely to be abridged by any *unsuccessful* direct effort to extend it, especially in a direction where it must encounter the most deeply-rooted prejudice that now afflicts humanity,—the sexual prejudice.[3]

Despite vigorous criticism from contributors to *Liberty*, such as James L. Walker, Tucker refused to mitigate his staunch opposition to becoming involved in any controversial or secondary cause that might damage labor reform. Under the circumstances it was not surprising that the debate over children's rights—or their lack thereof—arose almost accidentally, and continued only because it related directly back to a point of central dispute within philosophical egoism: namely, what is the status of those who cannot contract in a society based on contract?

Yet at least one of Tucker's mentors, the pioneering Josiah Warren, was well known for his strong and novel stand on the status of children.[4] He advocated making children both responsible for their own needs and capable of satisfying them at the earliest possible age. Indeed, in his household, Warren's own children contracted to exchange their labor in return for the food and the other necessities with which he provided them.[5]

In his book *Equitable Commerce*, Warren described approaching his daughter when she was "between seven and eight years old" with an economic question. After describing the many goods, including food and clothing, which she consumed, Warren asked the girl, "How much should you properly do for us for what you receive?" When his daughter was unable to answer, Warren—who owned a store—proposed: "Well, then, I will tell you what I have thought; that I would as soon buy and sell goods an hour as to wash dishes an hour; so if you will wash as many dishes as I or your mother would wash in an hour, I should consider that you had paid us for an hour of our labor."[6]

Warren claimed that his daughter "comprehended me and seemed to feel the justice of her position."[7]

The free love advocate Stephen Pearl Andrews, a contributor to *Liberty*, also acknowledged the extreme influence of Warren upon the issue of children: "the world will yet gladly confess its indebtedness, to the genius of Josiah Warren, of Indiana, who has been engaged for more than twenty years in testing, almost in solitude, the practical operation, in the education of children."[8]

But in championing Warren's Proudhonian views on economics, Tucker seemed determined to push away many of the social concerns that lent a more compassionate tone to his mentor's voice. Tucker's rather biting manner of discussing issues and his commitment to following "the plumb-line" of his logic, wherever that might take him, prompted more than one person to accuse him of being inhumane. Indeed, such accusations would never be more prevalent than when the venerable editor finally addressed himself to the status of children.

Perhaps the somewhat inhumane and cerebral tone of the eventual debate on the status of children under Anarchy accounts for one of the most remarkable features of that debate—women did not contribute a major voice to the core exchange on a topic usually considered to be of special interest to women.[9] The debate was sadly impoverished by their absence, because many of the male contributors displayed remarkable ignorance concerning the realities surrounding childbearing and children.

For example, Victor Yarros—writing under the name "Victor"—penned an article entitled "The Woman Question" in which he sketched what he considered to be the ideal relationship between man and woman.

"Women, in the first place, are the slaves of capital," Victor's argument began. Women also felt the social brunt of their sexual desires more keenly than men: "While man's part in the relation is pleasurable throughout, woman purchases her enjoyment at an enormous price." That price was the birth of a child, which placed the mother at a great disadvantage in providing for herself and her offspring. When "the equality of powers for self-support vanish," Victor claimed "all other equalities" were destroyed as well. Thus, the sexual impulse mixed with the oppression of capitalism, all to the detriment of woman.[10]

Instead of advocating the solution of fewer children, however, Victor suggested what he termed "independent homes." The man should "'make a home' for the woman he loves," providing the "means," while she educates the children and surrounds him with comfort.[11]

The subsequent issue of *Liberty* carried a fascinating and lengthy response from Zelm—the pen name of Sarah Holmes, an intimate of Tucker's—entitled "A Reply to Victor," in which she observed:

[O]n his [Victor's] theory of life . . . every Apollo will find his Venus before she is older than twenty-five. She has twenty years of child-bearing possibilities before her, and the simple gratification of by no means abnormal sexual impulses might result in her giving birth to ten children. And yet his plan involves that, during this time, when, he asserts, she "needs the care, support, and service of others and is therefore unable to support herself," she is nevertheless "educating the children and surrounding her lover with comfort"![12]

Zelm proceeded to enunciate some of the harsh implications that Victor's ideal relationship between the sexes had for women. But, in reference to children, the exchange between Zelm and Victor involved only the economic and social impact that childbearing had upon women.

The Debate Is Foreshadowed through the Women

The subject of children had arisen briefly in several forms within the pages of *Liberty* before the debate on children's rights erupted. For example, *Liberty* reprinted an exchange between Henry James, Horace Greeley, and Stephen Pearl Andrews, entitled *Love, Marriage and Divorce,* which discussed how a stable marriage related to the maintenance of offspring.

Moreover, the article by Zelm, which took Victor to task, hinted at tantalizing threads of discussion that were not subsequently woven into real arguments. For example, Zelm sketched a feminist argument for the day care of infants by unrelated third parties. Cognizant of how most members of society would be appalled by mothers voluntarily "abandoning" their children in order to work, Zelm preemptively defended herself:

"A true mother will never leave a young child, they will say. But I am almost certain that every mother who is thoroughly honest with herself will admit that it would have been better, both for herself and her child, if she could have left him in safe hands for a few hours each day."[13]

Unfortunately, Zelm's budding argument for day care centers was ignored in A. Warren's ensuing protest entitled "The Rights of Babies," which was offered in a well-intentioned manner. Warren picked up on an unrelated but more fundamental issue that had been raised by Zelm: the need to protectively control a child who had not achieved the age of reason and, thus, was unable to shield itself from dangers, such as a hot stove. In a patronizing tone, Warren complimented Zelm on the "sensitivity" which caused her to overlook the rights of children. "Her soul went out to the mother only." Warren explained Zelm's oversight. "I am sure that, when she comes to turn her attention to this branch of the subject, she will agree with me."

The point on which Warren expected Zelm to express agreement was as follows, "I do not deny the *right* of the mother to control her child . . . but it is not *her exclusive right.* It belongs to the father also, and to everyone else. The right to control children is not different from that to control adults. It is not derived from motherhood or fatherhood."[14]

Zelm offered an immediate—though rather unresponsive—reply, which was followed by a thoughtful article several issues later. There, with a diplomacy rare to the pages of *Liberty*, Zelm confessed "my own words express my thoughts so clumsily, it may easily be that theirs [her critics'] have at least in some degree failed also in revealing their own conceptions. That is, we may have mistaken each other." She graciously refused to consider another argument advanced by J. Wm. Lloyd to the effect that the child be required "to pay for its life." She preferred to believe that "Mr. Lloyd was dreaming of a glorious anarchical future."[15]

Sadly, it may have been Zelm's civility and tentativeness that doomed this seed of debate to never flower. Confrontations within *Liberty* seemed to require thick skins and a confidence bordering on ideological arrogance. Other women fared no better in their attempts to discuss children's rights.[16]

Subsequent to Zelm's foray, Clara Dixon Davidson, editor of the short-lived periodical *L'Enfant Terrible*, broached the issue anew in a *Liberty* article entitled "Relations Between Parents and Children." Davidson returned to the key question: what of infants who are too young to care for themselves? "Who shall decide upon the permissible degree of freedom?" she asked. "Who shall adjust the child's freedom to its safety so that the two shall be delicately, flawlessly balanced?" With an argument foreshadowing the debate that would erupt some hundred issues thereafter, Davidson contended that parents had no inherent or legal duty to support their children. Their only duty was to not aggress against them.

Abiding strictly by the principle of equal liberty, Davidson reasoned,

> While a cursory glance at the subject may seem to show a denial of equal freedom in the refusal of a parent to support his child, a more careful study will reveal the truth that, so long as he does not hinder the activities of any one nor compel any other person or persons to undertake the task which he has relinquished, he cannot be said to violate the law of equal freedom. Therefore, his associates may not compel him to provide for his child, though they may forcibly prevent him from aggressing upon it.[17]

Tucker declared the issue in which Davidson's article appeared to be "devoted to" the question of the status of the child under Anarchy. Announcing that Davidson's article had lain unopened in an envelope "for several months," he confessed to being "delighted to find that a woman had written such a bold, unprejudiced, unsentimental, and altogether rational essay on a subject which women are especially prone to treat emotionally." In the next breath, however, Tucker pushed the issue of children's rights into the background of Anarchism by observing, "In one view the question of the status of the child under Anarchy is a trivial one" whose chief value lay "in the light which it throws on the matter of equal freedom."[18] The concluding words of his article in the same issue, "Children Under Anarchy," restated the egoist position that rights resulted from contract, not from nature.

The issue of *Liberty* that Tucker declared "devoted to children" occasioned little comment in subsequent issues. Lillian Harman's piece questioning the legal age of consent also sparked little controversy.[19] Even a well-reasoned article by Mona Caird, entitled "Ideal Marriage," did not prompt open debate. In this piece Caird argued that mothers have a superior "claim" over their offspring: that is, superior to the father who, in turn, had a superior claim over any third party:

> [O]ver and above . . . unpaid labor, the wife has borne and reared the children, and from the very nature of the case has therefore a superior claim. An uncle or a friend might work for the children far harder than the father ever works, but he could not by that means assume rightful authority to direct their career, although the parents would naturally take the benefactor into their counsels. The mother's right rests upon her unique relationship to the child. . . . The breadwinner, of course, has a strong claim to be consulted.[20]

Other than a brief flurry of responses to Zelm's "A Reply to Victor," the contributions from women stirred little interest.

In short, although it was the women of *Liberty* who originally broached the subject of the status and treatment of children under Anarchy, the real exchange arose independent of their efforts. It was conducted by—or, perhaps more accurately, abandoned to—the men.

The Debate Appears

Liberty's debate over children's rights began almost accidentally on May 4, 1895, with the publication of excerpts from an article by the British Individualist and natural rights advocate J. Greevz Fisher, whom Tucker admired. Fisher's original piece had been published in the April issue of the London periodical *Personal Rights*, dated March 15th. Fisher argued along the same natural rights lines as Clara Dixon Davidson had. Accordingly, he maintained that parents could not be legally compelled to care for an infant offspring. The sole justification for invading the liberty of a person was to prevent him or her from molesting a third party, not to compel him or her to render assistance to a third party.

Although Fisher morally decried the act of neglecting an offspring, he emphasized, "Neglect is not attack. It is unsafe for an Individualist to avow a duty to punish neglect."[21] In other words, however an Individualist might emotionally or morally view the neglect of a child, he could not say that the child's rights had been violated thereby, for to say this would introduce a principle antagonistic to Individualism. It would be tantamount to saying that *not* acting to maintain another's life was legally equivalent to aggressing against him or her.

The application of this Individualist principle had a flip side. If parents had no inherent obligations to the child, neither could they claim any inherent right of control over the infant. Fisher continued with the speculation:

> If a person . . . alleging parentage, beats, enslaves, or defrauds a child, the Individualist has a perfect right to interfere. He can voluntarily associate himself

with the child in a mutual defence organization and may undoubtedly assume acquiescence by the child. No title to guardianship by a claimant parent ought to be admitted when the alleged guardianship is inimical to the minor. . . . Beyond this point it is unsafe to take one step.

If a parent abused a child, any third party could enter the situation and assume the guardianship. But legal action could not properly be taken against the parent who was merely neglectful: "We must not interfere to prevent neglect, but only to repress positive invasion." Fisher added, "Neglect can be better remedied by upholding liberty for anyone directly to supply the wants of the neglected. It cannot be safely dealt with by a third party to force someone, supposed to be responsible, to undertake the duty."[22] The best way to protect a neglected child was to maintain the right of third parties to assume care of the child, even over the parents' objections.

Tucker prefaced the reprinted excerpts from Fisher with a note stating that, although the two of them disagreed on monetary issues, he was pleased to endorse his colleague's position on "the question of parental responsibility for the support of children." Tucker was soon taken to task for his endorsement by other colleagues who had adopted Stirnerite egoism—a philosophy Tucker was supposed to share. If rights and obligations derived solely from contract, they demanded that Tucker explain to them where a third party acquires any right to interfere in a child-parent relationship. Where was the contract? Who was it between?

Tucker was made most sharply aware of his transgression of egoist principle by Henry Replogle, who often wrote under the pseudonym "H." Tucker duly acknowledged what he called H's "Sound Criticism." "In the latest issue of Egoism . . . H. very properly takes me to task editorially for my wholesale endorsement . . . of J. Greevz Fisher regarding the relation of parents to their children, and of outsiders to both." Tucker reiterated his belief in the "legal nonresponsibility of parents for the support of their children," but he admitted error in not having jumped upon another aspect of Fisher's argument. Namely, Fisher's contention that "No title to guardianship by a claimant parent ought to be admitted when the alleged guardianship is inimical to the minor."

Tucker hastened to concede H's point that a parent's prior claim to an offspring was "too obviously a proper thing" to admit of "a superior right of the community . . . even in the interest of those who suffer from parental abuse."[23]

Remaining consistent, Tucker maintained that infants who were too young to contract were absolutely without rights. He wrote, "the material with which the sociologist deals may be divided into two classes,—owners and owned." For philosophical egoists, the factor that allowed one to be an owner was solely the ability to contract. The factor that made something, or someone, property was the inability to contract.

Tucker expanded on this theme, "Now, under this classification the child presents a difficulty; for, while unquestionably belonging in the category of the owned, he differs from all other parts of that category in the fact that there is steadily developing within him the power of self-emancipation."[24] In other words, children were a form of property that had an expiration date. The ownership of the child expired the moment he or she was able to contract and, thus, to become an owner in his or her own right. Until the point of the child's emancipation, however, Tucker considered the only question to be whether the parents or the community owned the infant. Since the parents had produced the child, Tucker supported the parental claim.

The castigating editorial by "H" in *Egoism*, with which a repentant Tucker hastened to agree, had stated that the community must allow parents "to beat their children to all but death or permanent disablement." Tucker had not quoted this portion of the editorial within his own periodical but some subscribers to *Liberty* obviously read Replogle's publication as well. One of them was British John Badcock Jr., whose dissenting letter appeared in the August 10th issue of *Liberty* and had apparently been written before he had read Tucker's article agreeing with "H."

Badcock argued that "sentiency," and not merely the act of contracting, distinguished human beings from objects to be owned. He claimed, "it is suffering that is the prime mover for all ameliorating libertarian propaganda," and "if our liberty principles cannot be extended so as to shield the child and the animal, then they fall short of our requirements—the requirements of the sympathetic—and must be re-cast."[25]

In the same issue, Tucker responded to Badcock. While acknowledging that his friend would be horrified "to find me joining the enemy, bag and baggage," Tucker refused to budge an ideological inch: children who could not contract were "on a par with property." A world in which children were beaten was, admittedly, not a perfect one, but Tucker believed "Mr. Badcock and I have to put up with the best system we can devise, even though it does fall short of our sympathetic requirements."[26] He invited debate on the issue of children as property.

Debate swiftly ensued. Tucker's fellow egoist Steven Byington took up the challenge and argued that even a baby owns himself or herself by virtue of having a will of his or her own. In the absence of that condition, he questioned why it was better for a child to be owned by his or her parents, rather than by the community.

A Scot subscriber, William Gilmour, quoted Tucker to himself, noting that the editor was contradicting statements published in his work *Instead of a Book*. From page 135 of that work, Gilmour quoted Tucker's response to a question: "[I]n answer to the question: 'If a parent starves, tortures, or mutilates his child, thus actively aggressing upon it to its injury, is it just for other members of the group to interfere to prevent such aggression?' you said: 'If, instead of Is it just? he (the questioner) should ask, Is it Anarchist policy? I would make reply as follows: Yes.'"[27]

Also from across the Atlantic, Fisher reentered the fray with the observation that, if the child was "owned," nothing should prevent the parent from disposing of his or her property by killing the child.[28] Yet "H" had indicated that parents could beat their children to "all but death." Tucker himself had hesitated at acknowledging that infants could be killed by their parents.

He hesitated no longer. In a notorious article entitled "L'Enfant Terrible," Tucker commented gleefully on the "rumpus" he had stirred up. It was evidence, he declared, that "the child is likely to prove a very troublesome member of the Anarchistic family, especially in Queen Victoria's realm [England], whence most of the criticism has thus far come."[29]

To Byington's argument that children were self-owners because they had an independent will, Tucker replied, "Animals have wills and can make their volitions known, but they do not thereby become owners, and members of society." As to the accusation that he maintained it was better for the parents to own a child rather than the community, Tucker declared himself misinterpreted. True, he stood by the superior claim of the parent, but not because it was "better" for the child. Tucker argued, "I do not believe that it is better that children should be owned by their parents than by the community in any other sense than that in which I believe that it is better that potatoes should be owned by their producers than by the community."

In response to Gilmour's discovery of an apparent contradiction, Tucker maintained:

> If I had previously held that parental cruelty is indubitable invasion and therefore to be prohibited, my present argument would indeed show a complete revolution in my opinion on this subject. But Mr. Gilmour will find, on re-reading the articles from which he quotes certain sentences, that I explicitly stated therein that I considered it a matter of doubt whether parental cruelty is invasive, and that I justified interference with it in extreme cases only on the ground of that necessity which arises in the face of disaster immediately impending. The change, then, which my opinion has undergone consists simply in the substitution of certainty for doubt as to the non-invasive character of parental cruelty.[30]

Turning to Fisher's argument that, if the child is the property of the parent then the parent should be able to dispose of him or her absolutely, not merely to "all but death," Tucker seemed to acknowledge the point, and to restrict the right of disposal to the mother. He wrote, "Certainly the mother's title to the child while it remains in her womb will not be denied by any Anarchist. To deny this would be to deny the right to the mother to commit suicide during pregnancy, and I never knew an Anarchist to deny the right of suicide." If the pregnant mother could kill the developing infant by killing herself, then she could dispose of the infant in her arms "as freely as she may dispose of any other property belonging to her."[31]

Perhaps anticipating the backlash, Tucker prudently insisted, "I have the welfare of children as sincerely at heart as any of my critics, and that I believe that an observation of the principles here formulated would secure to children, on the whole, greater happiness than they have ever enjoyed, or than they ever can enjoy in any society neglectful of these principles."[32] Tucker believed that by making children the property of the parents, or mother, he was actually protecting them against aggression at large, for such aggression would be a violation of the parents' property rights, which society recognized and protected.

Predictably, one of the first questions asked of Tucker was whether he would stand by and let "a woman throw her baby into the fire as a man throws his newspaper." Tucker answered, "it is highly probable that I would personally interfere in such a case. But it is as probable, and perhaps more so, that I would personally interfere to prevent the owner of a masterpiece by Titian from applying the torch to the canvas. . . . If I interfere in either case, I am an invader, . . . And as such I deserve to be punished. . . . On my arraignment I should plead guilty."[33]

In other words, an emotional sense of horror might have impelled Tucker to save the child from immolation but, in doing so, he would have acknowledged that he was violating the mother's property rights. The mother would have had a right to take recourse against him and/or demand compensation.

The subsequent issue of *Liberty* revolved around the alleged "right" to kill a child. Tucker professed surprise at the extreme reactions his answer had provoked, and he declared Byington to be almost the only correspondent to "have preserved his equanimity and to be willing to discuss the matter on a purely rational basis, without insinuation or apparent suspicion that I was no longer possessed of the most ordinary instincts of humanity." Tucker, who later became a doting father, seemed truly disturbed by accusations of indifference to the pain of children.[34]

The only other correspondent he declared to have "equanimity" was the natural rights advocate J. Wm. Lloyd, who was astute enough to correctly judge Tucker's position as being the inevitable outcome of accepting philosophical egoism. Lloyd argued that as long as one looked upon contract as the only basis of rights, then Tucker's statements were unassailable. "I do not accept contract as the ethical basis of Anarchism in the first place, and, in the second, do not regard children as the property of anybody. . . . The parent has the right of defensive control over the child, and no other."

Lloyd dismissed the idea of property with an expiration date as "absurd." "My property is mine," he declared, "*always mine*."[35] In this, Lloyd was pointing out that either you own something or you don't. The idea of something being fully yours one day, and not at all yours the next, contradicted the entire basis of ownership.[36]

Indeed, the idea of "temporary ownership" seemed to support rather than contradict the early claims of Fisher who had introduced an important term into the discussion: trusteeship. Fisher had written: "during the whole period of control, the parent is not an owner at all, but, if legal jargon can solve a sociological question, a *trustee*."[37] Gilmour's letter to the editor had supported this view, "Further, I cannot . . . agree . . . 'the only question is: Who shall own him—the parent or the community?' and for the reason that I think that *guardianship, not ownership*, is the real question at issue."[38]

Lloyd correctly identified the issue as being larger than children's rights. Did *anyone* who could not contract have any rights? What of people in a coma or those who were mentally deficient? This question was the true battleground and became a direct continuation of the natural rights v. egoism debate, alas without the presence of the best of the natural rights advocates.[39]

Confronted with accusations of inhumanity from such fellow travelers as Badcock, who declared Tucker's arguments to be "obnoxious" and against human instincts, Tucker rallied in spirit. "The question," he declared, "is not whether the editor of *Liberty* is sensitive or callous, courageous or cowardly, man or demon, but whether a mother is the rightful owner of her infant child, and as such may do with it as she will; and I must ask my critics to confine themselves to the question."

In a three-page article entitled "What Is Property?" Tucker vigorously defended his position not only on children, but also on contract as the only source of rights. Stating the Stirnerite underpinnings of his stance, Tucker wrote, "[If] might is the measure of right everywhere and always, until, by contract, each contracting party voluntarily agrees to measure his right thenceforth, not by his might, but by the equal liberty of those whom he has contracted to protect, then my position is invulnerable."[40]

In answer to Lloyd's most compelling criticism—"My property is mine, *always mine*"—Tucker answered in a manner reminiscent of his rejoinder to Fisher in "L'Enfant Terrible,"

[N]o Anarchist will deny a mother's right to commit suicide during pregnancy. To admit this is to declare her the owner of the child in her womb. But, according to Mr. Matter and Mr. Lloyd, if the child is once her property, then it is always her property,—a conclusion which carries these gentlemen further than I ask them to go. All these considerations combine to expose the ridiculous weakness of the reasoning that, if a child is once property, it must be property as long as it lives.[41]

The question posed by A. S. Matter, in a letter to the editor, concerned the process by which the child would be emancipated—that is, when and how was a child's ability to contract to be recognized. Tucker explained that one might as well ask "at what age or condition a child may buy or sell a house. The age varies according to precocity. The matter is one for the jury in any given case of complaint."[42]

With highly developed editorial instincts, Tucker clearly sensed that the arguments were running ideologically dry. Unlike the natural rights v. egoism debate, however, the exchange on the status of children had no clear resolution, although it had a definite end.

Discussion Deteriorates into Silence

Aside from the advertisements it carried, the last words of the September 21st issue of *Liberty* were those of Tucker, who had been apparently experiencing a deluge of articles and letters. "I must ask my critics to refrain from writing further until my next article has appeared."[43]

The promised article appeared in the next issue and constituted a reply to Badcock on the question of "the determination of the prime motive that prompts defensive association." Badcock has argued for human "sympathy" as the prime motive, whereas Tucker argued egoistically for "the protection of self." Indeed, Tucker quoted Badcock's own words from his pamphlet *Slaves to Duty* which supported the self-defense argument.[44]

As Byington and Tucker went on to explore the subtleties of defensive associations, the debate took a souring turn with Lloyd announcing that—in consequence of the debate on the status of children—he could no longer call himself an Anarchist but would adopt the label of Free Socialist instead. Lloyd considered Tucker to be "my chief leader and teacher," to be "the accredited head of that philosophy [Anarchism]." If Tucker stated "that an Anarchist has a right to invade, that might is the measure of right everywhere and always, that slavery in Anarchy is a necessity and children, fools, and non-contracting individuals the fit subjects of such slavery," Lloyd declared himself willing to believe him. But, as a result of such belief, he could no share the same ideological name as Tucker.[45]

The editor's response hardly ameliorated the conflict. He wrote, "Mr. Lloyd, though denying property in babies, evidently believes in property in Anarchism. He regards me as the owner. . . . I am not the owner of Anarchism. . . . I can interpret it only for myself." This reasonable statement was quickly followed by the accusation—grounded or not—that Lloyd expected his rebellion to cause a wide scale defection of the "real" Anarchists from *Liberty*. Against this perceived threat, Tucker declared himself prepared to continue publishing *Liberty* by himself. He concluded, "My tired friend Lloyd may brand me 'an enemy of the people'; I spit upon 'the compact majority,' and 'stand alone, the strongest man.' He may 'decree' my death; I will 'demonstrate' that I am just beginning to live."[46]

Meanwhile, a refreshingly civil letter from Badcock in the same issue offered Tucker a sincere apology for any offense that he might have given. The debate had deteriorated into a clash of personalities. Tucker wrote a second piece on the status of children which was meant to address only Lloyd's arguments, not his motives. Nevertheless, Tucker could not resist making derogatory comments such as, "Your [Lloyd's] mind is one that accepts with very little evidence that which it wishes to believe. Mine is more exacting."[47]

After another exchange that bordered on outright viciousness, Lloyd seemed content to drop the issue of the treatment of children under Anarchy, as did Tucker. Other than a whimsical piece by Byington, *Liberty* basically moved on to other matters.

Notes

1. Tucker's championship of *The Leaves of Grass* occurred during the summer of 1882, approximately a year after the periodical's appearance. Tucker noted that Boston booksellers had been intimidated into taking this work off their shelves and hoped to ignite a spark of courage in them.

2. For a more extensive discussion of Tucker strategic vision, see chapter 3, "On Violence."

3. Benjamin R. Tucker, "Shoot Folly as it Flies," *Liberty* 7 (May 24, 1890): 6. Emphasis in original.

4. For an account of the arrangement, see Josiah Warren, *Equitable Commerce* (New Harmony, Ind.: n.p., 1846), 79-81, or James J. Martin, *Men Against the State* (Colorado Springs, Colo.: Ralph Myles, 1970), 35.

5. On a personal level, Tucker adopted the Warrenite approach to children. His only child, Oriole, later wrote, "Father, incidentally, believed in contracts. We had written contractual arrangements around the house. When I was eighteen, he wrote a whole contract about my paying a share of what I made from giving piano lessons. That might seem cold and calculating, yet it made everything clear and simple." Quoted in Paul Avrich, *Anarchist Portraits* (Princeton, N.J.: Princeton University Press, 1988), 151.

6. As quoted in Leonard I. Krimerman and Lewis Perry, eds., *Patterns of Anarchy* (New York: Doubleday-Anchor Books, 1966), 446.

7. Krimerman and Perry, *Patterns of Anarchy,* 447.

8. "The Science of Society: Part First. The true Constitution of Government" as reprinted in *Liberty* 4 (October 30, 1886): 6. Warren was acknowledged in Andrew's *Love, Marriage, and Divorce* as well, where he referred to his mentor as "the Euclid of social science."

9. Although an article by Lillian Harman entitled "An 'Age-of-Consent' Symposium" appeared during the exchange, it had no real bearing on the debate. Given the controversial nature of Harman's article, Tucker prefaced it with a rare—though predictable—disclaimer: "The appearance in the editorial column of articles over other signatures than the editor's initial indicates that the editor approves their central purpose and general tenor, though he does not hold himself responsible for every phrase or word." *Liberty* 10 (February 9, 1895): 1.

10. "Victor" [Victor Yarros], "The Woman Question," *Liberty* 5 (May 12, 1888): 6.

11. Yarros, "The Woman Question," 7.

12. Zelm [Sarah Holmes], "A Reply to Victor," *Liberty* 5 (May 26, 1888): 6.

13. Zelm, "A Reply to Victor," 6.

14. A. Warren, "The Rights of Babies," *Liberty* 5 (June 23, 1888): 7. Emphasis in the original.

15. Zelm [Sarah Holmes], "The Problem Which the Child Presents," *Liberty* 6 (September 1, 1888): 7.

16. Nor was their treatment within *Liberty* quite fair, as Tucker himself acknowledged. After Zelm's "A Reply to Victor," for instance, yet another piece by "Victor" appeared, responding specifically to Zelm's arguments. Tucker admitted the unfairness of

this in a note appended to Victor's second piece, "Individualism, Communism, and Love," *Liberty* 6 (September 15, 1888): 7-8:

> It was agreed between Victor and Zelm, in accordance with a proposal made by Victor himself, that he should write a statement of his views of the subject in question, and submit it in manuscript to Zelm; that she should then write a statement of her views as a contrast to his, and in turn submit it to him; that he should then revise his manuscript in the light of hers . . . that she then should have a similar privilege; and so on, until each should be content to let his or her statement finally stand for comparison with the other's. . . . The original articles were to end the matter between Victor and Zelm . . . [The arrangement's] purpose was to save *Liberty*'s space and to avoid controversy, to which Zelm is averse. She would not have entered into the arrangement on any other terms.

17. Clara Dixon Davidson, "Relations Between Parents and Children," *Liberty* 9 (September 3, 1892): 3.

18. Benjamin R. Tucker, "Children Under Anarchy," *Liberty* 9 (September 3, 1892): 2.

19. The circle around *Lucifer, the Light Bearer*—which included Lillian Harman—generally took a different tack on children's rights, preferring to acknowledge the sovereignty of the child. Lillie White, who edited the periodical for a short period said: "there is no person living more competent to decide the matter of association than the child itself. A fair acquaintance with both parents, freedom of choice, liberty to come and go, to visit or stay, will always be found, most convenient and effective in adjusting these relations."

20. Mona Caird, "Ideal Marriage," *Liberty* 7 (January 19, 1889): 7.

21. J. Greevz Fisher, as quoted in Benjamin R. Tucker, "Anarchism and the Children," *Liberty* 10 (May 4, 1895): 5.

22. J. Greevz Fisher, as quoted in Tucker, "Anarchism and the Children," 5. Within the originating issue of *Personal Rights*, the editor J. H. Levy had appended his reservations regarding Fisher's position. In essence, he claimed Fisher was expressing the Anarchistic, and not the Individualistic, view. "If a parent beats his (or her) child, we may constitute ourselves and the child a 'mutual defence organization, and may undoubtedly assume acquiescence by the child.' But if parent leaves his (or her) child to starve, we may *not* join in the defence of this and other children, and may not entertain the question of the child's acquiescence. If this were Individualism, the distinction between it and Anarchism would be merely verbal." This might well be an unsympathetic and inaccurate read of Fisher's position.

23. Years earlier, Tucker had made a somewhat similar comment in response to a question from "F. F. K." (Florence Finch Kelly). He wrote, "in regard to the control of the child I . . . anticipate a general recognition, in the absence of contract, of the mother's superior claim, and a refusal on the part of defensive associations to protect any other claim than hers in cases of dispute not guarded against by specific contract." "Not a Dream, But a Prophecy," *Liberty* 5 (April 28, 1888): 5.

24. Benjamin R. Tucker, "A Sound Criticism," *Liberty* 11 (June 29, 1895): 3.

25. John Badcock, Jr., "The Life More than the Creed," *Liberty* 11 (August 10, 1895): 8.

26. Benjamin R. Tucker, "The Creed Essential to Life," *Liberty* 11 (August 10, 1895): 4-5.

27. William Gilmour, "An Apparent Contradiction," *Liberty* 11 (August 24, 1895): 7.

28. The British Individualists, such as Fisher and Gilmour, who had not been deeply involved in the former debate on egoism v. natural rights, conducted the argument in a different manner than the American correspondents. They tended to simply say that Tucker was wrong, that human beings have rights and proceeded from that point.

29. The strongest pens opposing Tucker's position on children wrote from Britain, perhaps because many of the American natural rights advocates had been alienated from *Liberty* by the prior debate over egoism. Also, *Liberty* had treated the American individualist feminists with such disrespect, they may not have cared to participate.

The British opponents were at a decided disadvantage because they were not versed in the arguments of philosophical egoism, and assumed Tucker adopted his position out of expediency. To some degree—because the debate over children rested on the prior one over egoism—the British missed the point of Tucker's arguments.

30. Benjamin R. Tucker, "On Picket Duty," *Liberty* 11 (September 7, 1895): 1.

31. Benjamin R. Tucker, "L'Enfant Terrible," *Liberty* 11 (August 24, 1895): 4.

32. Tucker, "L'Enfant Terrible," 5.

33. Tucker, "On Picket Duty," 1.

34. Tucker's one offspring, a daughter Oriole, was born in late 1908 after the *Liberty* offices had been destroyed. A sense of his devotion can be gleaned from how he spoke of her room in a letter, "[it] is almost her castle . . . which her father rarely enters, except under stress of necessity." Quoted in Avrich, *Anarchist Portraits*, 148.

35. J. Wm. Lloyd, "The Anarchist Child," *Liberty* 11 (September 21, 1895): 6. Emphasis in the original.

36. Ironically, Tucker himself would use a similar argument against the possibility of ownership in ideas. He pointed out that copyrights with time limitations were absurd because property does not expire.

37. J. Greevz Fisher, "Children as Chattels," *Liberty* 11 (August 24, 1895): 6. Emphasis added.

38. Steven T. Byington, "The Status of the Child," *Liberty* 11 (August 24, 1895): 7.

39. In the same issue, A. S. Matter raised a similar point in asking whether a child who was "an idiot or a cripple" would ever be able to emancipate himself or herself. And who would adjudicate when the point of emancipation had come? "Are Children Property," *Liberty* 11 (September 21, 1895): 7.

40. Benjamin R. Tucker, "What Is Property?" *Liberty* 11 (September 21, 1895): 4.

41. Tucker, "What Is Property?" 5.

42. Tucker, "What Is Property?" 8.

43. Tucker, "What Is Property?" 8.

44. Benjamin R. Tucker, "What Is Property" (second use of this title), *Liberty* 11 (October 5, 1895): 3.

45. J. Wm. Lloyd, "Anarchist or Free Socialist?" *Liberty* 11 (November 2, 1895): 7.

46. Benjamin R. Tucker, "Mr. Lloyd's Departure," *Liberty* 11 (November 30, 1895): 3-4.

47. Benjamin R. Tucker, "Rights and Contract," *Liberty* 11 (December 14, 1895): 4.

Chapter 6

Intellectual Property

Intellectual property—as embodied in copyright and patent—was the subject of intense debate within *Liberty*. Benjamin Tucker flatly rejected the idea that legal copyright was conducive with Anarchism. The strength of Tucker's opposition to patents may be judged from his essay "State Socialism and Anarchism: How Far They Agree, and Wherein They Differ." Here, Tucker explained the key difference between Individualist Anarchism's position on intellectual property and that of the major competing radical school of his day—State Socialism: "The two principles . . . are AUTHORITY and LIBERTY, and the names of the two schools of Socialistic thought which fully and unreservedly represent one or the other of them are, respectively, State Socialism and Anarchism."

Tucker explained that "nearly all political economists" confined themselves to describing society as it existed. By contrast, State Socialism and Anarchism described society as it should be, and explored the means by which such an ideal could come about. Tucker observed, "This seems to have been done independently by three different men . . . Josiah Warren, an American; Pierre J. Proudhon, a Frenchman; Karl Marx, a German Jew." The "parting of ways" between Marx on one hand, and Warren and Proudhon on the other was their method of "striking down monopoly." Following the path of Authority, Marx accepted that "government must assume all the functions of the economy in order to protect it from monopoly. . . . First, then, State Socialism, which may be described as the *doctrine that all the affairs of men should be managed by the government, regardless of individual choice.*"[1]

Warren and Proudhon adhered to Liberty and "saw that monopoly rested upon Authority [government] and to destroy the former it was necessary to destroy the latter." The means they advocated was "to create as much competition as possible." Thus, they launched a frontal attack on the four monopolies of "principal importance,—the money monopoly, the land monopoly, the tariff monopoly, and the patent monopoly."[2] To Tucker, patent was one of the four mainstays of monopoly upon which Authority rested.

A debate on intellectual property within *Liberty* was, perhaps, inevitable. Lysander Spooner, one of Tucker's mentors, had written a work entitled *Law of Intellectual Property or an Essay on the Right of Authors and Inventors to a Perpetual Property in Their Ideas*. Moreover, Herbert Spencer, a thinker much quoted and respected by *Liberty*, argued vigorously for intellectual property. The stage was set for a clash of concepts.

As a topic of debate, intellectual property appeared in the July 7, 1888 issue of *Liberty* through a provocative article in which Tucker declared, "there can rightfully be no such thing as the exclusive ownership of an idea."[3] From this point, the twin issues of patent and copyright gradually blossomed into major debate through which the concept of "property" was finely honed.[4]

The Boundaries of the Debate

In a debate, it is natural to assume that the exchange of opinions swings back and forth between advocacy and denial. This is not a precise statement of what occurred in the debate on whether ideas could be property. Most of the positions held were more complicated. For example, the egoist James L. Walker, who wrote under the pseudonym Tak Kak, contributed heavily to the *anti*-intellectual property side. Yet he wrote: "My thoughts are my property as the air in my lungs is my property."[5] Clearly, Tak Kak did not object to copyright and patent on the grounds that ideas could not be "property" in some sense. Both sides of the debate acknowledged that an individual owned his own thoughts, which could be expressed or withheld entirely at his option.

Moreover, both sides believed that an idea could remain the property of its originator even after it had been imparted to others. Tak Kak maintained:

> If any person wishes to live by imparting his ideas in exchange for labor, I have nothing to say against his doing so and getting cooperative protection without invading the persons and property of myself and my allies. . . . Mr. Spencer [Herbert Spencer] is welcome to all the property in ideas that he can erect and maintain without government. No one can speak or write, and yet have the same advantage as if he were silent. . . . But whatever he can do by contract, cooperation, and boycotting . . . let him do so at his pleasure.[6]

Tak Kak restated his theme in different terms, "As long as Spencer has an idea in his brain, it is his, and it is not mine until it is in my brain."[7]

Note two key points in Tak Kak's position. The first is a restatement of the self-ownership principle: that is, every human being simply by being human has jurisdiction over his own body. By logical extension, self-ownership protected any idea within his mind. The second point is that "communicated" ideas—ideas that ceased to be solely within his mind and assumed a public status—no longer enjoyed the automatic protection of self-ownership. Any ownership of public ideas did not derive from natural rights, but from a contract or from what Tak Kak called "cooperative protection."

Tucker refined Tak Kak's second point. In distinguishing between an idea within your mind (private) and an idea that had been communicated (public), Tucker claimed that the ownership of a private idea did not result from originating it. The ownership resulted from the fact that the idea was protected by other rights. You owned an idea in your mind simply because it was impossible for anyone to access it without your consent unless they used force, such as torture. Thus, the "ownership" of private ideas was merely a by-product of self-ownership.

A public idea was not comparably protected by self-ownership. When an author or inventor publicized his idea, he relinquished what Tucker termed "a power which theretofore had been guarded by other rights—the right of inviolability of person, the right of privacy of domicile."[8] Tucker was clear: by publishing his work, an author or inventor did not relinquish his right to it for there was no right to begin with. There had been a protective shield provided by self-ownership. Publication removed that protective shield. If an idea was in the public realm, an individual could access and use it without violating any one else's "equal liberty."

Thus, Tak Kak and Tucker defined one boundary of the debate: the anti-intellectual property side (hereinafter, AIP). You own private ideas. They can be protected either through silence or through contracts similar to those currently used by computer companies to "license" software packages. But there was no "natural" right to a public idea.[9] In being communicated, it became the private property of anyone who held it in his mind thereafter. As J. Wm. Lloyd expressed it, "You cannot cut an idea bodily out of a brain as you might transplant a strawberry from one garden to another. If I think the same thought as my neighbor, very well; it is plain that I have taken and received nothing from him, for he still has his thought as strong as ever."[10]

Proponents of intellectual property (hereinafter, IP) insisted that copyright and patent were natural rights and deserved protection whether they were private or public ideas.[11] In general, these proponents maintained one of two positions. The most radical position was the claim that the discoverer of an idea became entitled not only to his specific instance of the idea (the private one), but also to all subsequent instances of it (the public ones) *without exception.*

The more commonly argued IP position was that the discoverer of an idea held exclusive ownership until and unless someone else substantiated his independent discovery of the same idea—for example, the discovery of how to store electricity in a battery. At that point, the independent discoverer acquired an ownership claim equal to that of the other originator. Such dual ownership would be far more likely to occur in patents than copyrights because inventors use the same state-of-art technology to address the same questions and, so, often come up with identical solutions.[12]

IP advocates insisted that ideas were property because they were the products of human labor, like chairs or tables, and every person rightfully owned what his labor produced. Lysander Spooner was widely quoted to support this argument, "the principle of individual property ... says that each man has an absolute dominion, as against all other men, over the products and acquisitions of his own labor."[13] In short, intellectual property was a natural right.[14]

Opponents of intellectual property countered by claiming that the proper reward for such labor was the specific idea produced.[15]

Although the discussion of intellectual property took many intricate twists within *Liberty*, it ultimately revolved around two key questions: What is property? and, What is an idea?

What Is Property?

IP advocates generally defined property as wealth whose ownership has been acquired either through discovery or through labor. Spooner stated, "Property is simply wealth, *that is possessed—that has an owner*; in contradistinction to wealth, that has no owner, but lies exposed, *unpossessed*, and ready to be converted into property, by whomsoever chooses to make it his own."[16] Spooner continued, "Any article of wealth which a man creates or produces by the exercise of any portion of his wealth producing faculties is . . . clearly his rightful property."[17]

Tucker addressed the question in more fundamental terms. He asked why the concept of property had originated within society in the first place. The logic behind this approach was his belief that concepts are problem-solving devices. Ideas arise only because they serve a need, they answer a question. To illustrate this, consider a universe parallel to our own, which runs along slightly different rules. In this alternate universe, you can satisfy needs simply by wishing for satisfaction. Food appears magically in your hand, clothes on your limbs, and a bed under your tired body. It is unlikely that the concept of money would evolve in such a universe, because that concept came about to solve the problem of transferring and storing wealth. Thus, in the parallel universe, the problem-solving concept of money would not arise because the problem did not exist.

Tucker used this approach to analyze the concept of property. He asked: what is it about the nature of our universe and of man that gives rise to property in the first place? What problem is being solved?

Tucker argued that the idea of property arose as a way to solve conflicts caused by scarcity. In the real universe, goods are scarce and this fact leads to inevitable competition among men for their use. For example, since one chair cannot be used in the same manner and at the same time by two individuals, it was necessary to determine who should use the chair. The concept of property resolved this problem. The one who could claim the chair as property should determine its use. "If it were possible," wrote Tucker, "and if it had always been possible, for an unlimited number of individuals to use to an unlimited extent and in an unlimited number of places the same concrete thing at the same time, there would never have been any such thing as the institution of property."

This argument had direct implications for copyright and patent. A public idea was not a scarce good, as it could be used by an unlimited number of individuals to an unlimited extent and in an unlimited number of places. According to Tucker, this meant that intellectual property as a natural right ran counter to the very purpose for which the idea "property" evolved.

In fact, intellectual property would create a scarcity where none naturally existed. It would create an unnatural monopoly. To claim all potential generators because you have built one yourself, Tucker argued, is comparable to "a claim on the part of a man who first struck oil to ownership of the entire oil region or petroleum product."[18]

What Are the Essential Characteristics of Property?

AIP advocates claimed that copyright and patent contradicted not only the purpose for which the idea of property evolved but also the essential characteristics of property.

What were these characteristics? Two related ones were claimed: alienability and transferability. In other words, to qualify as natural property, it has to be possible to alienate a good from one person and transfer it to another. Not all transfers had to be complete or final. For example, a homeowner might decide to rent out a room rather than sell the entire structure. But, *in principle*, it had to be possible to alienate and transfer a good in order to consider it "property."

Tak Kak applied this standard to ideas, "The giver or seller parts with it [property] in conveying it. This characteristic distinguishes property from skill and information. Bread is property." But the art of baking was not property; it was a skill that was not alienated in being transferred. "Monopoly consists in the attempt to make property of liberties, discoveries, sciences, and arts by a pretended or forced alienation."[19]

The idea that property must be capable of alienation was reminiscent of Thomas Jefferson's famous analogy between ideas and candles. Jefferson explained that, just as a man could light his taper from an existing candle without diminishing the original flame, so, too, could he acquire an idea without diminishing the original source. Jefferson wrote further: "If nature has made any one thing less susceptible than all others of exclusive property, it is . . . an idea, which an individual may exclusively possess as long as he keeps it to himself; but the moment it is divulged, it forces itself into the possession of every one, and the receiver cannot dispossess himself of it."[20]

The inalienability of ideas was a problem not only for the original owner, but also for anyone who received it. The recipient had no choice but to avail himself of the idea once it had been communicated to him—once he had heard or seen it. That is, the recipient had no means by which to pluck the information out of his head and return to a state of ignorance. Nevertheless, the enforcement of intellectual property prevented him from using what was in his own mind.

Lloyd further postulated that an essential characteristic of property was the ability to destroy what you possess. He commented, "the impossibility of destroying an idea, or withholding it from use . . . is excellent proof that there can be no property in ideas."[21]

What Is an Idea?

IP advocates argued from natural rights that an idea is the product of intellectual labor and, thus, a form of wealth.

The AIP egoist J. B. Robinson approached the issue differently. "What is an 'idea?'" he asked. "Is it made of wood, or iron, or, stone? . . . the idea is nothing objective . . . that is to say, the idea is not part of the product; it is part of the producer."[22] In other words, to own an idea in another person's mind reduced to a form of slavery because the ownership claim was over an aspect of another person's body. Ideas could not be owned by anyone other than the individual in whose mind the idea resided.

Thus, AIP advocates added another essential characteristic to property; it must be tangible. Tak Kak commented, "A convenient test [of property] is this: no ownership except in that which is embodied in tangible form, hence subject to wear and decay, for this is the general mark of products as distinct from that so-called production which can be imparted to others and become common property without the original owner having less than before."[23]

The Debate Debuts: The Question of Patent

In the July 7, 1888 issue of *Liberty*, Tucker critiqued an article by Henry George that had appeared in the June 23rd issue of the *Standard*. George claimed that ownership came from production, not discovery. This led him to reject patents, describing them as ideas that manipulated the laws of nature through machinery. He wrote, "No man can justly claim ownership in natural laws, nor in any of the potentialities which nature holds for it."[24] To those who protested that only the machine, not the natural law, was being claimed as property, George replied that the principles upon which the machines operated were intrinsic in nature. For example, a windmill was nothing more than an expression of how the force of wind pushing against a surface could produce power. Thus, every patent reduced to an ownership claim over an expression of nature.

George distinguished between two forms of labor that went into producing an invention. The first form was the mental labor of working out the operating principles of the machine: this was the labor of discovery. But since the principles existed in nature—for example, how X amps of electricity reacts to Y ohms of resistance—they were available for discovery by anyone and could not be claimed by one man. The second form of labor was the actual construction of a specific machine from raw materials: this was the labor of production. Thus, the specific machine a man produced, such as a wheelbarrow, could be claimed as his property but he could not prevent another man from producing his own wheelbarrow.

George then proceeded to distinguish between patents and copyright, and to argue that the latter was a defensible form of intellectual property. That is, he claimed that the labor of production expended on how to say something gave a man an ownership right to that arrangement of words and not merely to one specific instance of the arrangement.

In a response that bordered on an ad hominem attack, Tucker called George "one of the most dangerous men among all of those now posing as public teachers."[25] It was George's defense of copyright that elicited Tucker's scorn.[26] Henceforth, the topic of intellectual property would have two well-defined threads in which patent and copyright were addressed as separate issues.

Concerning patents, Tucker agreed that the act of discovery gave a man no more right to a principle, such as electricity, than simply stepping upon a continent gave him a right to that land mass. Only the labor of production endowed ownership. And, since the work of production is required afresh in the case of each particular thing, no particular thing can be claimed by anyone other than the individual who manufactured it.

Tak Kak then raised controversy by contending that the act of discovering the principle anew was not even required for someone to claim equal ownership to a specific machine, for the simple reason that such independent invention might not be possible. For example, Tak Kak disputed whether any man living in civilization had the ability to independently invent the steam engine; if a man had seen this machine, he was thereby deprived of the ability to conceive it anew. That is, a man who had seen a steam engine could not be totally original in inventing one even if he honestly attempted to be so. "This being the case," concluded Tak Kak, "a patent given to him [the inventor] puts the entire world at his mercy."[27]

Victor Yarros countered by claiming that there was an implied contract or obligation on the part of anyone who received another's idea to refrain from using it. After all, neither Tucker nor Tak Kak was forced to absorb the idea, even a popular one. Presumably, he did so of his own free will and, thus, he voluntarily deprived himself of the ability to discover the idea anew. "If Mr. Tucker wants to be the originator of everything he has occasion to use and enjoy in life, he is at liberty to abstain from reading and studying." Yarros continued, "All Mr. Tucker has the right to demand, is that these things shall not be brought to his own private house and placed before his eyes. . . . If he chooses to . . . walk in the public street and look at the display of goods in the windows, he does so at the risk of depriving himself of the liberty of originating certain things."[28]

Tucker responded, "Some man comes along with an invention and parades it in the streets; and we are told that, in consequence of this act on his part, we must either give up our liberty to walk the streets or else our liberty to invent. . . . Not so fast my dear sir! . . . Were you compelled to parade your invention on the streets? And why do you ask us to protect you from the consequences."[29]

Yarros conceded that "the man who parades a simple thing in the streets should not be protected in the monopoly of its use," but he maintained that complex creations should be protected since a duplicator would have to go out of his way "to stop and study the invention."[30]

Tucker countered that a man with great mechanical ability could understand a machine at a glance.[31] Thus, Yarros's standard of "complexity" made the enforcement of patent laws a purely subjective matter. A man who had to study a steam engine in order to duplicate it would be legally liable for such duplication, whereas an experienced engineer who understood the engine at a glance would be exempt. Thus, innocence or guilt would be purely a matter of the educational background or intellectual abilities of the accused.

Tucker extended his argument to include copyright, as well as patents. Presumably, a man with either a photographic or phonographic memory would able to remember verbatim literature that had been placed before his eyes or read aloud in his presence. But IP advocates would prove far less willing to concede points on the issue of copyright as opposed to patents.

The Question of Copyright

Although most contributors to *Liberty* viewed patents as discoveries of natural principles, many of them viewed copyright in an entirely different manner.

In Yarros's foray into ideological battle, he had stated, "Mr. Tucker's argument, entirely applicable to patent rights, is completely inapplicable to copyright."[32] Poetry and novels did not exist in nature to be discovered, like the principles of a generator. Indeed, advocates of copyright argued that it was impossible for two people to write the same short story independently, even though simultaneous and independent inventions were not uncommon.

The argument for copyright was two pronged. First, literature was pure creation rather than a discovery of existing principles. Second, independent creation of the same piece of literature was impossible.

These arguments led many of those who opposed patent laws into the advocacy of enforced copyright. Tucker had written, "The central injustice of . . . patent laws is that it compels the race to pay an individual through a long term of years a monopoly price for knowledge that he has discovered today although some other man . . . in many cases very probably would have discovered it tomorrow." This objection did not seem to apply to literature and copyright.

Nevertheless, Tucker maintained, "The same argument that demolishes the right of the inventor demolishes the right of the author." Patent and copyright were simply two expressions of the same principle.[33]

Tucker proceeded to answer the arguments for copyright. First, he denied that literature was pure creation rather than a discovery of existing principles. Literature was nothing more than an arrangement of the alphabet according to certain principles; both the alphabet and these principles preexisted any piece of literature and were available to anyone to use in any manner. If no one could reasonably claim ownership in a particular combination of the alphabet, then no one could own a style of expression.

The possibility of independently creating a piece of literature posed more of a problem. There were documented cases of simultaneous inventions of machinery, but not of literature. Although the general ideas expressed in a book might be duplicated—as in the instance of Walras, Jevons, and Menger, who all simultaneously "originated" theories of marginal utility—the duplication of the style of expression was considered beyond possibility.

Tucker staunchly defended this possibility. Even throwing letters randomly in the air a sufficient number of times would produce *Hamlet*, he argued, thus it was logically possible to independently reproduce a style of expression.[34]

Moreover, Tucker contended that a style of expression was a type of idea in and of itself. He made the somewhat Platonic assertion that all combinations of letters or words existed potentially, just as all combinations of raw materials existed potentially. Thus, one man had no more right to monopolize the arrangement of words in a poem than he had to claim ownership of the arrangement of raw materials that resulted in a generator.

Yarros considered such metaphysical talk to be "meaningless jargon." On the likelihood of anyone independently reproducing the exact words of an author, Yarros wrote, "Instead of being very probable, it is beyond all possibility . . . the method, the style, the manner, the peculiarities of all kinds due to his physical, mental and moral traits, these no other man might or would under any circumstances bring."[35] Copyright did not prevent anyone from writing a work that reflected the ideas of an author; it merely protected the work's unique style of expression, which could not be honestly duplicated.

In response, Tucker declared that discussions of probability or possibility were "improper," both in terms of forging law about copyright and of arguing its validity as a natural right. Regarding the making of law, he maintained, "the propriety of considering degree of probability . . . fails to distinguish between the weighing of evidence and the forming of laws. The question of probability rightly enters into the former, but not into the latter."[36] Besides which, the presumption of innocence would mean that an author who accused another of plagiarism would have to prove that independent creation had not occurred.

In terms of copyright as a natural right, Tucker wrote,

> To discuss the degrees of probability . . . is to shoot wide of the mark. Such questions as this are not to be decided by rule of thumb or by the law of chances, but in accordance with some general principle. . . . [A]mong the things not logically impossible, I know of few nearer the limit of possibility than that I should ever desire to publish *Liberty* in the middle of the desert of Sahara; nevertheless, this would scarcely justify any great political power in giving Stanley a right to stake out a claim comprising that entire region and forbid me to set up a printing press.[37]

In short, a question of rights must be determined by the general principles, not by probability.

Yarros' response to Tucker's argument of independent discovery of style was brief and empirical rather than theoretical: "Since men began to write, no such occurrence has taken place as the production of two similar quatrains, or two ten-line paragraphs by two independent men."[38] Unlike the patent dispute in which Yarros gave so much ground as to end up virtually agreeing with Tucker, the dispute between them concerning style remained unresolved.

Tak Kak picked up on Tucker's attack on protecting the style of literature. In an attempt at reductio ad absurdum, Tak Kak pointed to a large inconsistency in the pro-copyright arguments. They believed stylistic expression should be legally protected, yet they did not extend this protection beyond literature and art. Tak Kak observed that ideas and style are expressed in almost all aspects of our lives and, yet, it is only with regard to patent and copyright that laws are introduced to "protect" the originator.

"If a printer may not copy new books," commented Tak Kak, "of course the shoemaker may not copy new shoes." Such a denial, of course, would be widely considered a violation of the shoemaker's liberty. "[T]he shoemaker or printer with materials and tools in hand must copy what is in demand or starve. If he be not permitted to use his tools and his material in fashioning any goods that he knows how to fashion, and chooses to fashion, his liberty and his property are frustrated at one stroke."[39]

Chairs, hairstyles, clothing, flower gardens, room decor, and all other forms of expression have unique styles. The style of a flower arrangement may be as unique as the style of a sonnet, yet it was only with the sonnet, with so-called intellectual property, that special privileges of legal protection were demanded. Further, to be consistent, the copyright advocate would have to admit that all speech was a unique, personal form of expression. Therefore, a man should be entitled to legal protection for every sentence he uttered so that no one thereafter could speak that arrangement of words without his consent.

The advocates of copyright came close to adopting this latter position. The pro-copyright Lysander Spooner had previously written, "So absolute is an author's right of dominion over his ideas that he may forbid their being communicated even by human voice if he so pleases."[40] With lines so clearly and deeply drawn, neither side conceded many points on copyright.

Secondary Questions

Although questions of secondary importance tended to be dismissed quickly, they provide a sense of the complexity of the debate.

The AIP advocates attacked their opponents for being inconsistent on several points, especially on the advocacy of either a time limit or a territorial limit in law for copyright and patent. If the ownership of ideas was a natural right, critics inquired, why should it be so limited? Other natural property was not possessed only for five years or within a certain country. If ideas were property as a chair was, why were ideas being treated differently under the law? The impact of this argument was to make many who advocated copyright and patents so uncomfortable with time or territory limits that they conceded this point without changing their core position.

Purely utilitarian arguments were introduced by labor reformer Hugo Bilgram, who commented that the "only basis on which the question [copyright] must stand or fall is that of social expediency. . . . To this question only one answer appears possible, and this is an affirmative answer." The specific social expediency raised by Bilgram was the likelihood that no great literature would be written if authors were not granted a natural rights protection, and natural profit, for their published work. "Were it considered proper for any publisher to copy any new work without the author's consent, the authorized publisher . . . could therefore in no way afford to remunerate the author for his labour. And, authors having no earthly chance of being financially remunerated by any other means, they would simply not write."[41]

As a counter, Tucker pointed to the great literature produced by such writers as Shakespeare who had penned his plays a century prior to the first copyright law. Speaking as both a publisher and an author, he stated, "it is a rule, to which exceptions are very rare, that, even in the absence of copyright, competing editions are not published except of books the demand for which has already been large enough to more than reasonably reward both author and publisher for their labor." He also quoted the contemporary playwright and contributor to *Liberty*, George Bernard Shaw, who observed, "the cry for copyright is the cry of men who are not satisfied with being paid for their work once, but insist upon being paid twice, thrice, and a dozen times over."[42]

Tucker could have added that he did not advocate stripping authors and inventors of protection. He merely wished that protection to be placed upon a contractual basis. Elsewhere, he interjected the observation, "It must not be inferred that I wish to deprive the authors of *reasonable* rewards for their labor. On the contrary, I wish to help them to secure such, and I believe that there are Anarchistic methods of doing so."[43]

Tucker's appeals to his own personal experiences as a writer, editor, and publisher were difficult to refute. He referred to an earlier book published under the imprint of B. Tucker, "Why . . . did two competing editions of *The Kreutzer Sonata* appear on the market before mine had had the field two months? Simply because money was pouring into my pockets with a rapidity that nearly took my breath away. And after my rivals took the field, it came in faster than ever. . . . Competition in the book world is not to be shunned but to be courted."[44]

A latecomer in the debate, Joseph A. Labadie supported Tucker's point: "The question of recompense is not necessarily involved in the denial of the right to property in ideas."[45]

The argument from expediency was also used to defend patents, which were deemed to be socially necessary conditions to encourage inventors and scientists to create. Indeed, patents were presented almost as being necessary conditions for human progress itself. Lloyd replied to this claim by declaring precisely the opposite to be true:

> It is quite within the limits of possibility . . . that I could invent a hoe so superior to any other that not only all existing hoes, but all existing tools of cultivation were worthless by comparison . . . the practice of improved agriculture would then depend upon the manufacture and use of my hoes, yet the form of hoe thus expressed being exclusively mine, I would at once become an autocrat with tremendous power . . . and thus imperil human liberty without hope of redress, but I could at any time do something perhaps even worse—*refuse to make these hoes altogether, and forbid others to do so, and this for all time.*[46]

Some advocates of patents found this to be a convincing argument and conceded the right of independent invention; that is, so long as an invention resulted from the independent labor of an inventor, it could be claimed as property whether or not it duplicated any one else's similar independent effort. But, as the vigorous IP advocate Yarros explained, the onus of proof rested upon the second inventor to prove that his work had evolved independently. In other words, in asserting his claim, the second inventor would be considered guilty until proven innocent.

Tucker quickly pointed out that this reversal of legal process ran counter to all established methods of fair trial. He suggested that his sometime associate editor Yarros appealed to this argument because "to go to a jury on a question of independence of invention or authorship with the burden of proof on the complainant . . . would be sure victory for the defendant."[47]

Generally speaking, all aspects of the social expediency argument were dismissed with ease by Tucker whose career as a professional journalist and editor gave him a facility with examples and statistics as well as a background which may have intimidated his opponents more than it convinced them. Indeed, Tucker was not above stooping to ad hominem attacks and open ridicule. Regarding international copyright, Tucker charged that the other side consisted of authors who were arguing for their vested interests. He called them "free traders" who "declare for protection in the sphere which involves their special interest."[48]

In an article entitled "As Usual, Protection Only for the Rich," Tak Kak added a more reasoned observation. He claimed that a proposed international copyright law, which was being championed by the IP side, protected only the rich: "It allows any publisher to pirate the works of all authors who are not rich enough to invest a considerable sum in printing in this country or famous enough to get some American publisher—to do so for them."[49]

The Debate Closes

On the whole, the debate over intellectual property within the pages of *Liberty* was conducted with good will and with a minimum of personal attacks.[50] For example, when Tucker took exception to Yarros's use of the word "evasion" to describe one of his (Tucker's) arguments, Yarros hastened to defuse that word of any derogatory meaning. Tucker was equally, and uncharacteristically, generous. "If he [Yarros] has failed and, so far as I know it, such is the nearly unanimous verdict of the readers of *Liberty*,—the fault is not with the champion, but with his hopeless cause."[51]

With this remark, Tucker announced that "the discussion of property in ideas between Mr. Yarros and myself is now closed."[52]

Although the end of debate may have seemed abrupt or arbitrary, it is important to remember that the discussion spanned three years. It continued past its announced "official" closing date of May 1891 through to July 11th with articles by J. B. Robinson, Tak Kak, Lloyd, Wm. Hanson, and George Forrest. With the exception of a fairly neutral piece by Hanson, the contributions argued against intellectual property.

Tucker's AIP stance did not alter over the years, except perhaps to harden. He continued to view intellectual property as one of the four categories of usury through which monopolies were established by government. Although he considered the "banking (or money) monopoly" to be the most serious of the four, intellectual property—if carried to its logical conclusion—would be disastrous. One of Tucker's last statements on intellectual property remains his clearest:

> [H]ad it been in force in the lifetime of James Watt, [it would] have made his direct heirs the owners of at least nine-tenths of the now existing wealth of the world; and, had it been in force in the lifetime of the inventor of the Roman alphabet, nearly all the highly civilized peoples of the earth would be to-day the virtual slaves of that inventor's heirs, which is but another way of saying that, instead of becoming highly civilized, they would have remained in the state of semi-barbarism. It seems to me that these two statements, which in my view are incontrovertible, are in themselves sufficient to condemn property in ideas forever.[53]

Conclusion: Patent and Copyright by Contract

Tucker and the other contributors to *Liberty* who rejected intellectual property as a natural right were not hostile to copyright or patent enforced by contract. Nor did they deny a man's absolute right to exclusively use whatever ideas he privately held. The point at which this exclusivity was lost, however, came when the idea was communicated without the protection of contract. Tucker insisted that a man who wrote in the public realm abandoned all claim to his property just as a man who spoke publicly abandoned claim to his spoken words.

The natural rights side contended that the law must presume something to be property so long as it was valuable. If an idea had value, then it was presumed to be property whether publicly expressed or not. By contrast, Tucker advanced a theory of abandonment. That is, if a man publicized an idea without the protection of a contract, then he was presumed to be abandoning his exclusive claim to that idea.

If a man scatters money in the street, he does not thereby formally relinquish title to it . . . but those who pick it up are thereafter considered the rightful owners. . . . Similarly a man who reproduces his writings by thousands and spreads them everywhere voluntarily abandons his right of privacy and those who read them . . . no more put themselves by the act under any obligation in regard to the author than those who pick up scattered money put themselves under obligations to the scatterer.[54]

Perhaps the essence of Tucker's approach to intellectual property was best expressed when he exclaimed: "You want your invention to yourself? Then keep it to yourself."[55]

Notes

1. Benjamin R. Tucker, "State Socialism and Anarchism," *Liberty* 5 (March 10, 1888): 2. Emphasis in original.

2. Tucker, "State Socialism and Anarchism," 3.

3. Benjamin R. Tucker, "Ergo and Presto!" *Liberty* 5 (July 7, 1888): 4. This article was a hostile critique of Henry George's advocacy of copyright in his periodical the *Standard* of June 23, 1888. Nevertheless, Tucker approved of the politician's opposition to patent rights.

4. The debate lasted for almost two months past the May 29, 1891, issue of *Liberty* in which Tucker declared the three-year debate to be formally over.

5. Tak Kak, "Copyright.—III," *Liberty* 7 (March 21, 1891): 4. Although this statement occurred late in the debate, it is representative of the position taken consistently throughout by the AIP side. Note that, although Tucker was usually quite original in his titling of articles, the heading "Copyright" was used several times for different writers and may cause confusion.

6. Tak Kak, "Copyright.—III," 4. The "Spencer" critiqued by Tak Kak was the British classical liberal Herbert Spencer who claimed "exclusive use" of any idea he originated. Although Spencer was not party to the debate, he was much quoted and criticized in absentia by the disputants. The major proponent of Spencer was Yarros. Indeed, despite a brief lapse into philosophical egoism, Yarros was one of the main conduits of the radical Spencerian tradition in America.

7. Tak Kak, "Copyright.—III," 5.

8. Benjamin R. Tucker, "More on Copyright," *Liberty* 7 (December 27, 1890): 5.

9. Although this argument would seem to be a continuation of the egoistic rejection of natural rights and the embrace of contract, Tucker advanced the argument prior to his conversion to philosophical egoism. Indeed, his rejection of such monopoly predated *Liberty* and emerged during a period when he still espoused natural rights. The arguments can and should be considered on their own merits outside the context of egoism.

10. J. Wm. Lloyd, "Copyright," *Liberty* 7 (February 7, 1891): 6. Lloyd vehemently disagreed with the "Tucker-side" on both children's rights and egoism but aligned with Tucker on the issue of intellectual property.

11. The main proponents of intellectual property were Victor Yarros, A. H. Simpson, Wordsworth Donisthorpe, Hugo Bilgram, and M. Zametkin.

12. Even in purely theoretical—and, thus, more creative—realms, there have been many instances of "independent discovery." One of the most famous is the invention of calculus by both Sir Isaac Newton and Gottfried von Leibniz at approximately the same moment in time. Intellectual history tends to credit them equally.

13. Lysander Spooner, *Law of Intellectual Property or an Essay on the Right of Authors and Inventors to a Perpetual Property in Their Ideas* (Boston: Bela Marsh, 1855; reprint, Weston, Mass.: M&S Press, 1971), 17. A. H. Simpson was so fond of quoting Spooner that his submissions to Liberty were often as much Spooner as they were Simpson. Tucker's respect for Spooner cannot be doubted. His editorial at the death of this mentor, entitled "Our Nestor Taken From Us," is a moving tribute. Nevertheless he considered the *Law of Intellectual Property* to be "fundamentally foolish" and chastised Simpson for using his space to reprint it. Tucker found occasion to remind *Liberty* readers that Spooner "believed in God; he believed in religion; he believed in spirits; he believed in immortality; . . . he believed in land monopoly; he believed in marriage." *Liberty* 7 (March 21, 1891): 4.

14. Spooner and Spencer died before the debate on intellectual property erupted, but their presence was apparent through those who used their works as mainstays in their argument arsenal. (Spooner differed from Spencer in that he did not advocate a time limit on the ownership of ideas.) This arsenal also included an appeal to the Common Law tradition from which Individualist Anarchism as a tradition drew heavily.

15. The major opponents of intellectual property were Benjamin Tucker, James L. Walker, J. Wm. Lloyd, Joseph Labadie, and J. K. Ingalls.

16. Spooner, *Law of Intellectual Property*, 15. Emphasis in original.

17. Spooner as quoted by A. H. Simpson, "Spooner on Property in Ideas," *Liberty* 7 (March 21, 1891): 2.

18. Benjamin R. Tucker, *Liberty* 7 (December 27, 1890): 4. The "creation of scarcity" argument was not as applicable to copyright as it was to patent since the play *Hamlet*, for example, did not exist in nature and was not a physical relationship for all to discover equally. Nevertheless Tucker maintained that all combinations of the alphabet existed theoretically and that they were relationships that should be open to all.

19. "Copyright.—IV," *Liberty* 8 (May 30, 1891): 3.

20. As quoted in Dumas Malone, *Jefferson and the Rights of Man* (New York: Little, Brown, 1951), 284.

21. "Copyright," *Liberty* 7 (February 7, 1891): 6.

22. "A New Argument Against Copyright," *Liberty* 8 (May 16, 1891): 5.

23. "Copyright.—III," in *Liberty* 7 (March 21, 1891): 5.

24. As quoted in Tucker, "Ergo and Presto!" 4. Tucker reprinted this from George's single-tax paper, the *Standard*, June 23, 1888. During the entire run of *Liberty*, this is the only instance of Tucker commenting favorably on Henry George.

25. Tucker, "Ergo and Presto!" 4. Although the active debate may be (somewhat arbitrarily) dated from this article, the issue of intellectual property had arisen several times prior.

26. This was a reflection of Tucker's general opinion of Henry George. "Ergo and Presto!" began, "In Henry George may be seen a pronounced type of the not uncommon combination of philosopher and juggler." He ended with the observation, "He lies low till the excitement has subsided, and then, 'bobs up serenely' and suavely to hoodwink another crowd of greenhorns with the same old trick. Such has been juggler George's policy heretofore such it will be hereafter." *Liberty* 5 (July 7, 1888): 4. It is important to note,

however, that Tucker did not pass this harsh judgment onto others who disagreed on copyright. In fact, he made a point of exempting Yarros from any question of intellectual dishonesty. Benjamin R. Tucker, "More on Copyright," *Liberty* 7 (December 27, 1890): 4-5.

27. Tak Kak, "Copyright.—III," 4.

28. Victor Yarros, "The Right to Authorship," *Liberty* 7 (February 21, 1891): 4.

29. Benjamin R. Tucker, commentary on "The Right to Authorship," *Liberty* 7 (February 21, 1891): 5.

30. Victor Yarros, "Property and Equal Liberty," *Liberty* 7 (April 18, 1891): 2. With this concession, Yarros seemed to relinquish the claim that ideas became the originator's property through being produced by his or her labor and discovery. After all, a simple invention is produced in the same manner as a complicated one. Yarros appeared to adopt the very different position that ideas became property through labor and discovery *if and only if* they were sufficiently complex. If this is an accurate interpretation, his concession to Tucker reflected a major shift in the argument.

31. He dwelt with some satisfaction on the fact that hitherto Yarros had advocated property in all ideas, but now "neither perpetual nor temporary monopoly is to be allowed to any ideas except in the case of books and the few inventions which are either not to be seen or are too complex." This shift in the natural rights argument, Tucker claimed, "abandoned two thirds of it in theory." "The Knot-Hole in the Fence," *Liberty* 7 (April 18, 1891): 5.

32. Victor Yarros, "More on Copyright," *Liberty* 7 (December 27, 1890): 4.

33. Benjamin R. Tucker, commentary on "More on Copyright," *Liberty* 7 (December 27, 1890): 5.

34. As Tucker commented: "If an immense number of letters of the alphabet should be thrown into the air, there would be many billions of forms in which they might fall to the ground. One of these forms is the play of Hamlet . . . this at once disposes of the claim of logical impossibility." Tucker, "More on Copyright," 5.

35. "More on Copyright," 4.

36. Benjamin R. Tucker, commentary on A. H. Simpson, "Property in Ideas," *Liberty* 7 (January 24, 1891): 6.

37. Tucker's commentary on Yarros, "More About Copyright," 5.

38. Victor Yarros, "The 'General Principle' and Copyright," *Liberty* 7 (January 24, 1891): 5.

39. Tak Kak, "Copyright.—III," 5. J. Wm. Lloyd also emphasized the absurdity of claiming ownership in a style of expression: "we should have to pay a royalty for almost every thought and deed to the heirs of those first thinkers and doers,—an intolerable nuisance and slavery." J. Wm. Lloyd, "Copyright," 6.

40. Spooner, *Law of Intellectual Property,* 125.

41. Hugo Bilgram, "The Reward of Authors," *Liberty* 7 (January 10, 1891): 5.

42. Benjamin R. Tucker, commentary on "The Reward of Authors," *Liberty* 7 (January 10, 1891): 6. Tucker's quotation of Shaw occurred as follow-up commentary under the same article title as Bilgram's piece.

43. Tucker, "More on Copyright," 5. Emphasis in original.

44. Tucker, commentary on "The Reward of Authors," 6.

45. Joseph A. Labadie, "Cranky Notions," *Liberty* 7 (April 18, 1891): 3.

46. Lloyd, "Copyright," 6. Emphasis in original. Although Tucker contemptuously dismissed Lloyd concerning children's rights, he seemed particularly impressed by

Lloyd's arguments on intellectual property—perhaps because the two men were in agreement at last. On the same page of the same issue, he remarked, "To be forced to combat single-handed against five such gladiators as Yarros, Simpson, Donisthorpe, Fuller, and Bilgram develops one's faculties immensely. . . . Besides, I am no longer alone; Lloyd has come valiantly to my rescue. He is a host in himself, and with him at my side I have no notion of retreating."

47. Tucker, "Property in Ideas and Equal Liberty," *Liberty* 7 (February 7, 1891): 5. Tucker also speculated that Yarros misinterpreted Spencer, whom he had cited in support of his position.

48. Benjamin R. Tucker, "On Picket Duty," *Liberty* 5 (February 11, 1888): 1. Tucker, in fact, went further than mere ad hominem into direct accusation. In referring to international copyright, he observed: "It is simply a piece of political bribery,—the machinery of the ward room adopted by the preachers of 'pure politics.'" He ended with the plea, "Would that some modern Diogenes would explore the political arena with his lantern in search of an honest man!"

49. Tak Kak, "As Usual, Protection Only For the Rich," *Liberty* 5 (June 23, 1888): 7. This was published as an unattributed excerpt from *Galveston News* of which Tak Kak was an editor. Because his editorship was the attraction of that periodical for Tucker, I have attributed the reprint from *Galveston News* to Tak Kak.

50. An exception to this goodwill occurred in the exchanges between J. Wm. Lloyd and Victor Yarros. Lloyd described Yarros as "frank enough to express with regard to myself the most exalted contempt" and, in return, asserted that Yarros's ideas were "so crude, not to say idiotic," and "expressed in terms so unscientific as to be beneath notice." J. Wm. Lloyd, "Free Copyright and the Devil's Advocate," *Liberty* 8 (June 13, 1891): 5.

51. Benjamin R. Tucker, commentary on Victor Yarros, "The Latest Excuse for Government," *Liberty* 8 (May 2, 1891): 4.

52. Tucker, commentary on "The Latest Excuse for Government," 4.

53. Benjamin R. Tucker, "The Attitude of Anarchism Toward Industrial Combination," *Liberty* 14 (December, 1902): 3.

54. Benjamin R. Tucker, "The Knot-Hole in the Fence," *Liberty* 7 (April 18, 1891): 6.

55. Tucker, "The Knot-Hole in the Fence," 6.

Chapter 7

Trial by Jury

Nineteenth-century Philosophical Anarchism was not an expression of utopianism or a belief in the millennium: it did not seek to establish an ideal society through the perfection of man. Instead, as Victor Yarros explained, "The anarchists, as anarchists, work directly, not for a perfect social state, but for a perfect political system. A perfect social state is a state totally free from sin or crime or folly; a perfect political system is merely a system in which justice is observed, in which nothing is punished but crime and nobody coerced but the invader."[1]

Philosophical Anarchism sought both to eliminate the State and to establish in its place voluntary alternatives, such as private insurance and defense associations. Thus, its twin goals were the destruction of authority and the construction of a voluntary social system.[2]

The Philosophical Anarchists themselves tended to be practical men with experience in the real world of political radicalism. For example, as a young man Yarros had fled to the United States from his native Ukraine in order to escape arrest as a social revolutionary. Benjamin Tucker also had a background in civil disobedience. In August 1875, Tucker had been imprisoned for his Thoreau-like refusal to pay a poll tax, but his protest had ended quietly when a friend unilaterally decided to pay the fine.

Tucker came to believe, however, that civil disobedience was a poor strategy, except when it had an overriding educational value. The reason: until and unless a general foundation of Anarchistic education had been laid, acts of individual rebellion against unjust law were acts of martyrdom that drained the vitality of a movement and created a backlash of State violence against it. Instead, he urged Anarchists to strive vigorously to construct "a public sentiment" for freedom that would inspire too much popular resistance for unjust laws to be enforced.

In rejecting force in the form of both ballots and bullets, it was natural for such passionate radicals to channel their considerable talents into other strategies.[3] These strategies included education; printing books and translating foreign tracts; constructing parallel institutions; passive resistance to unjust laws; boycott; and strikes.

Perhaps the most fundamental strategy was to establish parallel institutions that provided necessary or valuable services to society, such as mail delivery or the settling of disputes—institutions that were monopolized by the State. These voluntary alternatives served two functions: they sped along the dissolution of the State by marginalizing its importance to society, and they provided a framework that would prevent society from dissolving into chaos without the State.

Among the parallel institutions Tucker stressed were private defense agencies or associations that would provide police and court functions, mutual insurance societies that ensured against hardships such as unemployment, and a free banking system by which every individual could issue his or her own currency. Tucker stressed the institutions that addressed economic concerns. As Steven Byington wrote, "Tucker himself would assuredly have given the emphasis . . . to the mutual banks." Nevertheless, the defensive associations that would replace the State police force were arguably the most discussed parallel institution in *Liberty*. Byington explained, "The defensive associations receive especially frequent mention [in *Liberty*] because of the need of incessantly answering the objection 'If we lose the State, who will protect us against ruffians?' but Tucker certainly expects that the defensive association will from the start fill a much smaller sphere in every respect than the present police."[4]

Moreover, since defense was merely another service being offered on the free market, the Philosophical Anarchists believed that several defensive associations would probably exist side by side. Tucker wrote,

> There are many more than five or six insurance companies in England, and it is by no means uncommon for members of the same family to insure their lives and goods against accident or fire in different companies. Why should there not be a considerable number of defensive associations in England in which people, even members of the same family, might insure their lives and goods against murderers or thieves? Defense is a service, like any other service.[5]

Under a competitive system, the best agency might well reap the majority of business, but it would do so through the quality of its service, not through the use of force.

The Anarchistic defense associations would provide court functions as well as police ones: that is, they would offer a format through which disputes could be tried and resolved. They would provide justice.

In the view of Tucker and other prominent Individualist Anarchists, one of the key elements of a free market justice system was "trial by jury." By this term, they meant that twelve randomly chosen members of society would sit in judgment on disputes and render a decision not only on the facts of a case but also on the justice of the law being applied to it. As a concept, American colonists had imported trial by jury from England, where it had acted as a safeguard against unjust laws and courts.

But trial by jury was more than merely a protection against overweening courts: it was a frontline defense against oppressive laws and, thus, against the State itself. The legal theorist Lysander Spooner argued that if a jury system that randomly selected jurors from the entire population had been in force within the United States, it was not likely that one-tenth of the legislation passed by the last Congress would have been enacted. Or, if the legislation had been enacted, it would not have been enforced.

Thus, Tucker declared in *Liberty*, "The truth is that jury service is of much higher importance than the right of suffrage; but our newspaper wiseacres and reformers are not aware of *that*."[6] He claimed jury nullification was "the principal safeguard against oppression."[7] Although trial by jury would not overturn the money monopoly and other attendant usuries that were the primary means of State oppression, some Individualist Anarchists believed that trial by jury would strike a blow at even these institutions. F. D. Tandy opined, "And I think it would not take much more propaganda to make it reasonably safe to refuse to pay rent. For if it came to such a test, most State Socialists and a goodly number of Single Taxers could be relied upon to give a verdict for the defendant."[8]

Other Individualist Anarchists fundamentally disagreed on the wisdom and propriety of trial by jury, and they argued vigorously within the pages of *Liberty* that juries were an expression of "thug" tyranny, of majority rule. In doing so, they challenged the moral and practical basis of trial by jury, and offered a competing vision of how anarchy would provide justice.

The Background of Trial by Jury

In the *Second Treatise on Government*, the seventeenth-century classical liberal John Locke argued that the need to protect the property of "life, liberty, and estate" led men to form a government.[9] In other words, the institution of the State arose as a shield against the conflicts that naturally occur when individuals accumulate property in a world of scarce resources. It arose through an explicit contract by which men relinquished to government the right to adjudicate their own disputes. As its part of the bargain, government agreed to regulate society in order to secure men's claims to their person and property. For example, it enforced inheritance procedures and laws that safeguarded the transmission of property from parent to child.

Locke developed a doctrine of tacit consent by which people were said to agree to the authority of Government even if they had not explicitly delegated the right to adjudicate their own case. In this manner, he explained how succeeding generations could be bound to the original social contract in which they had played no part. According to Locke, people who stayed within society and accepted its benefits—for example, the enforcement of contracts and inheritance—were tacitly agreeing to abide by the rules of that society. Of primary importance was their agreement to use the governmental court system.

But what protection did people have against unjust laws or courts? How could succeeding generations ensure that corruption did not creep into the legal system? In England, a tradition of trial by jury—the "right" to have one's case decided by a randomly chosen group—evolved as a bulwark against oppressive State law. If a jury were allowed to judge both the facts of the case being heard (the guilt or innocence of the accused) and the justness of the proceedings (the application of the law), then it was assumed that at least one jury member would refuse to convict on flimsy evidence or under unjust procedures.

In 1670, the right of a jury to refuse to convict was established when an English jury resisted a judge's instruction to find a defendant guilty and were imprisoned for their refusal. In ruling on the jury's imprisonment, the English high court stated that juries must be able to reach their own decisions without fear of punishment. The refusal of a jury to convict a defendant despite implicit or explicit instructions to do so became known as "jury nullification."

In his contemporary essay "The Jury: Defender or Oppressor," Michael E. Coughlin described how effective jury nullification can be.

> During the 19th century in England there were some 230 capital crimes, that is crimes which would result in capital punishment for the convicted. Because juries continually refused to convict many of the people charged with capital crimes, believing the punishment was far out of proportion to the crime itself, Parliament eventually was forced to reduce the number of capital crimes in England. Today you can count that number on one hand.[10]

In 1735, jury nullification was affirmed in America when jurors refused to convict the radical publisher John Peter Zenger for printing material critical of the governor of New York. Again, the jury ignored explicit instructions of the judge, who told them to consider only the guilt of Zenger under the law and not the justice of the law itself.[11] The importance of trial by jury to the colonies can be assessed with reference to the language of the Declaration of Independence, which read, in part, "The History of the King of Great Britain is a History of repeated injuries and usurpations, all having in direct object the establishment of an absolute Tyranny over these States." One listed injury was "depriving us in many cases, of the benefits of Trial by Jury."

Within the Individualist Anarchist tradition, Spooner is commonly considered to have penned the definitive work—*An Essay on Trial by Jury*,[12] which offered a revisionist history of the jury system from the Magna Carta through to nineteenth-century America. The essay's main contention was that any law or legal practice in the United States which contradicted common law was invalid and need not be respected.

The first chapter of the work set its main theme through the title "The Right of Juries to Judge the Justice of Laws." Spooner argued that three roles of juries had long been recognized: namely, to judge the facts of a case, the content of the law, and the intent of an accused. But he believed that a fourth role had been purposely sabotaged by the State: the right of a jury to judge the justice of the law and its application.

An Essay on Trial by Jury elaborated on the arguments Spooner had laid out in his earlier essay *A Defence of Fugitive Slaves, Against the Acts of Congress of February 2, 1793, and September 18, 1850* (1850).[13] In the earlier essay, he attacked the constitutionality of the Fugitive Slave Laws, which rendered those who assisted runaway slaves subject to arrest. Because the Fugitive Slave Laws were unjust, Spooner argued that a jury was under no obligation to convict anyone who was prosecuted under them. Instead, he urged juries to nullify such unjust laws by refusing to enforce them.

In *An Essay on Trial by Jury*, Spooner expanded his analysis and grounded jury nullification within history. The first line of chapter I, section I reads,

> For more than six hundred years—that is since Magna Carta, in 1215—there has been no clearer principle of English or American constitutional law, then that, in criminal cases, it is not only the right and duty of juries to judge what are the facts, what is the law, and what was the moral intent of the accused; *but that it is also their right, and their primary and paramount duty, to judge of the justice of the law, and to hold all laws invalid, that are, in their opinion, unjust or oppressive, and all persons guiltless in violating, or resisting the execution of, such laws.*
>
> Unless such be the right and duty of jurors, it is plain that, instead of juries being a "palladium of liberty"—a barrier against the tyranny and oppression of the government—they are really mere tools in its hands, for carrying into execution any injustice and oppression it may desire to have executed.
>
> But for their right to judge of the law *and the justice of the law*, juries would be no protection to an accused person, *even as to matters of fact*; for, if the government can dictate to a jury any law whatever, in a criminal case, it can certainly dictate to them the laws of evidence. That is, it can dictate what evidence is admissible, and what inadmissible, *and also what force or weight is to be given to the evidence admitted*. And if the government can thus dictate to a jury the laws of evidence, it can not only make it necessary for them to convict on a partial exhibition of the evidence rightfully pertaining to the case, but it can even require them to convict on any evidence whatever that it pleases to offer them.[14]

Chapter II, entitled "The Trial by Jury, as Defined by Magna Carta," continued the historical analysis within English common law by quoting and extensively analyzing "the language of the Great Charter" that established "the right and duty of the jury to judge of the justice of the laws." Chapter III, entitled "Additional Proofs of the Rights and Duties of Jurors," explored the "Ancient Common Law Juries" as "Courts of Conscience" in which such precedents as the "Right of Juries to fix the Sentence" were established.[15]

After dealing with "The Rights and Duties of Juries in Civil Suits" in chapter IV, Spooner moved on to "Objections Answered" in chapter V: for example, he answered the objection that "it is a *maxim* of the law, that the judges respond to the question of law, and juries only to the question of fact."[16] The titles of the next two chapters summed up the conclusions to which Spooner's arguments from historical precedent inexorably led: "Juries of the Present Day Illegal" and "Illegal Judges." The "free administration of justice" would be compelled through trial by jury.

In the words that end his argument, Spooner declares of trial by jury, "In short, government in practice would be brought to the necessity of a strict adherence to natural law, and natural justice, instead of being, as it now is, a great battle, in which avarice and ambition are constantly fighting for and obtaining advantages over the natural rights of mankind."[17]

Spooner put such confidence in trial by jury that he believed, without it, the people would have no alternative but armed resistance against an unjust State. This was particularly true with the growth of democracy—rule by the majority—against which the minority (the individual) had little defense. As legislation came increasingly to reflect "the voice of the people," the minority needed a powerful weapon with which to challenge intrusive laws. With trial by jury, one man in a panel of twelve could block an unjust law while not imposing any laws of his own on others. Trial by jury was an act of self-defense.

Tucker on Trial by Jury

Benjamin Tucker's belief that trial by jury was "the principal safeguard against oppression," which must be saved from usurpation by the State, defined his approach to the institution.

As the remedy, Tucker consistently advocated a return to the "jury in its original form" as described by Spooner in "An Essay on Trial by Jury." Tucker specified what he meant by this phrase, "Jury trial in its original form differed from its present form both in the manner of selecting the jury and in the powers of the jury selected. It was originally selected by drawing twelve names from a wheel containing the names of the whole body of citizens, instead of by putting a special panel of jurors through a sifting process of examination; and by its original powers it was judge, not of the facts alone, but of the law and the justice of the law and the extent and nature of the penalty."[18] Tucker repeatedly referred readers to Spooner's pamphlets on jury trial, including "Illegality of the Trial of John W. Webster," which was advertised in *Liberty*. This pamphlet addressed the methods by which the State could pack a jury by rejecting all those who were opposed to the law being enforced.

Over and over again, Tucker raged against juries as they were presently constituted, against juries on which men were forced to serve "at an expense to themselves and to the taxpayers, for no other purpose than to afford the bench an opportunity to place the responsibility for its own injustice on their shoulders."[19]

In the summer of 1897, Tucker reported on a special meeting held by the Central Labor Union for the Typographical Union No. 6 "to protest against the new special jury law"—Chapter 378 of the New York State laws of 1896. The new law established Special Jury Commissioners for some of the counties.

The Commissioners were authorized to select special jurors for those counties. Only those who agreed with both the law and the penalties being applied could serve as jurors. For example, people with doubts about enforcing the death penalty would be excused. This special jury law would be used "by judges, not only to pack the jury list itself, but also to pack, with impunity, the special jury drawn from the list for any given case."[20]

Tucker delivered an impassioned speech of protest and submitted several resolutions that were unanimously accepted by the Union meeting. Resolution 6 read, in part, "We call upon each and every citizen who may be drawn for ordinary jury duty to enter his individual, separate, and public protest, from his seat in the jury box, against being compelled to serve upon a jury."[21]

Only three hundred people attended the Union meeting, which constituted an extremely poor turnout compared with past gatherings. For Tucker, the "explanation" for the low attendance was "to be found in the apathy and blindness of the public" for whom the danger of the new jury legislation was "too remote as yet."[22] Nevertheless, he wondered aloud at the "apathetic silence on this momentous question thus far maintained by the New York dailies that champion the cause of the common people, with the single exception of the 'Daily News.'"[23] The laboring public and most of the voices that spoke for them did not seem to understand, as Tucker did, the important role that trial by jury played in securing the rights of labor.

Tucker had been battling vigorously and for years against special jury laws, most of which were aimed ostensibly at securing more educated jurors. For example, in 1894, the Massachusetts Legislature—the State from which the Boston periodical issued at that point—considered a law to secure "a better class of jurors." Quality would be ensured by having "selectmen and aldermen" prepare a list that included at one person per every hundred residents of an area. In Boston, Tucker observed that the list from which juries would be selected might be no more than four thousand people. He interpreted the bill as an attempt to pack the list of potential jurors with millionaires, their friends—in short, "men of quality and affairs."[24] The Senate had already passed such a bill.

In 1895, the Massachusetts legislature again was presented with a plan to establish a list of twenty-five hundred names, chosen from approximately five thousand, as a base from which to select Boston's juries, giving preference to "leading citizens." Tucker declared that such a list would consist "only [of] bankers, great merchants, and men of affairs." Tucker asked, "Would such a jury be inclined to deal fairly with a striker, boycotter, walking delegate, vagrant, Communist or any other 'enemy of society'?" Because the jury would represent only the privileged class, the interests of the great mass of people would be excluded. He marveled that those who advocated universal suffrage were among the voices calling for an "educated"—that is, restricted—jury. "[T]o adopt universal suffrage and restrict jury service to the few is to strain at a gnat after swallowing a camel."[25]

When the 1897 jury selection law passed in New York State, to which the *Liberty* offices had moved from Boston, *Liberty* published Tucker's impassioned speech in two segments in July and August 1897, and reprinted it as a pamphlet entitled "A Blow At Trial by Jury" which was offered, thereafter, for sale through *Liberty*'s offices. Therein, Tucker commented, "We are confronted now with a condition, not a theory."

He described the "condition" that was evolving as a result of the special jury law's passage. A jury commissioner and "sundry subordinates" were "examining the citizens of New York" to select potential jurors "who have sufficient disregard for individual liberty and common justice to be willing to do the bidding of power." The names selected to sit on a case were to be exempted from all other jury duty in the future, a fact that Tucker construed to be "a bribe offered to bankers and merchants . . . to tempt them to seek places on the panel." Reminding his readers of the main purpose of trial by jury, "the protection of the individual against the tyranny of government," Tucker declared the selection process to be a deathblow to the jury system.[26]

Tucker called for action. He urged men of good will to pursue "the policy of loud and steady protest, the policy of embarrassment, hindrance, blockade, and obstruction." He went on to explain the specific behavior that constituted such resistance regarding trial by jury. "If each and every one of you, on being placed in the jury box and before each trial begins, will rise in his place and say to the court: 'I most earnestly protest against having to serve on this jury . . . I serve here only on compulsion and in a spirit of indignant discontent,'" then —Tucker believed—a powerful contribution to Anarchistic propaganda could be made.[27]

Tucker was able to recount proudly a personal example of resistance that occurred upon his being called for serve on a jury in the criminal branch of the Supreme Court. He explained that the judge had instructed a pool of potential jurors to form two lines: one consisted of those men who were exempt from serving, and it was in this line that Tucker stood. When his time before the judge arrived, the editor explained that he had already been pronounced incompetent to serve as a juror in another case in New York State because of his radical views. After listening to Tucker expound, the judge questioned his "native Americanism." Apparently, only foreigners held such radical views. "Strange is it not?" Tucker asked his readers. If a man showed "mental independence," he immediately came "under suspicion of being a Pole, or a Russian, or a Hungarian, or some other awful monster."[28]

Within a few months, Tucker was summoned to another courtroom as a potential juror. Again, he joined the line of "those claiming legal exemption" and, so, had a private meeting to discuss his "excuses" before the judge. Tucker announced that he had already been declared incompetent. When asked the reason, he replied, "my convictions regarding trial by jury are such as to prevent me from accepting the instructions of the court on points of law as absolutely binding." The judge pointedly inquired whether Tucker thought he knew more than the court about the law, to which he responded, "I must judge for myself." The judge curtly informed him that he would have to serve, nevertheless. Tucker sat down to wait, "knowing perfectly well that the court was bluffing." Eventually, he was discharged with the pronouncement, "no such man as you is wanted on the jury."[29]

Thereafter, *Liberty* reprinted items from the popular press that described how people had been dismissed from jury duty because they insisted on their right to judge the law. For example, S. H. Randall recounted an incident wherein, having been called to jury duty, he asked the court to excuse him on the grounds that he had scruples against serving. As Randall explained to the court, he rejected most of the statutes he would be asked to enforce as a juror, because he rejected the legitimacy of the State to enact them. He concluded, "If pledged as a juror to their [the statutes] administration, right or wrong, I might be under the necessity of breaking my promise, or becoming a tool of iniquity."[30]

Such incidents were foreshadowed by a serialized essay in *Liberty*, announced as "An abridgement and rearrangement" of Spooner's treatise *An Essay on Trial by Jury*, which had been prepared by Victor Yarros especially for *Liberty*. Entitled "Free Political Institutions: Their Nature, Essence, and Maintenance," the abridgment and rearrangement appeared in the June 8, 1889, issue and continued through the next seven issues. Yarros introduced the abridgment as a work of political philosophy, rather than as the work of historical revisionism intended by Spooner. In essence, Yarros stripped out the history and obscure legal references, making it understandable and relevant to the average reader. Thereafter, "Free Political Institutions" became one of the stock items advertised for sale from Tucker's press.[31] Tucker described "Free Political Institutions" as "the best instrument for Anarchistic propaganda."[32]

Although most of those who formed the "*Liberty* circle" embraced trial by jury, a substantial number of contributors vocally disagreed with the procedure. Before moving onto the details of their disagreement, however, it is necessary to mention a fundamental question that was never adequately explored by Spooner or the pages of *Liberty*. Perhaps the most basic question regarding trial by jury was: how can a government or any other collective entity claim the right to adjudicate the case of an individual if that person does not first delegate the right? In other words, if an individual has a right to try his own case, as Individualist Anarchists generally insisted, then how can a jury claim any jurisdiction over a man who does not recognize its authority?

One of the key arguments used against electoral politics and the State revolved around the issue of "delegated rights." Tucker believed a free society had to be based upon voluntary association, and a legitimate government required the consent of every person over whom it claimed jurisdiction. Otherwise stated, without an individual's delegation of rights, the government had no legitimate claim over that person.

The delegation of rights was an arrangement that could not be presumed as Locke had done through his doctrine of tacit consent. In *No Treason, No. II*, Spooner wrote of government's need for an explicit delegation, "No one's consent could be presumed against him, without his actual consent being given, anymore than in the case of any other contract to pay money, or render service.

And to make it binding upon any one, his signature, or other positive evidence of consent, was as necessary as in the case of any other contract."[33]

What would this consent entail? Spooner clearly delineated the parameters regarding a delegation of rights to the State: the individual possessed the right being delegated, the delegation was explicit, it did not bind future generations, and the delegation could be withdrawn. With regard to the Constitution, he wrote, "Even those who actually voted for the adoption of the Constitution did not pledge their faith *for any specific time*. . . . Any one man, or any number of men, have had a perfect right, at any time, to refuse his or their further support; and nobody could rightfully object to his or their withdrawal."[34]

Logic would seem to dictate that—by the same argument they used to counter the legitimacy of government—Individualist Anarchists could not presume that another collective entity, called a jury, had any right to adjudicate the case of an individual unless he had delegated that specific right. A legitimate jury must have received a delegation of the right to try a case from the individual over whom they sat in judgment. Again, the question becomes, how can a jury properly try an individual who refuses to delegate that right or who withdraws such delegation?[35]

Spooner assumed that certain laws or societal conditions were so obviously beneficial that members of society would naturally agree to them. But he recognized the real possibility that some individuals would disagree with the *form* of trial by jury established through general consent and he insisted that "legitimate government can be formed only by the voluntary association, it can have for its objects only those things in which the members of the association are *all agreed*."[36] Without such agreement from an individual, "the objects of the association" did not apply to him. If an individual claimed to have "acquired a more extended knowledge of justice than is common to all . . . they must either form a separate association for that purpose, or be content to wait until they can make their views intelligible to the people at large."[37]

Spooner then specified the method by which it would be ascertained whether or not "all the parties to the government do approve of a particular law." Twelve men would randomly be chosen from the "whole people" and their unanimous decision on the facts and justice of a case would be taken as "representing the opinions of the whole." Spooner acknowledged "this mode is not theoretically accurate; for theoretical accuracy would require that every man, who was a party to the government, should individually give his consent to the enforcement of every law in every separate case," but he declared this requirement to be "impossible in practice." Instead, he concluded, "This system [trial by jury], it is assumed, will ascertain the sense of the whole people—'the country'—with sufficient accuracy for all practical purposes, and with as much accuracy as is practicable without too great inconvenience and expense."[38]

The abridgment and rearrangement of "An Essay on Trial by Jury" organized by Yarros for *Liberty*, entitled "Free Political Institutions: Their Nature, Essence, and Maintenance," opens with the statement, "The theory of government is that it is formed by the voluntary contract of the people individually with each other."[39]

Meanwhile, Tucker seemed to view "Trial by Jury" more as a strategic measure against State tyranny rather than as an issue to be resolved within Natural Law. Perhaps as a result of his adopting Stirnerite egoism, Tucker did not discuss the legitimacy of presuming consent by all to trial by jury but focused, instead, on how juries could be used as a weapon against illegitimate government.

The Debates in *Liberty*

The debates that flared around trial by jury in *Liberty* subsequent to the publication of "Free Political Institutions" had been foreshadowed several times. For example, an early discussion that occurred in *Liberty*'s first year had been sparked by the assassination of President James A. Garfield by Charles J. Guiteau in 1881. Tucker offered no defense of the act of assassination and clearly considered Guiteau to be mad. He wrote, "What may become of Guiteau is in itself a matter of little consequence. He represents a very low type of humanity."[40] Tucker focused, instead, on issues of principle. He used specific aspects of the court proceedings to highlight his theories of trial by jury and, in more general terms, he presented both the assassin and the assassination as results of statist oppression. The Guiteau case was particularly important because "Guiteau is the first man in the record of great trials who ever had a fair whack in open court at judicial liars and hirelings on the bench, legal thieves at the bar, and learned professional quacks and usurpers generally."[41]

Tucker analyzed the court proceedings as an expression of State control. He wrote, "The government experts, in Guiteau's case, seem to be having things very much their own way; and will probably succeed in getting him hanged, provided they succeed in getting the jury to accept their opinions as to his sanity, or insanity."[42] Tucker claimed that the medical experts utterly failed to render arguments or reasons to convince the "common man" of the accused's sanity and, therefore, his criminal guilt. Yet Guiteau was likely to hang on the strength of their testimony, on the basis of the government's experts.

Almost immediately, a contributor with the pen name "Basis" raised an objection that would reemerge in future discussions. In an article entitled "The Guiteau Experts," Basis argued that, if he were an accused assassin, he would prefer to have his case tried by experts rather than by twelve men who were ignorant of what constituted medical insanity. He considered a randomly chosen jury to be incapable of rendering "justice" in such a case because they were ignorant of science: it was absurd, he declared, to hang a man on the "mere opinion of twelve ordinary men." This was especially true regarding controversial cases in which the people tended to adopt a mob mentality rather than the dispassion of experts. Basis asked, "Would a jury of 'ordinary men,' unaided by expert testimony, be likely to come to a just decision, if an insane man of little character had killed with great deliberation a popular and beloved public servant?"[43]

On the same page, in a reply immediately appended to Basis' objection, Tucker set a tone typical of *Liberty*'s approach to dissent. Declaring that *all* of his editorials were serious ones—Basis had speculated to the contrary—Tucker declared, "In insinuating that [the non-seriousness] . . . he did not realize that he was offering us an insult which he would afterwards regret." After quoting testimony from the trial, Tucker suggested that Basis should read the experts in order to know what he was talking about "unless, indeed, he should suspect that these men, too, are not 'serious,' but 'merely showing off.'"[44]

Dealing with more substance, Tucker argued, "Absurd or not [to rely upon ordinary men], it is less dangerous than to make a human life dependent upon such *ex cathedra* utterances as are always purchasable in the expert market." In this, Tucker echoed a passage in "Trial by Jury" in which Spooner stated, "the powers of juries are not granted to them on the supposition that they know the law better than the justices, but on the ground that the justices are untrustworthy, that they are exposed to bribes, are fond of authority, and are also the dependent and subservient creatures of the legislature."[45]

Thus opened the debate on the wisdom of trial by jury.

The subject of an "educated jury" arose again in 1891 when George A. Schilling of Chicago questioned an article written by Yarros on the subject of majority rule. Schilling objected, "juries drawn from the body of the people impartially are not likely to be more just or intelligent than the *whole* body from which they are drawn." Acknowledging the validity of Schilling's point, Yarros explained that this was a strength of trial by jury, not a weakness. Because the jury represented "the country" in terms of intelligence, opinions, and state-of-knowledge, no State law that was vague or unpopular could be enforced. "A trial by such a tribunal is therefore in effect a trial by the country," Yarros declared.[46] In a later article, Francis Tandy added his agreement in saying, "In very few prohibition States could a jury of twelve men be found which would render a unanimous verdict to punish a man for selling liquor."[47]

Schilling also made an intriguing claim: to allow juries alone to have the final word on the law established them as a monopoly that served to strip other individuals of their equal right to judge the law in a particular case. If trial by jury was based on the right of every individual to judge the law, then juries seemed to rob the individual of the very right upon which they drew for justification. Yarros declined to argue the issue on a theoretical basis, shifting instead to utilitarian arguments. "If Mr. Schilling can point out a more perfect way of insuring 'government by consent,'" Yarros replied, "we are ready to accord it the most favorable consideration. All we assert is that reference of laws to juries is preferable to reference to majorities." Why? Because juries chosen at random are more likely to include representation of minorities and, thereby, truly represent the demographics of an area. Unfortunately, this thread of debate was not pursued.[48]

The serial publication of "Free Political Institutions: Their Nature, Essence, and Maintenance" began in June 1889. As previously mentioned, the series opened with the words, "The theory of government is that it is formed by the voluntary contract of the people individually with each other." Having set this stage and continuing to assume a legitimate government, the next installment of "Free Political Institutions" asked, "how shall this government instituted by the whole people . . . be confined to the accomplishment of those purposes alone which the whole people desire?" Yarros preserved the gist of Spooner's original answer that "The trial by jury is a *trial by the country*—that is, by the people—as distinguished from a trial by the government. . . . The object of this trial by the country . . . is to guard against every species of oppression by the government." In short, trial by jury provided an institutional procedure through which the people could pass judgment on the justice of government law and authority.[49]

What prevented such a powerful institution from becoming an instrument of arbitrary authority itself? In answering the objection that a jury could arbitrarily decide to take a man's life or property, Yarros suggested that juries should have the absolute right only to prevent such travesties from happening, not to commit them. Moreover, if a person's rights were violated, a retrial could be obtained.[50] In essence, he argued that trial by jury existed not to condemn the guilty but to protect the innocent.

The possibility of a mistrial was hardly the most prominent objection to trial by jury, however. Some contributors to *Liberty* objected to the very procedure itself. For example, Byington raised an objection to trial by jury based on one of the problems that "the rule of law" was designed to solve. In an article entitled "The Weak Side of Juries," Byington later wrote of "the need for certainty in some kinds of laws, where it has been reasonably said that certainty is sometimes more important than justice."[51]

Otherwise stated, if one purpose of the law was to provide a predictable society, then trial by jury introduced a large element of confusion and uncertainty. Could contracts be respected and enforced if they were subject to the will of twelve men rather than the letter of the law? For example, some publishers would prefer there be a clear and certain standard of obscenity by which they could predict the legality of works they published, rather than to depend on the unpredictable decision of twelve men who represented community standards. One "verdict" might be no more just than the other but—under the rule of law—predictability allowed publishers (and others) to decide which legal risks they wished to assume.

As for trial by jury protecting peaceful behavior and the equal liberty against State law, Byington expressed doubt. He believed that the prudery and other biases of the majority would intervene: he declared himself unwilling to wager $5 on the success of a peaceful defendant charged with walking naked down a public street.

The British Individualist Wordsworth Donisthorpe registered his agreement, declaring that "Juries 'hampered by law' were bad enough, but juries 'unhampered by law'—that is, left without the guidance of generalizations from thousands of cases—would be unbearable."[52]

Byington's objections to trial by jury were procedural as well as practical, including "the well known clumsiness of the jury system," which he believed would probably result in juries not being called often in "any society where things are done on a business basis." Instead of trial by jury, Byington imagined, in a rough and speculative manner, how a system of competing "defensive associations" would handle disputes. He wrote: "[D]efensive associations will have their judges, and their treaties as to the method of arbitration when two associations are on opposite sides of a case, and these tribunals of one or three professional judges will settle all cases where some one does not distinctly demand a jury. I suppose a case will almost never come before a jury except on appeal."[53]

Moreover, being practical men of business, those who ran the defensive associations would probably institute a policy stating that cases "clearly identical with ones" previously adjudicated required no jury. "If any defensive agency persistently followed the contrary policy, of demanding juries in such cases whenever its clients asked for them, it would go bankrupt with litigation."

Byington ended his article by candidly admitting, "I believe . . . I am plowing new ground, and am running that risk of error. . . . Such errors may be shown up by contradiction . . . and I guess the contradiction will come."[54]

Indeed, Tucker had written a one-paragraph response that preceded Byington's article, but he did not specifically address the "new ground" broken. He merely denied in advance that the jury system was "clumsy" or would be rarely used by a defensive association, and he seemed dismissive of Byington's other ensuing arguments, merely denying them rather than arguing against them.

Byington took up the debate once more by quoting from an editorial run by the "Times of Natal"—an English-speaking country in which racism made trial by jury for black defendants undesirable. Judgments could not be obtained against whites who committed acts of aggression against blacks. Byington claimed that in the presence of such prejudices, "trial by jury" became an instrument of injustice. Moreover, the prejudice would not need to be widespread for it to have a disastrous impact on the Anarchistic jury system. "If only ten per cent of the people were of this sort, more than sixty-four per cent of the juries would include one or more of these men to prevent a conviction. In order that there should be an even chance of twelve men taken at random being unanimously willing to judge according to certain principles, it is necessary that there be not so many as six per cent of the population who reject those principles."[55]

Byington declared it impractical to believe that any particular society would sufficiently adopt Anarchistic principles so as to allow for fair juries. He believed at least 6 percent of the people would always reject the law of equal liberty and, so, there would never be more than a 50/50 chance of a fair trial by jury. "Under certain circumstances," he declared, "juries are so certain to give a biased verdict that trials are little else than a waste of time."[56]

In response, Tucker seemed to move far from his initial reverence for trial by jury to a more pragmatic stance. He wrote, "those Anarchists who favor the jury system advocated by Lysander Spooner do not make it an essential of Anarchism. They offer it simply as a possible—and very good—means of securing an approximation to justice, in answer to those objectors to Anarchism who maintain that without government it is impossible to secure justice."[57]

Unfortunately, the reopening of this disagreement occurred in December 1907, in the second to last issue before *Liberty*'s demise.

Conclusion

Whether a jury system appears desirable seems to hinge on the observer's viewpoint. If the jury is seen to sit in judgment on the law, it may well be an effective strategy against oppressive government. If the jury is seen to sit in judgment on other and unconsenting human beings, the procedure seems to be at odds with Individualist Anarchism because it is difficult to understand where a collective entity derives such a right if it is not assigned by the individual.

Perhaps Byington resolved the debate by observing that, as a procedure, trial by jury had not evolved within a "society where things are done on a business basis," and any system of justice that did so evolve would be unlikely to embrace it. Moreover, to the extent a free-market justice system existed, the jury system's current function of mitigating oppressive laws might lose much of its value. In place of this strategic advantage, the disadvantages of trial by jury might loom large: its expense, the unpredictability of its verdicts, the problem of dissenting defendants, and the widespread tendency toward prejudice. In short, trial by jury may be a procedure that can be justified only in the presence of oppressive government. It may be an object lesson in how a free-market society should not look to structures and institutions that evolved in response to oppression, but seek instead to sculpt their own.

Notes

1. Victor Yarros, "An Exchange of Cordial Invitations," *Liberty* 8 (January 2, 1892): 2.

2. Some voices in *Liberty*, for example, Yarros, believed that alternate institutions would evolve naturally under conditions of freedom.

3. In his work *State Socialism and Anarchism*, Tucker wrote,

[E]ducation is a slow process, and for this reason we must hope that the day of readjustment may not come too quickly. Anarchists who endeavor to hasten it by joining in the propaganda of State Socialism or revolution make a sad mistake indeed. They help to so force the march of events that the people will not have time to find out, by the study of their experience, that their troubles have been due to the rejection of competition. If this lesson shall not be learned in season, the past will be repeated in the future.

As quoted in James J. Martin, *Men Against the State: The Expositors of Individualist Anarchism in America, 1827-1908* (Colorado Springs, Colo.: Ralph Myles, 1970), 274.

4. Footnote 87 in Paul Eltzbacher, *Anarchism: Exponents of Anarchist Philosophy*, trans. Steven T. Byington, ed. James J. Martin (Plainview, N.Y.: Books for Libraries Press, 1960), 134.

5. Benjamin R. Tucker, *Instead of a Book, by a Man Too Busy to Write One; A Fragmentary Exposition of Philosophical Anarchism* (New York: B. R. Tucker, 1893), 32.

6. Benjamin R. Tucker, "On Picket Duty," *Liberty* 11 (June 29, 1895): 1.

7. Benjamin R. Tucker, "On Picket Duty," *Liberty* 1 (March 4, 1882): 1.

8. F. D. Tandy, "The Importance of Trial by Jury," *Liberty* 10 (June 2, 1894) 2.

9. Although Locke requires each generation to "sign on," the institution he calls a Government retains a continuing territorial jurisdiction to the land which nonsignatories must leave.

10. As quoted in Michael E. Coughlin, Charles H. Hamilton, and Mark A. Sullivan, eds., *Benjamin R. Tucker and The Champions of Liberty* (St. Paul, Minn.: Michael E. Coughlin, 1986), 46.

11. Michael E. Coughlin, "The Jury: Defender or Oppressor," in Coughlin, Hamilton, and Sullivan, *Benjamin R. Tucker and the Champions of Liberty*, 46.

12. Lysander Spooner, *An Essay on Trial by Jury* (Boston: n.p., 1852).

13. Lysander Spooner, *A Defense of Fugitive Slaves, Against the Acts of Congress of February 2, 1793, and September 18, 1850* (Boston: n.p., 1850).

14. Lysander Spooner, *The Lysander Spooner Reader* (San Francisco: Fox & Wilkes, 1992), 121. Emphasis in original.

15. Spooner also detailed the internal mechanisms that would ensure a "legal" jury, such as proper selection methods.

16. Spooner, *The Lysander Spooner Reader*, 220.

17. Spooner, *The Lysander Spooner Reader*, 303. The last chapters of "Trial by Jury" were entitled, respectively, "The Free Administration of Justice," "The Criminal Intent," "Moral Considerations for Jurors," "Authority of Magna Carta," and "Limitations Imposed upon the Majority by the Trial by Jury."

18. Benjamin R. Tucker, "More Questions," *Liberty* 5 (January 28, 1888): 5.

19. Benjamin R. Tucker, "Not Content to Be Figureheads," *Liberty* 10 (June 2, 1894): 5.

20. Benjamin R. Tucker, "A Blow at Trial by Jury," *Liberty* 13 (August, 1897): 2. Anarchists were particularly sensitive to the implied support of the death penalty due to the Haymarket Affair in Chicago, which led to the hanging of several demonstrably innocent comrades. In the second part of "A Blow at Trial by Jury," Tucker wrote of "the judicial murder of August Spies and his comrades at Chicago."

21. Tucker, "A Blow at Trial by Jury," 5.

22. Benjamin R. Tucker, "The Special Jury Mass Meeting," *Liberty* 13 (July 1897): 4.

23. Tucker, "The Special Jury Mass Meeting," 5.

24. *Liberty* 10 (May 19, 1894): 5. Emphasis in original.

25. Benjamin R. Tucker, "On Picket Duty," *Liberty* 11 (June 29, 1895): 1. Tucker was well versed in Spooner's argument, "The second essential principle of the common law, controlling the selection of jurors, is, that when the selection of the actual jurors

comes to be made . . . that selection shall be made in some mode that excludes the possi-bility of choice *on the part of the government."* Spooner, *Trial by Jury,* 242.

26. Benjamin R. Tucker, "On Picket Duty," *Liberty* 13 (March, 1897): 1.

27. Benjamin R. Tucker, "A Blow at Trial by Jury," *Liberty* 13 (August, 1897): 5.

28. Tucker, "A Blow at Trial by Jury," 3.

29. "Half an Hour with Justice," *Liberty* 13 (December, 1897): 4-5. Tucker felt so strongly about refusing to return an "instructed" verdict that he even praised Henry George—a common target of *Liberty* insults —for opposing the orders of a judge while serving on a jury. In a rare statement, Tucker declared, "Others should follow Mr. George's example." Benjamin R. Tucker, "On Picket Duty," *Liberty* 8 (August 20, 1892): 1.

30. S. H. Randall, "Too Honest for Jury Duty," *Liberty* 10 (October 20, 1894): 6.

31. Because the focus is on the debate within *Liberty,* I am using this version of *An Essay on Trial by Jury* in the belief that it represents what Tucker and the *Liberty* circle considered to be essential about Spooner's arguments.

The "abridgement and rearrangement" of Spooner's original treatise was extensive. For example, portions of the original's appendix on "Taxation" appear at the beginning of Yarros's version. Although Spooner's wording is generally preserved, large portions of text are deleted, and there are occasionally words inserted within sentences that are oth-erwise entirely Spooner's. For example, the opening sentence of the fourth paragraph of the appendix begins, "All government is a mutual insurance company . . ." In the fifth paragraph of Yarros's rearrangement, this opening becomes, "All legitimate government is a mutual insurance company . . ." Clearly, however, this was Spooner's meaning and not a sleight of hand by Yarros. Much of the deleted material dealt with the Magna Carta and other historical precedents in the English common law.

32. Benjamin R. Tucker, "On Picket Duty," *Liberty* 7 (September 13, 1890): 1.

33. Lysander Spooner, "No Treason No. II, The Constitution," chap. in *The Ly-sander Spooner Reader* (San Francisco: Fox & Wilkes, 1992), 59.

34. Spooner, "No Treason No. II," 60. In "No Treason," Spooner rejected the idea that by voting, you give sanction to the State. He argued that voting could be a means of self-defense, but it is not clear that Spooner advocated voting defensively. Arguing against a negative is not the logical equivalent of advocating a positive.

Spooner was something of an annoyance to George Bradburn who, as an abolition-ist, had heralded the antislavery Liberty Party. Although Spooner fully shared a commit-ment to abolitionism, he refused on principle to vote for Liberty Party candidates.

35. For more on the problem of delegation of rights, see chapter 2.

36. Spooner, *The Lysander Spooner Reader,* 225.

37. Spooner, *The Lysander Spooner Reader,* 225-226.

38. Spooner, *The Lysander Spooner Reader,* 227.

39. Victor Yarros, "Free Political Institutions," *Liberty* 6 (June 8, 1889): 2. This was the first segment. The last segment ran in *Liberty* 6 (December 28, 1889): 2.

40. Benjamin R. Tucker, "Guiteau, the Fraud-Spoiler," *Liberty* 1 (January 21, 1882): 2.

41. Tucker, "Guiteau, the Fraud-Spoiler," 2.

42. Benjamin R. Tucker, "The Guiteau Experts," *Liberty* 1 (January 7, 1882): 2.

43. Basis, "The Guiteau Experts" (second use of title), *Liberty* 1 (April 15, 1882): 3. As a counter, Tucker insisted that randomness in the selection of jurors would eliminate the "mob mentality." For example, in the Haymarket court case, he believed that a jury

drawn from Chicago's entire population would have ensured that workingmen were sworn in and their presence would have prevented a miscarriage of justice.

44. Benjamin R. Tucker, commentary on Basis, "The Guiteau Experts," *Liberty* 1 (April 15, 1882): 3-4.

45. Victor Yarros, "Free Political Institutions," *Liberty* 6 (September 7, 1889): 2.

46. Victor Yarros, "Juries and Majorities," *Liberty* 8 (October 24, 1891): 2.

47. F. D. Tandy, "The Importance of Jury Trial," *Liberty* 10 (June 2, 1894): 2.

48. Tandy, "The Importance of Jury Trial," 2.

49. Victor Yarros, "Free Political Institutions," *Liberty* 6 (June 29, 1889): 6.

50. Yarros, "Free Political Institutions," *Liberty* 6 (June 29, 1889): 6. In 1895, Yarros again picked up the theme of trial by jury in a series of articles, defending the original institution and attacking its current abuses.

51. Steven T. Byington, "The Weak Side of Juries," *Liberty* (December 1907): 49-57.

52. Wordsworth Donisthorpe, as quoted in Benjamin R. Tucker, "On Picket Duty," *Liberty* 8 (May 16, 1891): 1.

53. Steven T. Byington, "The Engenderment of Laws," *Liberty* 14 (April 1904): 4.

54. Byington, "The Engenderment of Laws," 5.

55. Byington, "The Weak Side of Juries," 52.

56. Byington, "The Weak Side of Juries," 50.

57. Benjamin R. Tucker, "On Picket Duty," *Liberty* (December 1907): 4.

Chapter 8

Economics: The Money Debate

"[L]iberty, to be effective, must find its first application in the realm of economics and nowhere has that been emphasized more continually than in this journal," declared Benjamin Tucker early in the seventh year of *Liberty*'s run.[1]

Tucker's overriding commitment to economic matters was apparent from *Liberty*'s first appearance.[2] His editorial in the first issue on August 6, 1881, declared that the purpose of *Liberty* was "Down with Authority!" by which he referred primarily to the State. An article in the same issue quoted a question from the *New York Truth*, which focused in on the area of economics that would occupy much of Tucker's attention for the next twenty-seven years: namely, usury. The *New York Truth* asked, "Somebody gets the surplus wealth that Labor produces and does not consume. Who is the Somebody?"

Like most nineteenth-century Individualist Anarchists, Tucker subscribed to a version of the labor theory of value with its corresponding theory of surplus wealth, which was wealth over and above what the laborer received for his product. According to the labor theory of value, if a worker produced a product that sold for $1.50, for which he was paid only $1.00, the "surplus" $0.50 was wealth that had been taken from him because men deserved the full fruit of their labor. Tucker considered the question of who received the surplus, and how, to be crucial.

In typical fashion, Tucker began to answer "Who is the Somebody?" by posing a more fundamental question. What were the ways people came into possession of property in the first place? He concluded that there were not many ways: "work, gift, discovery, gaming, the various forms of illegal robbery by force or fraud, usury." Unlike illegal robbery by force or fraud, usury was legalized robbery, which existed in three basic forms: interest on money, rent paid on land and houses, and profit in exchange. These were the dominant forms of legal robbery practiced by an elite class within society, the Somebodies.

But where did the Somebodies get the power to rob with impunity? Tucker answered, "From monopoly . . . Usury rests on two great monopolies,—the mo-

121

nopoly of land and the monopoly of credit."[3] These monopolies had been legally created by and were being steadfastly protected by the State, which had formed an alliance with business to rob the common man.

Tucker believed that this particular exercise of State Authority—the establishment and protection of monopolies—was the main means by which the working man was oppressed by government and big business. In the second issue of *Liberty*, he explained how the State could be eliminated in nine steps by destroying monopoly. Tucker detailed the sequence by asking a series of rhetorical questions that were directed at B. W. Ball, a contributor to *The Index*, who had been writing on Anarchism. Tucker responded within *Liberty*:

> When next he writes on anarchism, let him answer these questions:
> [1] Are not the laboring classes deprived of their earnings by usury in its three forms,—interest, rent, and profit?
> [2] Is not such deprivation the principal cause of poverty?
> [3] Is not poverty, directly or indirectly, the principal cause of illegal crime?
> [4] Is not usury dependent upon monopoly, especially upon the land and money monopolies?
> [5] Could these monopolies exist without the State at their back?
> [6] Does not by far the larger part of the work of the State consist in establishing and sustaining these monopolies and other results of special legislation?
> [7] Would not the abolition of these invasive functions of the State lead gradually to the disappearance of crime?
> [8] In that case, would not the State have been entirely abolished?
> [9] Would not this be the realization of Anarchy and the fulfillment of Proudhon's prophecy of "the dissolution of government in the economic organism"?
> To each of these questions we answer: Yes.[4]

Thus, the overriding goal of Individualist Anarchism was to expose and to destroy the monopolies created and maintained by the State in order to eliminate the State itself. Of these monopolies, the most destructive and, therefore, the most important to destroy, was the monopoly on money. "It [*Liberty*] believes that the first point of attack should be the power of legally privileged capital to increase without work. And as the monopoly of the issue of money is the chief bulwark of this power, *Liberty* turns its heaviest guns upon that."[5]

Throughout its twenty-seven years of publication, *Liberty* devoted more space by far to economic matters than to any other set of issues. Analyzing the intricate facets of the economic theory advanced by *Liberty* would require a book length treatment of its own and is beyond the scope of this volume. To render a sense of *Liberty*'s approach, however, it is valuable to examine the one aspect of economics that Tucker viewed as his *bete noire* —monopoly banking.

Before examining in detail Tucker's opposition to centralized banking, it is necessary to review the general background from which *Liberty*'s economic policies were drawn, with emphasis upon monetary theory.

Background: The Contribution of Josiah Warren

In 1833, the pioneering Anarchist Josiah Warren began publication of *The Peaceful Revolutionist*, the first Individualist-Anarchist periodical to appear in America.[6] He called for a voluntary society based on respect for individual autonomy and operating in accord with the labor theory of value. His vision was hard won, coming from his disillusioning experiences in several utopian communities that had failed. In the May 1848 issue, Warren reported on the structure of a new community, Utopia:

> Throughout the whole of our operations . . . everything has been conducted so nearly upon the Individual basis that not one meeting for legislation has taken place. No Organization, no indefinite delegated power, no 'Constitutions,' no 'laws' or 'bye [sic] laws,' 'rules' or 'regulations' but such as each individual makes for himself and his own business.[7]

Over decades of attempting to combine a philosophy of radical Individualism with community building, Warren had constantly confronted the problem of how to achieve the social advantages of community without sacrificing individual rights and choice. His quest for a just society had started in February 1826 when he became one of the original settlers of the famous Owenite community of New Harmony. Other experimental communities had followed through which Warren had observed how social theories operated when they were put to the test of functioning in the real world.

Through conducting such experiments, he evolved two principles that he considered key to the proper organization of society: 1) the Sovereignty of the Individual and 2) Cost is the Limit of Price. These principles, especially as popularized in *The Science of Society* by Warren's brilliant student Stephen Pearl Andrews, formed the broad base of theory from which nineteenth-century Individualist Anarchism evolved.[8]

Sovereignty of the Individual

In developing a philosophy of radical Individualism, Josiah Warren distanced himself theoretically from his mentor, the Socialist Robert Owen, who had been the main force behind the New Harmony Community of Equality. Like most Owenite communities, New Harmony stressed community ownership and collective decision making, both of which Warren came to believe were counter to human nature itself. For two years, Warren watched New Harmony deteriorate. It seemed to him that dissent and differences of opinion grew within the community in exact proportion to its demands that individuals conform. From this experience, he concluded that a successful community must never absorb the individual into a collective, but always respect private property and personal autonomy. Only through the institution of private property would members of a community deal with each other for mutual advantage—that is, they would co-operate—rather than quarrel constantly.

In his book, *Practical Details*, Warren sketched an alternate arrangement that preserved the health both of the individual and of the society:

> Society must be so converted as to preserve the SOVEREIGNTY OF EVERY INDIVIDUAL inviolate. That it must avoid all combinations and connections of persons and interests, and all other arrangements which will not leave every individual at all times at liberty to dispose of his or her person, and time, and property in any manner in which his or her feelings or judgment may dictate, WITHOUT INVOLVING THE PERSONS OR INTERESTS OF OTHERS.[9]

Thus, Sovereignty of the Individual was a theory of radical individual rights and responsibilities based on human nature, which was designed to achieve co-operation rather than conflict within society. The individual remained the primary unit of the community.

Cost the Limit of Price

The second mainstay of nineteenth-century Individualist Anarchism was the principle of Cost the Limit of Price. This was a version of the labor theory of value, which Warren believed was a necessary prerequisite to ensure an equitable reward for labor to the laborer.

For better or worse, after leaving the Owenite community of New Harmony, Warren retained at least one aspect of Owen's philosophy. He adopted the economic doctrine of cooperation that was expressed through the formula of "labor for labor." He used the doctrine to resolve the perceived social dilemma of how the full value of one man's labor could be exchanged for the full value of another's under current conditions. Warren realized that just having each man claim his own labor and its products would not lead to an advanced society. There could be no division of labor and flowering of wealth without a medium of exchange: that is, society needed some form of currency that would enable it to rise above the level of either brute barter or the need of each person to provide for his own needs. Warren believed that part of the answer lay making labor the basis of a circulating currency that he called "labor notes."[10]

In using cost as the limit of price, Warren was specifically objecting to the use of value as a standard of measurement. If subjective value were the limit of price, he believed that a good would rise to whatever level the seller was able to charge. Price would be determined by the desperation of the buyer. For example, a loaf of bread might cost ten thousand dollars to a starving man, or a bottle of medicine might cost twenty thousand to a mother who needed it for her child. Thus, a pricing system based on value allowed the seller to extort profit from the needy buyer.[11]

Instead of a subjective measure setting the price, Warren proposed to have cost be the objective measure and the limit. Thus, for a loaf of bread, a baker should charge only what that good had cost him, including such costs as the labor expended, the "rent" of his oven and other tools, taxes, etc. Cumulatively, these factors constituted the entire cost of the bread, which was its price. With this sort of calculation, pricing became an objective, scientific matter.

In an article entitled "The Labor Dollar," Warren's popularizer Stephen Pearl Andrews attempted to measure labor, cost, and price in a scientific manner. For example, with regard to labor, Andrews wrote, "Work of any kind, in order to be accurately and completely defined, must be determined in three aspects:— First, as to the length of time; Second, as to the degree of its intensity or severity; Third, as to the degree of acquired skill, or ability previously accumulated by other work preparatory to the work now in hand; and as to certain other minor considerations."[12] Warren attempted to bring objectivity to what he must have viewed as the chaos of the free market.

And, as always, Warren sought to test his theory in a real community.

On May 18, 1827, in Cincinnati, Warren opened what he called a Time Store, which the historian James J. Martin has dubbed, "the first scientific experiment in cooperative economy in modern history."[13] Warren's store worked on the basis of exchanging staple commodities, such as flour, priced at his own cost for the labor notes of customers. Upon opening his Time Store, with three hundred dollars worth of staple goods within, Warren posted a bill for public view, stating what each good had cost him and adding a 7 percent fee for overhead expenses such as shipping. This posted bill constituted the cost of the goods. In exchange, Warren received a labor note from the purchaser, which represented an equitable amount of the purchaser's time.[14] One of the advantages of the system was that people were far less inclined to bargain at length over prices because they were paying for the shopkeeper's time. Warren explained the process: "A clock was in plain sight to measure the time of the tender in delivering the goods which was considered one-half of the labor, and purchasing, etc. the other half."[15]

The exchange was more sophisticated than a mere hour for hour basis, however. Warren exchanged what he called "equivalent labor." "I have placed emphasis on the idea of equivalent labor, because it appears that we must discriminate between different kinds of labor, some being more disagreeable, more repugnant, requiring a more COSTLY draft upon our ease or health than others. The idea of cost extends to and embraces this difference."[16] Interestingly, this led Warren to the conclusion that the most disagreeable work, such as cleaning sewers, should be among the highest paid in society. Of course, factors such as "repugnance" were subjective matters—embodying the same subjectivity that Warren objected to in value as the measure of price. This meant that each individual must set the price for his own labor because each person is best able to estimate his own costs.

As Andrews phrased it, "Assuming, then, that by the prevalence of equity . . . we had a full supply of everybody's estimates of every kind of work in respect to its relative repugnance or attractiveness,—its intensity, in fact, as hard or easy work,—it would be easy to strike an average which should be very exact—the true par of labor intensity."[17]

Warren uses the example of coat making. Two coat makers with different levels of skill and working habits would probably set entirely different prices for a new coat. A fast working coat maker who produced a mediocre product might charge twenty hours of labor for a new garment. A slower coat maker who produced an exceptional garment might charge forty hours.

Warren also seems to have considered the problem of opportunity costs regarding interest: namely, if someone loans out money to another, he is thereby foregoing other investment opportunities for that same capital. "If you sacrifice twenty dollars (to which you are equitably entitled) in lending me a hundred, then . . . twenty dollars, or twenty per cent together with pay for your labor would be your proper compensation."[18]

Despite such problems, Warren believed that labor notes—and Cost the Limit of Price in general—would guarantee both equitable reward for the laborer and a harmonious society. "Costs being the limit of price, everyone becomes interested to reduce cost,—to lighten each other's burdens! Then, every man's hand acts with instead of against every man, and HUMAN INTERESTS ARE HARMONIZED!"[19]

Warren closed the Time Store after three years, convinced (along with many others) that "labor for labor" and Cost the Limit of Price had proven to be a viable economic arrangement.[20] Tucker referred to Warren as his "teacher" and wrote,

> It was his misfortune that he so long lacked a truth-soldier. It is true that one did appear for a time, and a master he was,—Stephen Pearl Andrews. . . . Two decades or more passed before new soldiers appeared. Then a few of us took up the fight, and by our persistent aggression more has been accomplished in the last ten years for Josiah Warren's ideas than was accomplished in the entire half century which elapsed between his discovery of them and the beginning of our warfare.[21]

Background: Lysander Spooner's Contribution

Lysander Spooner, whom Tucker called "Our Nestor," prolifically addressed the issue of money reform, focusing more upon opposing a legal monopoly and less upon instituting private currency than Warren did. Coming from a legal background, Spooner argued that the bank monopoly was unconstitutional because the Constitution did not give anyone the right to provide a national currency that the public was obliged to accept. The power to coin money did not imply a right to enforce its universal acceptance and use.

In *A New System of Paper Currency*, Spooner wrote, "[G]overnment has constitutionally no more right to forbid men's selling an invested dollar [private currency based on land or other capital] than it has to forbid the selling of a specie dollar. It has constitutionally no more power to forbid the sale of a single dollar, invested in a farm, than it has to forbid the sale of the whole farm."[22]

It is not possible to understand Spooner's emphasis on monetary theory without placing it in the context of the Legal Tender Acts and the National Banking Act of 1863, which the Union used to finance the Civil War. Through these measures, Congress guaranteed the notes of authorized bankers and legally protected them from liability for debt. The Act also established a national tax of ten percent for all money not authorized by Congress. Spooner believed that this Act established a de facto and unlawful monopoly by Congress over what was arguably the most important industry to the American economy—banking.

He also believed that the government monopoly of money and the establishment of bank charters were infringements of the right to contract in at least two manners. First, they prevented individuals from issuing money to those who would accept it. Second, they freed individual bankers from personal obligations through the act of incorporation. Thus bankers had "the advantage of two legal natures,—one favorable for making contracts, the other favorable for avoiding the responsibility of them."[23]

Spooner did not view banks as collective entities or impersonal mechanisms; he held the individual men who ran the banks personally responsible and legally liable for their policies. In his work *A New Banking System*, Spooner explained, "The 'National' system so called, is in reality no national system at all; except in the mere fact that it is called the national system and was established by the national government. It is, in truth, only a private system; a mere privilege conferred upon a few, to enable them to control prices, property, and labor, and thus swindle, plunder and oppress all the rest of the people."[24]

As early as 1843, Spooner advocated the issuance of private currency as the right of every individual. In his work *Constitutional Law Relative to Credit, Currency and Banking*, Spooner wrote, "To issue bills of credit, that is promissory notes, is a natural right. . . . The right of banking, or of contracting debts by giving promissory notes for the payment of money is as much a natural right as that of manufacturing cotton."[25] He considered the idea that government was providing money to people by prohibiting any and all competition in that area to be as absurd as saying that government provided people with food or clothing by refusing to let individuals grow food or make clothing, except as the government licenses them to do so.

Why was the right to privately issue currency of primary importance? Such issuance was not merely a natural right, it was also necessary to ensure equity to labor. Spooner also adopted a version of the labor theory of value. In *Poverty: Its Illegal Causes and Legal Cure*, Spooner argued that men deserve the full fruits of their labor. He believed that the most likely way this would happen was by each man becoming his own employer—that is, to work for himself in some direct manner. But to be a "self-employer," workers usually required access to capital in order to buy tools and otherwise establish a business. For this loan service, the monopoly banks charged what, for many, were prohibitive interest rates that shut them out of the possibility of self-employment.

Even low interest rates, if they were fixed by law, acted to deny some laborers the right to pursue credit. For example, if the capital that a laborer pledged against a loan was risky, then fixed low rates prohibited him from paying a greater rate of interest to offset the risk and secure a loan. Thus, any control on credit and interest rates—however such measures may be sold to the public as protection for the laborer—actually worked to disadvantage the working man. To put credit under the control of a banking elite only killed the ability of the poor to rise out of their poverty.

The solution to poverty? Allow each individual to access to his own capital or, at least, to access credit based upon his own capital through the issue of private currency. Spooner proposed not merely to remove restraints but to institute a parallel banking structure in which currency would be an "invested dollar" rather than a "specie dollar." That is, the dollar would be backed by "property of a fixed and permanent nature" such as a house instead of being backed by gold or silver.[26]

Spooner explained what he meant by an invested dollar in *A New System of Paper Currency*, in which he wrote, "The currency here proposed is not in the nature of a credit currency . . . it constitutes simply of bona fide certificates of Stock, which the owners have the same right to sell that they have to sell any other Stocks."[27]

In defending his rather unusual view of what constituted a dollar, Spooner attempted to demystify money by likening it to any other commodity in the market place. It was not a unique or mysterious commodity that required governmental intervention to produce. He explained,

> Perhaps we may conclude that money is simply property that is cut up, or divided, into such pieces or parcels as are convenient and acceptable to be given and received in exchange for other property; and that any man who has any property whatever that can be cut up, or divided, into such pieces of parcels, has a perfect legal and moral right thus to cut it up, and then freely offer it in the market in competition with all other money, and in exchange for any other commodity, that may there be offered in competition with, or in exchange for, it.[28]

As for the fluctuation in the value of currency from which the government allegedly protected the public, Spooner demystified that process as well. The invested dollar would have "no more true or natural market value than the property with which it is to be redeemed."[29] Rather than this leading to chaotic conditions in which no one could judge the worthiness of one money against another, Spooner claimed there was no reason to believe that money would function differently in the free market than any other commodity. "[N]amely, that free competition in producing it and offering it in the market is the sure, and only sure, way of guaranteeing to us the greatest supply, the best article and on the best terms."[30]

Free banking would improve both the quantity and the quality of money available to the common man. Moreover, it would bring the rate of interest "within the reach of everybody whose business and character should make him a reasonably safe person to loan to."[31] Instead, under monopoly banking, labor was being cheated out of its earnings by legislation that fixed artificial interest rates. A fixed high interest cheated laborers who could not afford to borrow the capital necessary to invest in themselves. Low interest rates denied opportunities to laborers with risky credit because, if they could contract freely on loans, they could pay higher rates to compensate for the risk. Although Spooner believed that interest rates would be lowered by free competition because money based on mortgages would be more plentiful than money based on specie, he also thought that high interest rates serve an economic function.

The depth of Tucker's commitment to Spooner's positions may be judged by the fact that, upon his Nestor's death, he purchased all his printed pamphlets and unpublished manuscripts from the heirs. He offered the pamphlets for sale within *Liberty*, donating the proceeds to the Spooner Publication Fund that he established to publish Spooner's manuscripts.

Background: William Bradford Greene's Contribution

Of the money reformer, William Bradford Greene, Tucker wrote, "I am indebted to Col. Greene's 'Mutual Banking' more than to any other single publication for such knowledge as I have of the principles of finance—the most compact, satisfactory, keen and clear treatise upon mutual money extant."[32] Although Warren sketched the broad framework of Individualist Anarchism and Spooner provided a well of theory from which Tucker drew, it was to Greene that he turned on monetary theory.

It is sometimes difficult to distinguish Tucker's commitment to Greene's monetary theories, however, from his admiration of Pierre Joseph Proudhon's ideas, especially Proudhon's Bank of the People. Although the banking system advanced by the two thinkers were quite similar, Tucker pinpointed a key difference between the two men. Tucker credited Proudhon with placing the issue of free banking in a larger radical framework that made him appreciate its revolutionary potential. Greene seemed to have little interest in the general theory of Anarchism and restricted himself to the single issue of banking.[33]

Just as Spooner had been deeply influenced by the centralization of banking that accompanied the Civil War and continued thereafter, Greene was impacted by the Great Panic of 1837, which has been called America's first Great Depression. In 1837, the real estate market began to collapse on a national scale and banks started to suspend payment in specie. Then, in the face of widespread bank failures, as many as nine out ten factories closed their doors. Farms across the nation were abandoned for lack of credit and the unemployed homeless roamed the cities en masse, where they often starved in the streets. The subsequent depression lasted through the early 1840s.

James J. Martin commented on one impact that the economic upheaval had upon the intellectual landscape of the United States.

> Few instances in American history have created as much curiosity concerning economic and financial matters among amateurs and members of the general citizenry as the panic of 1837. . . . Banking abuses came under concentrated scrutiny and gave rise to many proposed radical remedies. William Beck's plan for inducing the business world to adopt credit and employ it so as to perform the functions of money by utilizing a complicated system which generalized credit in account, was broached in 1839.[34]

Greene, who had been impressed by Beck's pamphlets, became one of those "amateurs" whose curiosity drove him to construct a radical remedy that would prevent another depression from devastating society. He first presented his theories in 1849 through a series of articles that appeared in the *Palladium*, a newspaper from Worcester, Massachusetts. These articles formed the basis of Greene's book *Equality*, which, in turn, was reissued in altered form as *Mutual Banking*.[35] Meanwhile, the government was slowly beginning to establish centralized banking, also as a response to the Great Panic.

Greene believed that government control and the centralization of banking did not protect the common man but was the cause of great poverty and misery. Government authorized banks prevented competition between capitalists who would have stayed in the jostle of the free market had they not been able to pool their interests through monopoly banking. In doing so, they effectively barred competitors from offering credit. By fixing interest rates, they also prevented borrowers from playing banks off against each other to obtain better terms.

To Greene, the only proper purpose of a bank was to bring lenders and borrowers together, yet monopoly banks tended to drive the two parties apart. The artificial scarcity of money caused by a monopoly created conflict between lenders and borrowers, who resented the resulting high interest rates. Moreover, government banking privileges created a class of people—shareholders—who made a profit without having to produce anything or take a risk. Greene declared such banks to be "nothing but conspiracies and combinations to defraud the public."[36]

Another effect of monopoly banking was to drive up the price of gold and silver, making them scarce commodities because they were legally designated as the basis of value for the legal tender. This meant that specie was able to purchase more of other commodities, which drove down the prices of those commodities.

Additionally, monopoly banks inevitably issued more paper dollars than they could redeem in terms of the specie they held. Through this and other processes, the money of a nation eventually consisted of little more than paper dollars that circulated because they were backed by the government, but which had no other underlying basis of value. At the same time, those who held stores of specie—most often, governments and banks—profited from its steady or increasing value.

Greene described how government banking did not prevent depressions but manufactured them. The monopoly banks issued more money than they could redeem, which drove prices upward. At that point, capitalists sold their goods and reaped huge profits. Then, the banks drew in their issues, partly by recalling loans, upon which money grows scarce and prices decline. Whereupon, "the community becomes distressed for money, individuals are forced to sell property to raise money—and to sell at a loss on account of the state of the market: then the capitalist buys what he desires to buy, while everything is cheap."[37]

Greene's solution to the economic injustice was mutual banking. People became members of a bank by pledging a mortgage on real property that they owned: bills of exchange, equaling one-half of the value of the property, were issued against the mortgage. "Anything sold under the hammer may be a basis for the issue of money," Greene declared.[38] All members of the bank contracted to accept the money issued at par when it was presented by fellow members. The rate of interest charged was expected to be only enough to pay the expenses of the bank itself, which were estimated at 1 percent. As for the valuation of the monetized property, Greene suggested that it judged against the silver dollar as a standard of value because it was "less fluctuating, more universal, and more definite, than anything else."[39] But silver would not be the basis of issue for the dollars. That is, the mutual bank bills themselves would not be redeemable in specie or, at least, not in specie only but in all commodities. Indeed, redemption in specie occasioned the payment of an extra fee.

Greene wished to wean society away from redeeming dollars in specie because he believed that, when redemption was limited to specie and when courts recognized only monopoly money for the payment of debt, those who controlled specie could "levy a tax on all transactions except such as take place without the intervention of credit."[40] Instead of making exchanges easier, therefore, the use of specie as the sole medium of exchange or basis of redemption gave a tremendous advantage to one side and created conflict.

Greene suggested land as the best basis of value for mutual money.[41] There was precedent in American history in the "land banks" that were proposed in Massachusetts in the eighteenth century, one of which operated successfully before being quickly and forcibly dissolved by the British authorities.[42]

He detailed how a mutual bank based on land would operate. By pledging real estate to a mutual bank, a person became a member of the bank who could borrow a maximum of three-quarters of the value of the property so pledged. Each member could withdraw his membership at any time upon payment of his debt.

Greene claimed that anyone who lived from wages, rather than from profit, would benefit from a system of mutual banking. How else was a working man of good reputation, but who was just starting out, to raise the capital necessary to start a business and become independent? Under mutual banking, even a young man with no basis of personal credit could find an associate—perhaps a more solvent man without good reputation—to pledge land that would be the pre-requisite for a mutual loan.

Monetary reform was seen to be a working man's issue.

Tucker's Background

Tucker synthesized the economic theories of Warren, Spooner, and Greene.[43] This synthesis had a certain inevitability about it, given Tucker's background. Tucker began his antistatist career in the spring of 1872 at the age of eighteen, largely as the result of meeting Warren and Greene at a gathering of the influential New England Labor Reform League (NELRL). The *Declaration of Sentiments* of this organization drew heavily upon the economic philosophy of Warren. The *Declaration* called for, "Free contracts, free money, free markets, free transit, and free land—by discussion, petition, remonstrance, and the ballot, to establish these articles of faith as a common need, and a common right, we avail ourselves of the advantages of associate effort."[44]

The NELRL was established through the efforts of Ezra Heywood as a means of pursuing less traditional ways for improving the economic conditions of working people. In turn, the NELRL inspired Heywood to publish one of the most influential periodicals of nineteenth-century libertarianism—*The Word: A Monthly Journal of Reform* (1872-1893), to which Warren contributed. The prospectus of *The Word* declared:

> THE WORD favors the abolition of speculative income, of woman's slavery, and war government; regards all claims to property not founded on a labor title as morally void, and asserts the free use of land to be the inalienable privilege of every human being—on having the right to own or sell only his service impressed upon it. Not by restrictive methods, but through freedom and reciprocity, THE WORD seeks the extinction of interest, rent, dividends, and profit, except as they represent work done; the abolition of railway, telegraphic, banking, trades-union and other corporations charging more than actual cost for values furnished, and the repudiation of all so-called debts the principal whereof has been paid in the form of interest.[45]

In correspondence with Heywood, Tucker informed the editor, "I hope to do some work for the Labor Cause but first wish to study the question that I may thoroughly understand it."[46]

In 1874, under Greene's influence, Tucker made his first trip to France in order to study the manuscripts of Proudhon. Upon his return to the United States in 1875, Tucker became the associate editor of *The Word*. At the age of twenty-one, Tucker's status as a serious thinker was established within the Anarchist community by his 500-page translation of Proudhon's "What Is Property?" which was published in 1876.[47] Disillusioned by Heywood's drift toward free love and away from labor reform, he resigned from *The Word* in December 1876 and began to publish the *Radical Review* (1877-1878), which stressed freethought and labor.[48]

Then, in 1881, *Liberty* was born to provide a pure vehicle for Anarchism that emphasized economics, especially the money issue. As mentioned previously, the incredible diversity and longevity of *Liberty*, coupled with Tucker's prolific pen, makes it difficult to organize a general analysis of his economic views. For the purposes of this chapter, the subject of usury is broken into three very broad categories: money and interest, land and rent, and trade and industry.[49] The connection that linked and sustained all three forms of usury was the support of the State, upon which all coercive monopolies rested.

Trade and Industry

Tucker's analysis of profit taking with regard to trade fell into two categories, which were defined by the recipient of benefits: namely, the laborer and the businessman. In terms of the laborer, Tucker's attitude toward strikes was indicative of his general approach to labor reform. In terms of business, his stand on tariffs was indicative. In both cases, his approach was consistent: the first step in curing the problem was to remove coercion—especially in the form of the State—from the situation. The State could not be part of the cure.

With regard to labor, Tucker staunchly advocated strikes as a strategy so long as the use of force was eschewed. He wrote, "Strikes, whenever and wherever inaugurated, deserve encouragement from all true friends of labor. They give evidence of life and spirit and hope and growing intelligence. They show that the people are beginning to know their rights, and knowing, dare maintain them."[50]

Twelve years later, as strikes were being successfully utilized by the mainstream labor movement, *Liberty*'s position remained consistent. In 1894, Tucker wrote of the "great railroad strike" (the Pullman strike) and lamented the fact that "sentimental editors" were using it as a reason to call for legislation. To him, the demand for legislation as a labor cure-all only masked the important issues raised by labor agitation, issues such as the federal encroachment upon labor's rights and the propriety of using violence in response. Tucker condemned the violence on both sides but left no doubt as to where his sympathy lay. "To those who shriek that labor is criminal, we say that capital is far more criminal." To those who decried disorderly strikes, Tucker advised them to work for conditions that allowed orderly strikes to function unmolested by the authorities.[51]

Tucker's antipathy toward labor laws led him to oppose many popular labor organizations of his day, such as the Knights of Labor who called for "proworker" legislation and supported "pro-labor" political candidates. *Liberty*'s refusal to deal with the Knights sparked several altercations within its pages. For example, F.F.K.—a synonym for Florence Finch Kelly—contributed an article entitled "Use Them Instead of Abusing Them" in which she objected to

Tucker's constant criticism of the Knights. While admitting "there is much in their methods and their intentions that is repulsive to an Anarchist," Kelly pointed to their "good impulses and right tendencies." She believed it was "a great mistake not to make use of every possible opportunity of making people familiar with Anarchistic principles." In short, she called for the infiltration of the Knights of Labor by Individualist Anarchists for the purpose of spreading their ideas among the membership.[52]

In typical fashion, Tucker responded to her admonishments in an article entitled "A Great Idea Perverted." He detailed a petition that the Knights of Labor had voted to send to Congress regarding monetary policies of the nation. One section of the petition called for imprisonment and forfeiture of all wealth as well as forfeiture of citizenship for the crime of privately selling gold and silver coin. Tucker concluded with high irony, "A beautiful organization, these Knights of Labor, for an Anarchist to belong to!"[53]

Tucker was no less harsh with businessmen who appealed to the State for protection or privilege. In particular, he attacked those businesses who benefited from the protection of tariffs, official duties, and customs imposed by government on imports or exports. Such measures infringed the right of an individual to buy and sell without being held up by "a highwayman" whenever he crossed an artificial, State-created line known as a border. By raising the price of goods that might compete with homemade products, tariffs forced consumers to pay a premium to business whenever they made a purchase.

The ill effects of the tariff monopoly were not limited to levying an invisible tax on consumers. It also distorted the natural allocation of capital and material that occurred in a free market by legally "fostering production at high prices and under unfavorable conditions." Thus, uncompetitive businesses which produced an inferior product enjoyed a market share that was legally protected by a government who visited "the penalty of taxation [tariff]" upon "those who patronize production at low prices and favorable conditions." Sheltered from competition, protected business drove up prices and encouraged the misallocation of resources.[54]

The Land Monopoly

Tucker considered the land monopoly to be second in importance only to the money monopoly. This monopoly rested upon the legal enforcement of government titles to land. Rent was the "tax" levied by the land monopoly, and Tucker believed rent would be driven down toward zero if titles were based on the principle of occupancy and use instead of governmental authority.[55]

After the natural rights versus egoism debate of 1886 within *Liberty* and Tucker's rejection of natural rights, he did not accept the idea of property in anything except as acquired through contract. Through the act of contracting, an individual voluntarily bound his will and granted a "right" to the other party. Without a contract, "rights" were merely social conventions.

This definition of rights posed a problem for land ownership. The fact that no one had produced the land itself meant that no one had a superior claim to possess any particular parcel nor to transfer it through contract. Nevertheless, because land was limited in quantity and much in demand, it was necessary to find some method by which to determine whose claim was superior. Tucker adopted the standard of occupancy and use. A person's claim to a piece of land resulted from his brute possession of it—that is, from his occupancy and use of the land. Or, more accurately, he established a claim to land by virtue of the use he made of it, for example, by building a house upon a lot. The man could then claim the lot itself by virtue of possessing the house resting upon it.

Tucker used the phrase "land for the people" to describe his policy on land. By this phrase, he advocated "the protection . . . of all people who desire to cultivate land in the possession of whatever land they personally cultivate, without distinction between the existing classes of landlords, tenants, and laborers, and the positive refusal of the protecting power to lend its aid to the collection of any rent whatsoever."[56]

Thus, Tucker called for the existing status quo of "ownership" to be recognized to the extent that it was based upon occupancy and use. The inequities of current land ownership would quickly and naturally fall away once the State ceased to enforce rent agreements. Indeed, rent and landlordism would be virtually eliminated.

Much of *Liberty*'s discussion of land was in the context of Tucker's fundamental disagreement with Henry George in that area. George and his followers, called Georgists, agreed that no one could rightfully claim land because it had been produced by no one. Yet some land was clearly more desirable perhaps because of soil conditions. If everyone had an equal right to own this unproduced good, how could it be just for one man to claim the very best parcel and deprive others of its advantages? This seemed particularly unjust to Georgists when the value of the land derived from the improvements that others in the community had made that benefited the owner. For example, the community may have built roads that allowed easy access from the land to markets, schools, and other desirable destinations. George's solution was a tax levied upon property owners by their community, which he called "the Single Tax."

Tucker utterly rejected this proposal, referring to the Single Tax as a State Socialist measure. "In the first place, if I have a right to a share of the advantages that accrue from the possession of superior land, then that share is mine; it is my property . . . no man, no body of men, is entitled to decide how this property shall be used." If the property was not his by right but only possessed by him, Tucker considered it "impertinent, dishonest, and tyrannical" for any one either to take it away from the "land-occupant" or to demand taxes.

Tucker denied that members of a community had a collective claim upon any land within the community that they did not personally occupy. Indeed, he did not believe an entity known as "community" existed at all.

That there is an entity known as the community which is the rightful owner of all land Anarchists deny. I . . . maintain that "the community" is a non-entity, that it has no existence, and is simply a combination of individuals having no prerogatives beyond those of the individuals themselves. This combination of individuals has no better title to the land than any single individual outside it.[57]

The Single Tax was merely the community exerting its "right of might" over the individual. And, if the government—whether it was called a community or a State—could collect rent, then what would prevent it from collecting interest and other forms of usury? Tucker declared, "There was never anything more absurd than the supposition of some Single-Taxers that this tax can be harmonized with Anarchism."[58]

Although the land monopoly was often discussed as an issue separate from that of money, Tucker did not think the two monopolies could be disentangled from each other. After all, land and houses were the most commonly suggested commodities to form the basis of currency from mutual banks. Thus restricting land ownership deprived people of the capital they needed to participate in mutual money. In the same manner, removing restrictions from the money monopoly would have salutary effects upon land ownership, because it would cause a fall in interest rates and a fall in rent would follow. "For no one who can borrow capital at one percent with which to build a house of his own will consent to pay rent to a landlord at a higher rate than that."[59]

As important as free land might have been, however, the most important monopoly upon which the State rested was that of money.

The Money Monopoly

In building an argument for mutual banking, Tucker drew clear definitions and hard distinctions. For example, he distinguished between money and capital.

Representative money [a paper dollar] is not capital, it is only a title to capital. He who borrows a paper dollar from another simply borrows a title. Consequently he takes from the lender nothing which the lender wishes to use; unless, indeed, the lender desires to purchase capital with his dollar, in which case he will not lend it, or, if he does, will charge for the sacrifice of his opportunity,— a very different thing from usury, which is payment, not for the lender's sacrifice, but for the borrower's use; that is, not for a burden borne, but for a benefit conferred.[60]

Further, Tucker believed that capital and product were one and the same thing and did not constitute different kinds of wealth. They were "simply alternative conditions or functions of the same wealth" that "undergoes an incessant transformation from capital into product and from product into capital."[61] Thus, a house could be the product of a man's labor and then be used as the capital he uses to borrow or issue money. This meant that any commodity produced could be the capital upon which currency was based.

Not surprisingly, Tucker's argument for mutual banking proceeded along lines very similar to those of his mentors. To restate the position briefly: money was a necessary aspect of a society if it wished to rise above the level of brute barter because money provided a medium of exchange that allowed the division of labor. Money was worthless except for the capital it represented and for the willingness of people to accept its value. The buyer took money, which represented the title to capital, into the marketplace and traded with those who accepted its value for real capital, such as tools and shoes. Those who required money to purchase capital borrowed it from lenders who charged a fee to cover the risk and expense involved in the loan: this fee was called interest. Under free banking, the lender would be a private individual or entity and the interest rate would be quite low. But the right to issue money had been monopolized by government-authorized banks who used the law to penalize competitors. The monopoly resulted in a scarcity of money that drove interest rates up to an artificially high price. In turn, this stifled productivity because working people could not or would not borrow at such ruinous rates. The monopoly banks thrived while the working man and the consumer were systematically defrauded.

The solution was simply and immediately to abolish the money monopoly. "For . . . if the business of banking were made free to all, more and more persons would enter into it until the competition would become sharp enough to reduce the price of lending money to the labor cost, which statistics show to be less than three-fourths of one percent."[62]

The foregoing is the basic outline of *Liberty*'s position on money. One of the best and more detailed expositions occurred in an article written by Hugo Bilgram, "Is Interest Just?" With this article, Bilgram assumed the honor of occupying the first page of *Liberty*, which was customarily reserved for Tucker. Bilgram began by defining the key term "interest" as "the premium paid for the loan of money." He eliminated from his discussion that portion of "interest" that acted as insurance against the risk that a lender must assume, a payment which he did not find improper. "Interest proper is therefore only that part of the gross interest which constitutes, in the grand average, a persistent net income to the lender of money." Thereafter, his use of the word "interest" excluded the payment for risk by assuming a theoretical loan in which there was no risk of default.

In the context of such a loan, Bilgram inquired into the cause of paying interest to the lender. He dismissed the contention that interest was paid on loans because of the opportunity cost imposed upon the lender. That is, because the lender diverted money into the loan, it was not available to him to invest in another profit-making arena. Therefore, he should be reimbursed for the opportunity cost. Bilgram insisted, "The reason why interest is paid on money loans must be treated independently of the profit-bearing power of invested capital." If the lender had wished to use the money in another manner, he would have done so.

Bilgram then proceeded to define a term that would soon arise in his argument against interest—"justice." He considered "justice" to be a synonym for "the absence of violent unilateral interference." Thus, every voluntary contract between two people was perfectly just whether or not it involved the folly of paying high interest rates. But such contracts did not exist in current society because the State, through legislation, acted as a violent third party who denied the very possibility of free contracts. This fact alone rendered all current loan contracts unjust because they could not pass the test of his definition of justice. This form of direct interference in the ability to freely contract Bilgram called a "personal monopoly."

Next he described an "impersonal monopoly" through an analogy, "Suppose the government prescribes the number of shoes in the country, forbidding the making of new shoes except for replacing those worn out." If the number of shoes produced in this manner was less than the number of people in the country, then some people would have to go barefoot. Moreover, some people undoubtedly would come to own more than one pair of shoes, if only through inheritance. This would make the number of barefoot people rise even further. "Those who have more shoes than they need will find it profitable to hire their surplus shoes to those who have none, say at the rate of $25 a year." The obvious parallel to the monopoly in shoe production, and the resulting scarcity of shoes, was the monopoly in the issue of currency. Some people would receive more scarce currency than others, who would be forced to pay for the privilege of borrowing it. This form of State control and State-induced scarcity Bilgram called an "impersonal monopoly." It, too, interfered with individuals freely contracting with each other for shoes or for money.

The groundwork had been laid for an exploration and advocacy of mutual money, which offered a solution to the scarcity of currency caused by State monopoly. Bilgram observed, "Fortunately it has been found that promissory notes which constitute liens on the wealth possessed by the issuer will answer as well as the metals. By this means the amount of money can be vastly increased."[63]

But how exactly was money "made" or issued? The first prerequisite for money was wealth that could serve as the basis for issue; the second prerequisite was a token—a coin, a paper dollar, a promissory note—by which the title of ownership to the wealth could be transferred from hand to hand in the course of exchanges; and, the third prerequisite was people's agreement to accept the tokens as valid representations of wealth. Ideally, as with gold coin, people's acceptance would be universal. It was the last prerequisite of money—the people's acceptance—through which the State enforced its monopoly, through laws against circulating private currency, and through courts that recognized only authorized dollars as legal tender with which to pay debts.

After he explained how money was made, Bilgram explained the basics of how a loan occurred. He postulated a manufacturer who had received a promissory note that was due in three months and redeemable in goods that he would receive from the issuer at that time. The note represented a legal claim, due three months hence, on the future property of the person who issued it. The manufacturer then took the note to a bank, endorsed it over and, so, converted it into a claim, not only on the future property of the original issuer, but also on his own property in case the issuer failed to satisfy its terms.

The banker had a different type of promissory note—paper money—representing a claim on property, which had been ensured through bonds deposited in the national treasury. The paper dollars were redeemable on demand in gold, but they functioned on an implicit understanding that few people would actually seek to so redeem them. A loan occurred when the banker exchanged paper dollars for the endorsed promissory note under specific terms. After three months, if the manufacturer wished to reclaim the original note by paying off the loan, the note would be returned to him. If the banker demanded more than the note itself, plus his costs in handling, the excess was called interest.

According to Bilgram, the only reason the banker could charge interest was the "monetization" of the banker's promissory notes. That is, by law they were endowed with the privilege of general acceptance. Thus, Bilgram concluded, "It is true, the right to become a banker is not denied to me. . . . I possess the necessary money, the note. I am willing to pay an adequate insurance to cover the probable loss from risk, thereby making the security offered by me as good as that securing the bank notes; but, in order to use it as money, I must go to the usurer and pay him for a temporary exchange of notes a tribute." In this manner, government became "the principal actor" in a "conspiracy through which the producers are robbed of about one-half of the results of their labor."[64]

The Debate on Money within *Liberty*

Due to sheer volume, it is difficult to isolate the discussions and debates that raged around monetary theory within *Liberty*.[65] Among the most interesting of the debates were those that occurred between the American Individualist Anarchists and the British Individualists who included Auberon Herbert, Wordsworth Donisthorpe, Joseph Greevz Fisher, Albert Tarn, Joseph Hiam Levy, John Badcock, Jr., and Henry Seymour.[66]

Both sides of the debate shared a common belief in individual freedom within economic and social exchanges, but they disagreed on many points such as Anarchism versus limited government. As the contemporary voluntaryist Carl Watner has written, "Benjamin R. Tucker defined anarchism as the doctrine that the State should be abolished and all the affairs of men be carried out on a voluntary basis. More than likely, Herbert, Donisthorpe, Tarn, Seymour, and Badcock would have accepted this statement as an expression of their own political beliefs. J. H. Levy definitely would not have."[67]

Even in focusing in on the debates between the two sides of the Atlantic, however, it is necessary to further refine the voluminous discussion down to a representative few exchanges.

The First Debate with J. Greevz Fisher

In 1891, Tucker and Fisher began a debate on the money monopoly, which focused on the topic of gold. Gold was the traditionally accepted standard of value for money but, according to Tucker, by legally declaring gold to be the standard of value *and* basis of currency, the State had artificially driven up the price of gold and forced it from the marketplace as a commodity. The rise in value had benefited the owners of gold, who were most often the State and the bankers, to the disadvantage of everyone else. By contrast, mutual banking would lower the price of gold because it would no longer enjoy a legal monopoly as a basis of issue, thus making it less valuable.

Liberty's debate with Fisher over gold started with an editorial commentary in which Tucker critiqued a letter Fisher had written to the London periodical, the *Herald of Anarchy*. In his letter, Fisher had asserted that "government does not, and never can, fix the value of gold or any other commodity," and denied that government even affected "such value except by the slight additional demand which it creates as a customer." Tucker agreed that government could not *fix* the value of gold or of any other commodity, because its influence—even when translated into draconian law—was only one of several factors that governed value within society. For example, even if gold were outlawed, a black market in the commodity would spring up.

Nevertheless, Tucker maintained that the government's power to influence the value of gold was far out of proportion to its importance as a mere consumer of the commodity. This was because government could create a false utility for gold—namely, its value in redeeming paper money—as a matter of "arbitrary decree." Tucker drew several analogies. The first was meant to demonstrate the effect of prohibiting private currency, "When the government prohibits the manufacture and sale of liquor, does it not thereby reduce the value of everything that is used in such manufacture and sale?" Equally, a prohibition on the issuance of currency devalued the capital of all nonbankers.

Another analogy sketched the affect of government control on prices and value. "If government were to allow theatrical performances on Sundays [which were then prohibited under Blue Laws], would not the value of every building that contains a theatre rise?" If government were to withdraw from the business of stating what capital could legally be the basis of currency, all capital would rise in value.

But Tucker's commentary contained more than a mere difference of theory. Clearly, the editor was irritated by Fisher. He claimed that Fisher had lectured the editor of *Herald of Anarchy* in a "dogmatic, know-it-all style which only those are justified in assuming who can sustain their statements by facts and logic."[68]

Three issues later, Fisher responded in a letter to the editor that Tucker captioned "The Power of Government over Value" and to which he appended a response.[69] Fisher denied that the analogy drawn between prohibiting Sunday performances and gold was valid. In the case of the theater, the effect of government prohibition served to "diminish demand and to prolong or retard consumption." Although opening Sunday theaters might increase the value of buildings containing them in the short term, others would quickly construct more theaters to share in the profit and the price would level out. In the case of gold, however, government interference had little impact in increasing consumption because government did not "collect it to consume it, but simply to sell it." You could not compare a prohibition on consumption with a prohibition on a medium of exchange.

From England, Fisher observed, "beyond specifying this metal as the vehicle of value in contributing to the revenue, the interference appears to be limited to a restriction of the liberty of citizens to exchange promises of delivery of gold to bearer on demand." This was a restriction in form "only and not one in quantity" because people were able to circulate "checks, drafts, and promissory notes other than to bearer on demand" in unlimited quantity. Because they were transferable, they functioned as currency even though they had next to nothing to do with the consumption of gold. Finally, Fisher argued that government was not responsible for making gold the universally accepted standard of value. Rather, "the portability, divisibility, and recognizability" of gold forced itself "upon the attention of every one who avails himself of the services of others."[70] Gold had simply been the only logical choice.

Tucker's response was unfriendly. Fisher had opened his letter with an acknowledgment of the validity of Tucker's accusation of dogmatism; he had directed no personal comments toward Tucker; and, he signed himself "Respectfully Yours."[71] Nevertheless, Tucker accused Fisher of "addressing the Anarchists upon finance as if they were babies and he a giant." He asked Fisher to consider the theater analogy once more. Not all theaters would be allowed to show Sunday performances, but only certain theaters would be so allowed. Others would be legally constrained from competing on that day. That was the true analogy to the money monopoly. Moreover, Tucker claimed that the very fact Fisher acknowledged that a rise in theater values would follow a release from Sunday prohibitions utterly destroyed his contention that government could not materially influence prices.

In conclusion, Tucker accused Fisher of belittling "the restrictions placed upon the issue of paper money" and asked whether England would permit a mutual bank to exist.[72]

Fisher's response in the next issue of *Liberty* highlighted the difference in approach to government that defined the two men. Fisher contended that most governmental interference was well intentioned, although injurious in consequence. The response also revealed a diminution of civility. Fisher opened his letter by lamenting that liberty was being wounded within its own house of *Liberty*. He accused Tucker of viewing freedom as a panacea for all social wrongs when "there is no more philosophical reason for believing that all men can be equal, rich, and happy than for believing that all animals can be equal, including, of course, that they should all be equal to men."[73]

Continuing in this vein, Fisher commented on the error of considering governmental interference in "our existing systems of currency" to be any "more pernicious than in many other matters." He argued that the contrary was true because of the ineffectiveness of government in the area of currency. "[T]here is scarcely anything which more completely illustrates the powerlessness of government to establish code in opposition to custom than the unvarying failure of unsound currency enactments."

Thus, Fisher rejected the entire basis of Tucker's call for free banking. He wrote, "Low rates of interest depend upon the magnitude of the mass of capital competing for investment rather than upon the presence or absence of the really trifling interference of governments with the modes in which debt can be incurred." He called free trade in banking nothing more or less than a cry for unlimited liberty to create debt under the label of money. Credit, unlike currency, did not represent title to capital, it did not represent wealth but only a promise. Fisher referred to Tucker as a "currency-faddist."

As for the price of gold being too high, Fisher inquired after the practical evidence upon which Tucker based his empirical claim that displacing gold from currency would reduce the price of gold "as long as its cost and utility remain what they now are." The reason that gold would maintain its price, according to Fisher, was that "Gold is valuable; it does not merely represent value. The value represents an estimate of the comparative labor necessary to produce the last increment needful to replenish the stock of gold at a rate equivalent to its consumption,—this consumption depending upon the comparative utility of gold in relation to its own value and that of other commodities."[74]

Tucker replied that free trade in banking did not mean "*only* unlimited liberty to create debt" but also "vastly increased ability to meet debt," which made it a "blessing." Moreover, it was "not erroneous to label evidence of debt as money. . . . When evidence of debt circulates as a medium of exchange, to all intents and purposes it is money." Here Tucker was saying that anything that served as an accepted medium of exchange *was* money because that was the definition of what constituted money.

As for Fisher's statement that displacing gold from currency would not reduce its price as long as its cost and utility remain what they now are, Tucker declared it to be absurd. It was comparable to saying that "displacing flour as an ingredient of bread would" not "reduce the price of flour as long as its cost and utility remain what they now are. The utility of flour consists in the fact that it is an ingredient in bread." The utility of gold consisted in the fact that is was the legal standard of value. The value of gold would be reduced by stripping it of "that exclusive monetary utility conferred upon it by the State." But by how much, Tucker was unwilling to speculate.[75]

The next "exchange" was rather summarily dismissed by Tucker who dealt with Fisher's rejoinders only in his editorial comments on the first page, referring to the arguments as "a string of assumptions" most of which were untrue. Although Tucker proceeded to contradict various facts presented in Fisher's article, printed on page three of the issue, he gave the impression that the arguments did not merit more than the brevity of dismissing them.[76]

The exchange on gold was winding down. The next volley covered little new ground, with Fisher making points that Tucker claimed were based on misrepresentations of his position. The only issue of significance broached was that of risk: namely, the claim that interest was a payment to the lender for the risk of lending money that might never be repaid. Tucker agreed that everyone who delayed the consumption of money incurred a risk but, then, so did anyone who held onto currency. After all, gold might plummet and drastically reduce the value of the currency being hoarded.

Of Fisher's rejection of loans without interest, Tucker parodied his opponent's position,

> "Credit without remuneration!" shrieks Mr. Fisher in horror. But, if credit is reciprocal, why should there be remuneration? "Debt without cost!" But, if debt is reciprocal, why should there be cost? "Unlimited or very plentiful money without depreciation!" But if the contemplated addition to the volume of currency contemplates in turn a broadening of the basis of currency, why should there be depreciation? . . . Mr. Fisher has been so inveterate a drinker of bad economic whiskey that he has got the economic jim-jams and sees snakes on every hand.[77]

The Second Debate

Fisher and *Liberty* entered debate again in 1894. The spark was the 1893 publication of Bilgram's article "Is Interest Just?" previously mentioned, which had been first delivered as a speech before the Friendship Liberal League of Philadelphia on Sunday, April 9. Bilgram had drawn particular respect from Tucker who praised his work *Involuntary Idleness* and compared it in importance to Greene's *Mutual Banking*. It may be assumed that Bilgram expressed the editor's views.[78]

At first, Bilgram's article occasioned little comment. For example, the money reformer J. K. Ingalls phrased his criticism of the article within a more general endorsement of it, calling Bilgram to task only for ascribing interest entirely to scarcity of money when other factors, such as patent right entitlements, contributed as well.[79] Bilgram responded that he had limited himself only to the money supply due to time and space restraints.

In March 1894, *Liberty* noted that a criticism by Fisher of Bilgram's article had appeared in the Manchester *Times* in England.[80] Responding in *Liberty*, Bilgram claimed that Fisher had not used his carefully spelled out definitions but had criticized his argument according to other definitions of key terms such as "interest."[81]

Regarding Fisher's claim that instruments such as checks and promissory notes could circulate like money, Bilgram denied stating that government restricted credit. What he had said was that government restricted the "monetization of credit"—that is, government controlled which form of credit was legally and, thus, universally accepted. Bilgram asked, "Can Mr. Fisher deny the existence of an unjust discrimination?" Under current conditions, checks could not substitute for legal money. For example, employees would not accept them as wages because they could not use them in stores that did not recognize the issuer of the check; by contrast, paper dollars were universally accepted as the legal tender. Thus checks were not fit to perform what Bilgram called "the money work." Nor were other forms of personal liens.

To illustrate his point, Bilgram inquired whether Fisher would accept gold coin or paper dollars equaling one hundred dollars in exchange for a similar value of goods? He believed Fisher would. But Bilgram doubted if his opponent would accept a lien on his (Bilgram's) personal property in the same amount, even though Fisher might have no question about Bilgram's reputation or financial standing. What was the difference? "[T]he government has assumed the guarantee and has authorized the use in circulation of the banker's notes." Bilgram demanded to know why the law had been introduced to give preference to one form of credit—banker's notes—over his own promissory note. If the former was so clearly preferable, why did the government not leave the judgment to Fisher himself?

Bilgram also called Fisher to task for dismissing the significance of the fact that bank notes were only nominally redeemable on demand. Bilgram pointed to the fact that banks kept only fractional reserves of gold as conclusive evidence of the impossibility of their being able to redeem every single note in circulation. Yet the full redemption of every dollar was the implicit contract that banks extended to customers. Apparently, Fisher disagreed. Bilgram asked, "Is he really ignorant of the fact that only a portion is so redeemable? No bank can carry a redemption fund equal to the issue of its notes. Nothing but the willingness of the people to circulate them for an indefinite period renders possible their issue in excess of the amount of true coin."[82] Implicit in Bilgram's analysis of fractional reserve banking was that a fraud upon the people was being committed.

Bilgram's critique prompted a direct response from Fisher, again in the form of a letter to the editor of *Liberty*. Fisher cut to the core question of interest, "What is necessary in order to establish the justice of interest is to show that in the absence of any restriction upon the issue of instruments of credit, and in the utter absence of laws of legal tender, interest would still be paid." In essence, Fisher was saying that Bilgram and the other "currency-faddists" were dealing in pure speculation with no empirical evidence to support their theories. Indeed, empirical evidence seemed to contradict the theory. He believed that "the deeper draught of knowledge, which it seems so difficult to take, is that the circulation of instruments of exchange bearing no interest is strictly finite." Although he agreed that no laws should restrict credit, he doubted whether that removal of such restrictions would greatly influence the practice of charging interest.

Fisher likened banks to "gold or money shops." He argued that just as a boot merchant tries to keep the minimum necessary boots in stock to allow for anticipated sales and no more, so too do businessmen attempt to keep on hand the minimum necessary money for anticipated needs and no more. "Gold in stock is as barren as boots in stock," he argued, meaning that uninvested gold is not productive. Banks could be viewed as "gold or money shops" that provided the valuable service of holding the money that people had not anticipated needing.

This touched on the main reason that paper dollars, and not Bilgram's personal notes, would be able to circulate as money even if there were no laws on currency. Bankers could redeem notes upon demand in gold specie, which made them highly and easily convertible into real wealth. On the other hand,

> [I]f Mr. Bilgram tries to issue a $100 note, secured in some fashion, upon his own supposed ample property, he will naturally find it a wholly different problem. Property is indefinite and slow of salability. Dollars are gold, they are definite; they possess the maximum of salability. All the world knows . . . that the banker has some gold ready if need be to cash the notes instantly. Few can know that Mr. Bilgram will be similarly prepared. He says "but look at the property." The note-holder says, "how can I use it?"[83]

Paper dollars not only had wide acceptance but they represented liquidity: that is, the bearer could almost instantly acquire the commodity—the wealth—upon which the dollar was based: gold. But a note constituting a mortgage on Bilgram's house could not be converted into spendable wealth except through the comparatively long process of finding a third-party buyer. Even if Bilgram's notes were universally accepted, they would be far less useful than a paper dollar backed by gold.[84] Fisher ended by repeating that government interference in matters of currency did little damage. In essence, he said the State could not significantly impact economic laws such as supply and demand.[85]

Fisher expanded on this theme in the next exchange with Bilgram, disputing that the law prevented private notes or checks from circulating as money. Checks actually did circulate as money despite the law, because the law could not control the principles of trade. It was the superiority of paper dollars as a medium of exchange that gave them dominance: the liquidity of paper dollars gave them a natural advantage over promissory notes, and this advantage constituted one of the justifications for charging interest.

But it was not the only justification for interest. The banker had to be prepared to redeem his notes immediately, which required him to hold a "mass of wealth" aloof "from productive application just in the same portable form in which it is by the note promised to be producible on demand." The interest the banker received was a just compensation for the wealth he was required to hold out of productive use. Fisher offered a different definition of interest from that of Bilgram, "Interest is the hire of commodities separated from their owner and entrusted to another person. The time of separation is a privation to the one party . . . and a benefit to the other party." Interest was a payment for that privation.[86]

Although the debate on interest continued, the content deteriorated under the weight of exasperation on both sides. Fisher concluded by accusing the Individualist Anarchists of becoming entangled in crank notions rather than leading the fight for freedom. "Mutual banking would be all right if it propounded a method of lending wealth. When it proposes to create it by getting people to handle pieces of paper and laments that it is the want of liberty alone which prevents this being done, it is a curse to the cause of liberty, and must be spurned as a faulty weapon and a treacherous friend."[87]

Given that mutual banking formed the economic basis upon which the Individualist Anarchists sought to build freedom, Fisher's spurning of mutual money as a "faulty weapon" was not well received. Bilgram replied, "the sooner we conclude this farce of a debate, the better."[88]

As an interesting footnote, Ingalls later provided insight into whether or not mutual banks would have been able to evolve without laws. Ingalls wrote about a proposed mutual bank that would have functioned through pure cooperation, "Col. W. B. Greene informed me forty-five years since that he was pressed by borrowers to form his mutual bank, but found no lenders, except a few philanthropists who would lend their money without interest anyway, and these he was unwilling to risk sacrificing in an untried experiment."[89]

Were the Individualist Anarchists Really Socialists?

In his book *Equality*, William B. Greene commented on the system of Socialism, "In socialism, there is but one master, which is the state; but the state is not a living person, capable of suffering and happiness. Socialism benefits none but demagogues, and is, emphatically, the organization of universal misery . . . socialism gives us but one class, a class of slaves."[90]

And yet it was commonplace for nineteenth-century Individualist Anarchists to call themselves "Socialists." Their widespread adoption of the labor theory of value and dislike for capitalism—often considered to be hallmarks of Socialism—only strengthened their apparent connection with the left. Moreover, Josiah Warren—arguably the founding figure of the tradition—had ideological roots deep within the socialistic Fourierite movement, and was a student of Owen's. These ties continued well into the days of *Liberty*. For example, the First Workingman's International consisted largely of Bakuninists (Communist Anarchists) and Individualist Anarchists. Despite their many attacks upon capitalism, however, the Individualist Anarchists consistently advocated the free market as the remedy for the capitalist system.

Insight into this seeming contradiction within nineteenth-century Individualist Anarchism can be gleaned from the words of key figures of that tradition. Moses Harman, for example, answered whether he was a Communist with the words,

We have never advocated the abolition of private property. We have always maintained that the development of the highest and truest individualism in human character requires the possession and therefore the existence of personal property. But while stoutly maintaining the right of each individual to his own earnings—the right of each individual to an equitable share of natural material upon which to create property by labor—we have also contended for the principle of Mutualism, the principle of Co-operative Communism.[91]

One reason why Individualist Anarchists sometimes adopted the label "Socialist" is that the meaning of the term has changed with time. In the nineteenth century, a common meaning of the term "Socialist" was "one who advocated an organization of society that allowed laborers to receive the full product of their labor." Within Individualist Anarchism, this goal was stated as Cost the Limit of Price.

But Individualist Anarchists also advocated Sovereignty of the Individual—that is, they were committed to creating a voluntary society in which the basic unit was the autonomous individual. Indeed, in the theoretical construction of Individualist Anarchism, Sovereignty of Individual preceded Cost is the Limit of Price and served as its foundation. Thus, although the *Liberty* circle agreed that profit was theft and big business had allied with government to promote usury, their primary commitment was to a voluntary society and to the right of contract. Tucker described the ideal society as "society by contract."

This commitment to contract led the Individualist Anarchists to vigorously oppose State-supported usuries, such as interest and, yet, defend the practice of charging interest in the context of a free market. Paying interest on a loan might be foolishness and akin to helping a thief rob your house, but—as long as the interest resulted from a voluntary contract—they defended the practice.

Tucker wrote,

> The monster that *Liberty* invites true reformers to help battle down and exterminate is the State, whose purpose is, first, to enforce unjust contracts through forcible defense of monopoly, and, second, to make effectual protest impossible by defending ill-gotten property from the natural retribution which attends tyranny and theft.
>
> "Liberty, therefore, must defend the right of individuals to make contracts involving usury, rum, marriage, prostitution, and many other things which it believes to be wrong in principle and opposed to human well-being. The right to do wrong involves the essence of all rights.[92]

All that Tucker required was that the "wrong" result from contract and not from force. In the presence of a contract, everyone had the right to make a foolish, self-destructive decision, and no one had the right to interfere in the voluntary process.

Although the Individualist Anarchists sometimes referred to themselves as Socialists, they adamantly rejected the school of Socialism that rose to dominance and which is almost a synonym for Socialism proper today: State Socialism. In an essay entitled "State Socialism and Anarchism: How Far They Agree, and Wherein They Differ," Tucker captured the difference between Individualist Anarchism and State Socialism.

Tucker opened by stating that there were two extremes battling within the Socialist tradition, each of which adhered to a principle antithetic to the other. "The two principles referred to are AUTHORITY and LIBERTY, and the names of the two schools of Socialistic thought . . . are, respectively, State Socialism and Anarchism. . . . [T]here is no half-way house between State Socialism and Anarchism."[93] These two forces were flowing from the very center of the Socialist tradition and an ultimate conflict between them was inevitable. On one side would stand the State Socialists who wished to use government to institute justice for labor: these factions included the eight-hour men, the trade-unionists, the Knights of Labor, the land nationalists, and the greenbackers. On the other side would stand the Anarchists who wished first and foremost to eliminate the State.

Before detailing the battle to come, Tucker explored the common ground shared by the opposing groups. "The economic principles of Modern Socialism are a logical deduction from the principle laid down by Adam Smith in the early chapters of his 'Wealth of Nations',—namely, that labor is the true measure of price." But Smith never examined the social and political implications of that observation. That task was left to "Josiah Warren, an American; Pierre J. Proudhon, a Frenchman; Karl Marx, a German Jew." Each of them reached common conclusions that led them to condemn usury, especially in its three most dominant forms—interest, rent, and profit. Moreover, they each recognized that usury survived due to an alliance between business and the State, which resulted in monopoly privileges being granted to an elite class of society. This point of agreement, however, was also the juncture at which State Socialism and Anarchism parted ways. "Here the road forked. They found that they must turn either to the right or to the left,—follow either the path of Authority or the path of Liberty. Marx went one way; Warren and Proudhon the other. Thus were born State Socialism and Anarchism."

State Socialism became the doctrine "that all the affairs of men should be managed by the government, regardless of individual choice." Marx's solution to the various monopolies was to create one vast monopoly known as the State, which would absolutely control individual action. Although State Socialists maintained that only the economic sphere would be controlled and not the private sphere, Tucker disputed the very possibility of limiting State intrusion. In a passage predicting the Communist State, he wrote that State Socialism was "doomed" to end in "a State system of hygiene, prescribing what all must and must not eat, drink, wear, and do"; a code of State morals, schools, hospitals, nurseries that raised children at public expense, and finally "a State family." The latter would consist of "scientific breeding, in which no man and woman will be allowed to have children if the State prohibits them."

This stood in stark contrast to Anarchism, the doctrine "that all the affairs of men should be managed by individuals or voluntary associations, and that the

State should be abolished."[94] Thus, Individualist Anarchism can be said to have branched off economically from the Socialist tradition and become an ideological movement in its own right. What made it branch away was the fact that its basis was not economic, but moral, and it was a morality of radical Individualism.

In the final analysis, it is not clear that Individualist Anarchism ever had a rightful place within the Socialist tradition as we use the word "Socialism" today. Indeed, a philosophy of Individualism that was so radical as to deny the very existence of society cannot be considered collectivist in any politically meaningful sense. With its stress upon contracts and voluntary society, Individualist Anarchism constituted an entirely original and distinct tradition upon the American landscape.

Notes

1. Benjamin R. Tucker, "Fiat Lux!" *Liberty* 6 (September 1, 1888): 5.
2. Tucker's commitment was apparent in 1873 when, at the age of nineteen, he engaged in a vigorous exchange of letters with the acerbic Francis Abbot, editor of *The Index*. The letters and replies ran in Abbot's freethought periodical between February and November 1873.
3. Benjamin R. Tucker, "Who Is the Somebody?" *Liberty* 1 (August 6, 1881): 3. Elsewhere Tucker defines the four great State monopolies as land, credit or money, tariff, and intellectual property (patent and copyright).
4. Benjamin R. Tucker, "Where We Stand," *Liberty* 1 (August 19, 1882): 2.
5. Benjamin R. Tucker, "Anarchy Necessarily Atheistic," *Liberty* 3 (January 9, 1886): 4. Among the heavy guns turned on the issue of money reform were Alfred B. Westrup, William Trinkhaus, Hugo Bilgram, and Henry Cohen.
6. Tucker stated that *Liberty* was "the foremost organ of Josiah Warren's doctrines," however, he also made similar statements about others who had influenced him, including Greene and Proudhon. When Spooner died, Tucker's tribune to him was entitled "Our Nestor Taken From Us." Such multiple statements of acknowledgment probably arose from generosity on Tucker's part rather than from insincerity.
7. *Peaceful Revolutionist* 2 (May 1848): 5.
8. The full titles of Andrews' two-volume work were: *The Science of Society* (No. 1. The True Constitution of Government in the Sovereignty of the Individual as the Final Development of Protestantism, Democracy, and Socialism) (New York: Fowler & Wells, 1852); and *The Science of Society* (No. 2. Cost the Limit of Price: Scientific Measure of Honesty in trade as One of the Fundamental Principles of the Solutions of the Social Problem) (New York: Fowler & Wells, 1852).
9. Josiah Warren, *Practical Details* (New York: n.p., 1852), 13. Capitalization is in the original. The full title is *Practical Details in Equitable Commerce, Showing the Workings in Actual Experiment, During a Series of Years, of the Social Principles Expounded in the Works Called "Equitable Commerce," by the Author of This, and "The Science of Society," by Stephen Pearl Andrews.*

10. Robert Owen acquainted Warren, his protégé, with the idea of "labor notes"—that is, of private currency that represented a stated amount of labor rather than an amount of specie. These were bills signed by an individual that promised "x" number of hours of labor would be performed at "x y z" tasks upon being produced for redemption. Many theorists had explored the possibilities of labor-based currency but Warren was the first one to put it into practice.

11. Warren seems to assume that a seller of bread could isolate a needy buyer from other competitors who would underbid the price of a loaf.

12. "The Labor Dollar," *Radical Review* II, 292. For an index of the *Radical Review*, see www.blancmange.net/tmh/articles/radicalrevindex.shtml [12 May 2002].

13. James J. Martin, *Men Against the State: The Expositors of Individualist Anarchism in America, 1827-1908* (Colorado Springs, Colo.: Ralph Myles, 1970), 13.

14. Martin, *Men Against the State*, 17, described the exchange,

> The customer was first to pay this cost price, plus the seven per cent, which was to defray shipping cost and general overhead of the store. But for the portion which represented his own labor, Warren merely required the customer to present him with a labor note. This note promised to repay an equal amount of time, in the customer's occupation, to the storekeeper, as he had consumed of the storekeeper's time in effecting the transfer of the merchandise. The principal distinction between Warren's store and those of his neighbors was this simple feature, the separation of the merchant's compensation from the cost of the goods sold.

15. *Quarterly Letter* I, 6. An interesting aspect of Warren's evaluation of labor in the exchange of labor notes was his belief that women's labor was undervalued.

16. Josiah Warren, *Equitable Commerce. A New Development of Principles as Substitutes for Laws and Governments, For the Harmonious Adjustment and Regulation of the Pecuniary, Intellectual, and Moral Intercourse of Mankind Proposed as Elements of New Society* (New York: Burt Franklin, n.d.), 42-43.

17. "The Labor Dollar," *The Radical Review* II, 296.

18. Josiah Warren, *True Civilization an Immediate Necessity and the Last Ground of Hope for Mankind. Being the Results and Conclusions of Thirty-nine Years' Laborious Study and Experiments in Civilization As It Is, and in Different Enterprises for Reconstruction* (Boston: n.p., 1863), 81.

19. Warren, *True Civilization*, 83.

20. Decades later, Warren's currency experiment was the subject of debate within *Liberty*, with Tucker vigorously defending his mentor. "Apex or Basis?" *Liberty* 1 (December 10, 1881): 2-4.

21. Benjamin R. Tucker, "The Truth-Soldier's Method," *Liberty* 7 (April 19, 1890): 6-7.

22. Lysander Spooner, *A New System of Paper Currency* (Boston: n.p., 1861), 17.

23. Lysander Spooner, *Constitutional Law Relative to Credit, Currency and Banking* (Worcester, Mass.: n.p., 1843), 21.

24. Lysander Spooner, *A New Banking System: The Needful Capital for Rebuilding the Burnt District* (Boston: n.p., 1873), 19-20.

25. Spooner, *Constitutional Law Relative to Credit, Currency and Banking*, 24.

26. At this time, the gold standard was still employed in the United States.

27. Spooner, *A New System of Paper Currency*, 17. According to James J. Martin, "The plan of this bank had actually been written in 1860, but was published along with 'A New System of Paper Currency' a year later as 'Articles of Association of a Mortgage Stock Banking Company.'"

28. Lysander Spooner, "Our Financiers: Their Ignorance, Usurpations and Frauds," *Radical Review* I, 153.

29. Spooner, "Our Financiers," 153. Three of Spooner's economic works: "Our Financiers, Their Ignorance, Usurprations and Frauds," (issued as a separate pamphlet in the same year, 1877), "The Law of Prices," and "Gold and Silver as Standards of Value," were first published in Tucker's *Radical Review*.

30. Spooner, "Our Financiers," 155. Among the features of the system Spooner proposed were certain safeguards against the fraudulent or bad dollars that the deregulation of currency might encourage. For example, the basis of all dollar-backing was to be a matter of public record so that people could judge the reliability of the private currency for themselves.

31. Lysander Spooner, *Poverty: Its Illegal Causes and Legal Cure* (Boston: n.p., 1850), 15.

32. Benjamin Tucker, "On Picket Duty," *Liberty* 6 (January 5, 1889): 1.

33. Indeed, Greene strenuously objected to the wider socialism of Proudhon. To the extent that he placed the issue of money within a broader context, that framework was religion.

How much of his theories Greene developed independently is a matter of debate. Bowman Newton Hall II opines, "Strangely, Greene's 'Equality' (1849) contains no references to any well known political economists. Even more surprising is that 'Mutual Banking' published the very next year quotes John Stuart Mill, Proudhon, and [William] Beck several times and contains two or three references to Adam Smith and Malthus." Bowman Newton Hall II, "A History and Critique of American Individualist Anarchists' Economic Theories," (Ph.D. diss., Duke University, 1971). In *Mutual Banking*, Greene provides a detailed critique of Proudhon.

34. Martin, *Men Against the State*, 128.

35. Martin calls *Mutual Banking* "the most widely reprinted of all anarchist financial publications written by a native American." Martin, *Men Against the State*, 128.

36. William Bradford Greene, *Equality* (West Brookfield, Mass.: n.p., 1849), 8.

37. Greene, *Equality*, 13.

38. William Bradford Greene, *Mutual Banking* (West Brookfield, Mass.: n.p., 1850), 51.

39. Greene, *Mutual Banking*, 45.

40. Greene, *Equality*, 35.

41. Hall observes that Greene "somewhat surprisingly for his time . . . effectively refutes the labor theory of value." He quotes *Mutual Banking*,

It is affirmed by some, that *labor* is the only true measure of value, that every thing is worth precisely what it costs in labor to produce it, and that the price of every thing ought always to be determined by the relative amount of labor expended in its production. We would remark, in answer to these affirmations, that there is such a thing as misdirected labor; and that a man may produce an article for which there is no demand, and which has, consequently, no exchangeable value.

Hall, "A History and Critique," 110.

42. The historian James J. Martin claims "The influence of closing the land bank in creating colonial unrest has generally been neglected by historians. It was the opinion of John Adams that 'the act to destroy the Land Bank Scheme raised a greater ferment in this province than the stamp-act did.'" Martin, *Men Against the State*, 133 (note 115).

43. Other influences on Tucker's economic theories include Proudhon, Ingalls, and Andrews (who largely reiterated Warren).

44. As quoted in Martin, *Men Against the State*, 109.

45. *The Word* (May 1872): 1.

46. *The Word* (February 1873): 3. Among Tucker's contributions to early issues of *The Word* included articles on interest, labor reform, Josiah Warren and Wm. B. Greene.

47. Tucker explained the origin of this translation. After reading Proudhon and discovering that the French radical "had not, like Warren, confined himself to the bare elucidation of the principles, but had discussed . . . their revolutionary light," Tucker was caught up by enthusiasm. "And I said to Colonel Greene: 'Why don't you translate What Is Property?' His answer was: 'Why don't *you*?'" Benjamin Tucker, "Announcement Extraordinary!" *Liberty* 4 (January 1, 1887): 4.

48. Volume I (May 1877) of the *Radical Review* lists the Office of Publication as 45 Purchase Street, New Bedford, Mass. The four issues serially featured "System of Economical Contradictions: or, The Philosophy of Misery" by P. J. Proudhon, translated from the French by Tucker. It included such articles as "The Labor Dollar" by Stephen Pearl Andrews, and "The Law of Prices: A Demonstration of the Necessity for an Indefinite Increase of Money" by Lysander Spooner.

49. This is the categorization used by Hall who, in turn, explained his categorization with reference to that used by Clarence Lee Swartz, editor of Benjamin R. Tucker, *Individual Liberty* (New York: Vanguard Press, 1926), a collection of Tucker's writings. Tucker himself referred to four monopolies and I tend to agree with James J. Martin's subdivision into those four categories—including patent and copyright as the fourth. However, because intellectual property absorbs an entire chapter of this volume, I will adopt the Hall/Swartz divisions. For analysis of patent and copyright, see chapter 6 of this volume.

50. Benjamin Tucker, "On Picket Duty," *Liberty* 1 (April 15, 1881): 1.

51. Victor Yarros, "The Strike and the Editors," *Liberty* 10 (July 28, 1894): 3-4.

52. F.F.K. [Florence Finch Kelly], "Use Them Instead of Abusing Them," *Liberty* 4 (June 19, 1886): 7. Others contributors, including Dyer D. Lum and Henry Appleton, argued along the same lines.

53. Benjamin R. Tucker, "A Great Idea Perverted," *Liberty* 4 (June 19, 1886): 5.

54. Benjamin R. Tucker, "State Socialism and Anarchism: How Far They Agree, and Wherein They Differ," *Liberty* 5 (March 10, 1888): 3.

55. Tucker's views were undoubtedly influenced by his great admiration for the Irish Land League, which staged a series of highly successful boycotts against English landlords. The early issues of *Liberty* publicized and lauded these actions and several contributors wrote to the Land League's periodical as well.

56. Benjamin R. Tucker, *Instead of a Book, by a Man Too Busy to Write One; A Fragmentary Exposition of Philosophical Anarchism* (New York: B. R. Tucker, 1893), 299.

57. Benjamin R. Tucker, "Protection, and Its Relation to Rent," *Liberty* 6 (October 27, 1888): 4-5.

58. Benjamin R. Tucker, "Economic Rent," *Liberty* 9 (November 5, 1892): 2.

59. Benjamin R. Tucker, *Individual Liberty* (New York: Vanguard Press, 1926), 11. http://flag.blackened.net/daver/anarchism/tucker/tucker.html [18 May 2002].

60. Tucker, *Instead of a Book*, 193. Tucker seemed inconsistent on this point. He also wrote, "Here is my argument. *Major Premise*. Everything not labor that plays a part in production is capital. *Minor Premise*. Money is a thing not labor that plays a part in production. *Conclusion*. Money is capital." Benjamin Tucker, "The Capital Contoversy," *Liberty* 9 (August, 1893): 2. Of course, he may have meant that only "representative money" was not capital yet representative money also plays a role in production.

61. Tucker, *Instead of a Book*, 10.

62. Tucker, *Individual Liberty*, 9-10.

63. Hugo Bilgram, "Is Interest Just?" *Liberty* 9 (April 22, 1893): 1.

64. Bilgram, "Is Interest Just?" 1.

65. Personally, I found the discussion of Henry George's defense of interest to be valuable but limited in scope. See Benjamin R. Tucker, "Economic Hodge Podge," *Liberty* 5 (October 8, 1887): 4-5.

66. Herbert was the founder of a philosophy known as "voluntaryism," an author of works including "A Politician in Sight of Haven" and editor of *Free Life*. Donisthorpe was editor of *Jus: A Weekly Organ of Individualism* and author of works including "In Defense of Anarchism." Fisher founded the Parents' Defense League to counter the compulsory schooling of children and authored works including "Voluntary Taxation." Tarn published *Herald of Anarchy* and *Free Trade*. Levy edited the *Personal Rights Journal* and authored works, including "Outcome of Individualism." Badcock was the author of works, including "The Money Fame." Seymour published *The Anarchist* and *Revolutionary Review*.

67. Carl Watner, "The English Individualists as They Appear in Liberty," chap. in Michael E. Coughlin, Charles H. Hamilton, and Mark A. Sullivan, eds., *Benjamin R. Tucker and The Champions of Liberty* (St. Paul, Minn.: Michael E. Coughlin, 1986), 193. Even though the aforementioned British Individualists might have accepted the principle enunciated by Tucker, some of them rejected the label of "Anarchist." Watner acknowledges this, "According to his [Herbert's] understanding, Anarchists would not retain any form of organization to repress aggression or crime. They would not maintain any sort of defense agencies to function as police or courts. . . . [H]e would retain such organization in his ideal society, but . . . he would not force those disapproving of the police or courts to pay for them." Watner, "The English Individualists," 194.

68. Benjamin R. Tucker, *Liberty* 8 (May 16, 1891): 3.

69. Fisher was far from the only contributor with whom Tucker debated the money issue during this period. In the same issue, on page two, there is a Letter to the Editor from Alfred B. Westrup, publisher of *The Auditor* (1891), a paper devoted to free banking. The letter began "It is not only a delusion, but a misuse of language, to talk of a 'standard of value.'"

70. J. Greevz Fisher, "The Power of Government over Value," *Liberty* 8 (June 27, 1891): 3.

71. Fisher wrote to excuse himself that "dogmatism of manner must often be adopted to avoid verbosity; it is not necessarily an assumption of infallibility."

72. Fisher, "The Power of Government over Value," 4.

73. J. Greevz Fisher, "Free Trade in Banking," *Liberty* 8 (July 11, 1891): 3. Although Fisher referred almost exclusively to an article by Alfred B. Westrup that had

appeared in *Liberty*, it was clear from context and from the editor's reaction that the comments were directed equally at Tucker. Indeed, Tucker responded to the "attack" in Westrup's stead.

74. Fisher, "Free Trade in Banking," 3. Elsewhere, Fisher commented pointedly on the prospect of "mutual bankism" reducing the price of gold. "If prices fell 90 per cent, then one dollar or one pound sterling would do ten times as much monetary work as at present. The evils wrought by such an unsettlement would be fearful, but they would be merely temporary. . . ." J. Greevz Fisher, "Interest Is Just," *Liberty* 10 (July 28, 1894): 8.

75. Benjamin R. Tucker, commentary on J. Greevz Fisher, "Free Trade in Banking," *Liberty* 8 (July 11, 1891): 4.

76. Benjamin R. Tucker, "On Picket Duty," *Liberty* 8 (August 15, 1891): 1.

77. Benjamin R. Tucker, "The Equalization of Wage and Product," *Liberty* 8 (August 22, 1891): 2-3. At the same time, Tucker's other debate with Alfred B. Westrup continued.

78. Philadelphia, 1889. Bilgram also authored *The Iron Law of Wages*, n.p., n.d.; and *A Study of the Money Question*, New York, 1895.

79. J. K. Ingalls, "Interest Just and Unjust," *Liberty* 9 (June 10, 1893): 1.

80. Although this seems like a large time gap, there was a gap in *Liberty*'s publication that made the February 24, 1894, issue follow directly after the August 1893 one.

81. Hugo Bilgram, "Interest Is Unjust," *Liberty* 9 (March 10, 1894): 11.

82. Bilgram, "Interest Is Unjust," 11. In his commentary, Bilgram refers favorably to volume I of Bohm Bawerk's *Capital and Interest* as having destroyed the fructification theory of interest, which Fisher apparently advances.

83. J. Greevz Fisher, "Interest Is Just," *Liberty* 10 (May 19, 1894): 8.

84. Elsewhere, Fisher distinguishes between banker's notes or paper dollars and Bilgram's notes by labeling the former as "demand notes" and the latter as "time bills." "Interest Is Just," *Liberty* 10 (July 28, 1894): 8.

85. Fisher, "Interest Is Just," *Liberty* 10 (May 19, 1894): 8.

86. J. Greevz Fisher, "Interest Is Just" (second use of title), *Liberty* 10 (July 28, 1894): 8.

87. J. Greevz Fisher, "Interest Is Just" (third use of title), *Liberty* 10 (November 17, 1894): 4-5.

88. Fisher, "Interest Is Just," *Liberty* 10 (November 17, 1894): 5.

89. J. K. Ingalls, "The Interest Question Narrowed to a Point," *Liberty* 10 (March 9, 1895): 4. Other contributors to *Liberty*, such as Steven T. Byington, weighed in on the issue of mutual banks. Often, their input was directed at exploring how such banks would function, however, rather than at fundamental objections. See, for example, Steven T. Byington, "The Value of Mutual Money," *Liberty* 10 (March 23, 1895): 8, in which Byington discusses "mutual bank notes were to be kept at par mainly by redemption at the bank after default of the borrower."

90. As quoted in Martin, *Men Against the State*, 136.

91. *Lucifer, the Light Bearer* (May 8, 1885), 2.

92. Benjamin R. Tucker, "Right and Individual Rights," *Liberty* 1 (January 7, 1882): 3.

93. Benjamin R. Tucker, "State Socialism and Anarchism," *Liberty* 5 (March 10, 1888): 2.

94. Tucker, "State Socialism and Anarchism," 2.

Appendix 1

Periodicals Associated with *Liberty*

The extent to which *Liberty* monitored, reprinted, and commented upon other periodicals—as well as being commented upon by them—may be judged by scanning a representative "On Picket Duty" column by Tucker, which generally introduced each issue of *Liberty*. "On Picket Duty" for the May 12, 1888, issue (selected at random) included the following observations:

> G. Bernard Shaw describes *Liberty* as "a lively paper, in which the usual proportions of a halfpennyworth of discussion to an intolerable deal of balderdash are reversed" . . .
>
> I print the extract from Henry Courtney [extracted from *Our Corner*] chiefly because it aptly puts the case for the Egoists . . .
>
> In Mrs. Annie Besant's magazine, "Our Corner," G. Bernard Shaw has published the first of a series of two articles in reply to my paper on "State Socialism and Anarchism."[1] After the buffoonery of the "Workmen's Advocate" and the superficiality of "Der Sozialist," it is pleasant to be critiqued by a man of brains and wit. . . . From the fact that so much space is devoted in her magazine to an examination of my arguments, I infer that Ms. Besant, who but a year ago "could support Mr. Benjamin Tucker's strictures with perfect equanimity," has discovered that equanimity alone is scarcely adequate to the task.[2]
>
> The London "Anarchist" and the Chicago "Alarm" have suspended publication. The former will appear again on July 1; the fate of the latter is uncertain. . . . [A review of the significance of the "Alarm" followed]
>
> Will Hubbard-Kernan, the eccentric editor of the prairies, in connection with S. F. Wilson, George Frances Train's lecture agent, has come to the surface with another journal, 'The Free-Lance." [A review of "The Free-Lance" and subscription information followed.]

An examination of the complicated network of connections between *Liberty* and virtually every other Individualist periodical issued in English during its publication span would require a book-length treatment. Indeed, a comprehensive list would include periodicals issued in French, German, Italian, and Yiddish as well. Thus, the following discussion provides merely a taste of some of the more important periodicals that associated with *Liberty*.[3]

Of equal importance, the discussion offers insight into the earlier periodicals from which *Liberty* ideologically drew. In November 1872, Tucker wrote to Ezra Heywood. "I hope to do some work for the labor cause," he stated, "but first wish to study the question that I may thoroughly understand it."[4] Shortly thereafter Tucker began publishing in *The Word*, which was then still a labor reform paper. Through *The Word*, he became conversant with Warren's labor theory of value and William B. Greene's theory of mutual banking.[5] Of Greene, Tucker wrote: "I am indebted to Col. Greene's *Mutual Banking* more than to any other single publication for such knowledge as I have of the principles of finance."[6] In 1873, he defended the Warren-Greene theory of money and interest in the pages of the *Index*, and engaged in a debate with the editor on the issue. Upon resigning from *The Word* Tucker declared: "I wish to give myself first and emphatically to the advocacy of justice to labor."[7] This statement was the raison d'etre of the *Radical Review*; it applied equally to the later *Liberty*.

Thus, from the beginning of his career in Individualist Anarchism through to the demise of *Liberty*, Tucker was acutely aware of and closely associated with other periodicals.

Labor Reform

Tucker's first love was the labor reform movement.

Tucker's association with Lysander Spooner undoubtedly strengthened this commitment to labor. Three of Spooner's economic works—*Our Financiers: Their Ignorance, Usurpations, and Frauds*; *The Law of Prices: A Demonstration of the Necessity for an Indefinite Increase of Money*; and *Gold and Silver as Standards of Value*—first appeared in Tucker's *Radical Review*. Tucker was also acquainted with Spooner's *What Is a Dollar?* and *Financial Impostors* published in the *New Age*, a weekly edited by J. M. L. Babcock, later a contributor to *Liberty*.

When *Liberty* appeared, Tucker maintained his connections with labor periodicals. *The Age of Thought* (1896-1898), edited by Edward H. Fulton was directly inspired by *Liberty*. The first two issues of this eight-page weekly discussed land and money from an Anarchist perspective. Francis Tandy, William Holmes, and Henry Cohen—referred to by Tucker as the "Denver circle"—were contributors to *Liberty*, as was William Trinkhaus. Tucker's announcement of the *Age of Thought* encouraged readers to "send a dollar . . . for a year's subscription." Of Fulton, he wrote approvingly: "He is young and ardent, and, situated as he is in the west, where the financial battle is waging, he will be able to lend more efficient aid to Cohen, Tandy and other comrades."[8]

The *Auditor*, a free banking paper, was another labor-economic periodical, published from Chicago (1891) by Alfred Westrup, a contributor to *Liberty* and the corresponding secretary of the Mutual Bank Propaganda of Chicago. The stated purpose of the organization was "the establishment of an equitable monetary system as an essential factor in economic science."[9] Westrup's works, *Citizens' Money* and *The Financial Problem; or, the Principles of Monetary Science*, were advertised in *Liberty*. Also considered an ally was the weekly *San Franciscan* edited by J. Goodman and A. McEwan.

In 1886, the most frequent contributor to the first volumes of *Liberty*, Henry Appleton, became editor of *The Newsman*, the monthly organ of news dealers published by the Mutual News Company of Boston. Although *The Newsman* was not specifically a labor paper, Tucker emphasized this aspect of it.

Liberty's connection with labor papers was often based upon the editor being a contributor to *Liberty*. For example, the Anarchist Joseph Labadie was an editor of the *Advance and Labor Leaf*. Similarly, the architect John Beverly Robinson had published the *Free Soiler* (1884), an organ of the American Free Soil Society.

A class of labor periodical toward which *Liberty* was hostile was Single-Tax journals. Tucker severely criticized Henry George, the founder of the Single-Tax movement, and he devoted considerable space in *Liberty* to refuting George. The two Single-Tax papers significantly mentioned in Liberty were the *Philadelphia Justice* and Henry George's *Standard*.

Freethought

There was a long history of intersection between Individualism and freethought. The freethought periodical *The Free Enquirer* (1828-1832), originally entitled the *New Harmony Gazette* (1825-1828), was edited by the freethinking reformers Robert Dale Owen and Francis Wright, both of whom were associates of Josiah Warren. George Henry Evans' *The Working Man's Advocate* coupled land and labor reform with freethought through advertising such freethought classics as Palmer's *Principles of Nature* and Voltaire's *Philosophical Dictionary*. The Individualist Anarchist Spooner, whose freethinking deism was unpalatable to the more religious abolitionists, first published *A Deist's Reply* serially (1836) in the *Cleveland Liberalist*. Another pamphlet by Spooner was entitled *The Deist's Immortality*.

Robert Reitzel's periodical *Arme Teufel* (Poor Devil), which was launched on December 6, 1884, from Detroit, blended freethought with Anarchism. The German-American publication spoke out against organized religion and religious thought. Reitzel considered Tucker to be a fellow-traveler, who shared an enthusiasm for the egoism of Stirner. In turn, Tucker called *Arme Teufel*, "*Liberty*'s brave and brilliant Detroit contemporary."[10] Like Tucker, Reitzel inspired disciples, and *Arme Teufel* clubs sprang up in cities with large German-speaking populations such as Toledo and Cincinnati.[11]

As a young man Tucker began reading two important freethought periodicals: the *Boston Investigator* and the *Index* (formerly the *Free Religious Index*). The first paper, the *Boston Investigator*, was a weekly founded by Abner Kneeland in 1831, and it remained one of the most prominent freethought periodicals until it merged with the *Truth Seeker* in 1904.[12] *The Boston Investigator*, edited by Horace Seaver (1839-1889) and published by J. P. Mendum, impressed Tucker.

The second paper, the *Index*, was also a weekly, published from Toledo (1870-1872) and then from Boston (1873-1886), edited in turn by Francis Abbot, W. J. Potter, and B. F. Underwood. Tucker published his first defense of the labor theory of value in the pages of the *Index* (1873). During *Liberty*'s life span, Tucker reprinted articles from both papers and reported upon their progress. In turn the freethinking *Boston Investigator* welcomed the first issue of *Liberty* in 1881 with the words: "Liberty is one of the grandest words in the language; and of course it is a grand name for a paper . . . we mean such as Mr. Benj. R. Tucker's *Liberty*. . . . As Mr. Tucker has ability and industry, radicalism and independence, he will make an interesting and suggestive paper."[13]

Of the *Investigator*, Tucker declared: "The paper has a glorious record, and all Liberals should unite in rewarding its valiant struggle against superstition by stanch support in its honorable and still vigorous old age."[14]

But Tucker later criticized the *Investigator*'s relatively conservative editor Seaver for his refusal to extend religious freedom to Mormons on the issue of polygamy. A hostile exchange followed, which ended with Seaver accusing Tucker of advocating polygamy and with Tucker retorting that Seaver was a peevish old man.

From his early association with the *Index*, Tucker's opinion of that periodical also seemed to decline. On the occasion of Underwood's assuming the editorship of the *Index*, Tucker observed: "The new editor, Mr. Underwood, has reconstructed its anatomy to advantage. If, in addition, he will infuse some blood into its colorless veins, it will become a readable and valuable journal."[15] This hope—in Tucker's opinion—was not realized.

The importance of freethought to Tucker's development can also be gauged by his observation upon the quarterly *Radical Review* (1877-1878), his first periodical, of which only four issues appeared, and which published Stephen Pearl Andrews, Ezra Heywood, Ingalls, William Greene, and Spooner. "I once published a magazine called the *Radical Review*," he wrote later, "which many competent judges pronounced . . . the handsomest freethought magazine ever published in America."[16] Tucker thus considered the *Radical Review* to be, at least substantially, a freethought periodical.

The *Truth Seeker* (1873-still published), the most prominent American freethought paper—which numbered Mark Twain among its subscribers—was connected with *Liberty* in several ways.[17] Most conspicuously, *Liberty* reprinted its articles and Tucker commented upon its editor, D. M. (De Robigne Mortimer) Bennett. For example, when D. M. Bennett upbraided the birth control crusader Ezra Heywood for his "bad taste" in being arrested under the federal postal obscenity law of 1873, the Comstock Act, Tucker bristled: "In this connection we must express our indignation at the cowardly conduct of D. M. Bennett . . . who prates about Mr. Heywood's taste and methods . . . It is not a question of taste, but of Liberty, and no man who fails to see this and act accordingly can ever fairly call himself a Liberal again."[18]

The third editor of the *Truth Seeker* was George E. Macdonald, an Individualist Anarchist and a contributor to *Liberty*. A personal friend of Tucker, Macdonald referred to him as "my uncle Benjamin"—an allusion to a book published by Tucker entitled *My Uncle Benjamin*. In response, Tucker called Macdonald "my nephew." Macdonald also coedited a San Francisco magazine entitled *Freethought* (1888-1890) with Samuel P. Putnam, which elicited mixed reviews from Tucker, who disliked Putnam. Nevertheless, *Freethought* was quoted fourteen times within the pages of *Liberty*.

A small but subsequently significant freethought paper was the *Valley Falls Liberal*, an organ of the Kansas Liberal League. Moses Harman and A. J. Searle informally directed the first issues. The periodical soon became the *Kansas Liberal* under the controversial editorship of Moses Harman. In 1883, again under Harman, its title changed again to *Lucifer, the Light Bearer* (1883-1907), and under that name this Midwestern journal evolved into the foremost free love periodical in America as well as an important vehicle of Individualist thought.[19]

The freethinker Edwin Cox Walker, who had been contributing articles to *Liberty*, began to write also for the *Kansas Liberal*, of which he became coeditor with Harman. He continued the association when the periodical evolved into *Lucifer*.

The link between the freethought movement and Tucker's *Liberty* was further demonstrated by the many freethought works advertised by *Liberty*. A partial list includes: *Church and State* (Tolstoi); *The Deist's Immortality* and *A Deist's Reply* (Spooner); *Dieu et Etat* ("Bakounine"); *Freethinkers' Magazine* (H. L. Green, T. B. Wakeman, editors); *The Freethought Directory*; the *Boston Investigator* (Horace Seaver); *Three Dreams in a Desert* (Schreiner); and the *Kansas Liberal* (Moses Harman, editor).

Free Love

The free love periodical with which Tucker was most closely associated was Ezra and Angela Heywood's *The Word* (1872-1890, 1892-1893), issued first from Princeton and then from Cambridge, Massachusetts. After the Civil War, the abolitionist Ezra Heywood had turned his attention toward the labor movement and, eventually, toward free love. The Heywoods' *The Word*—subtitled "A Monthly Journal of Reform"—was connected to radical Individualism both through its editors and through its contributors, who included Josiah Warren, Benjamin Tucker, and J. K. Ingalls. Initially, *The Word* presented free love as a minor theme, which was expressed within a dominant labor reform format. But the publication later evolved into an explicitly free love periodical.

In April 1875, Tucker became an associate editor of *The Word*, but as the paper de-emphasized economics to stress free love he grew dissatisfied. Finally, Tucker resigned in December 1876 and established the *Radical Review*.

Tucker's relationship with Heywood grew more distant.[20] Yet, when Heywood was imprisoned from August to December 1878 under the Comstock laws for circulating his pro-birth control pamphlet *Cupid's Yokes*, Tucker abandoned the *Radical Review* in order to assume editorship of Heywood's *The Word*.[21] After Heywood's release from prison, *The Word* openly devoted itself to free love. Tucker's disapproval of this policy stemmed from his conviction that "Liberty, to be effective, must find its first application in the realm of economics."[22]

This difference of emphasis did not prevent Heywood from welcoming Tucker's budding *Liberty* into the radical Individualist movement. In response to the first issue, Heywood wrote: "*Liberty* is intelligent and vigorous, has opinions, character and will command attention from its first issue; a bright, smart, timely journal to which live people will find it unsafe not to subscribe."[23]

As noted previously, the most important American free love journal was *Lucifer, the Light Bearer* (1883-1907) edited by Moses Harman first from Valley Falls, Kansas, then from Topeka (1890), and finally from Chicago (1896). Tucker's relationship with *Lucifer* started well. At one point, he exclaimed:

> I say, Messrs. Harman and Walker, editors of "*Lucifer*," I wish you wouldn't make absolutely every number of your paper so good and true and live and keen and consistently radical . . . since your advent, you have kept me in a state of perpetual doubt and anxiety lest *Liberty*'s light be dimmed by *Lucifer*'s. In mercy's name, let up a little, and give a toiling torch-bearer an occasional chance to recuperate.[24]

Gradually, however, the relationship between the two periodicals became strained over disagreements that revolved around the question of what was the proper strategy in advancing liberty.

As he grew older, Tucker became increasingly hostile to civil disobedience as a strategy. He became firmly committed to the strategy of education rather than civil disobedience, especially when that disobedience was likely to result in martyrdom or more stringent and repressive laws. With the Chicago Haymarket incident (May 4, 1886) and the hysterical repression of radicalism that followed it, Tucker observed first-hand the disastrous consequences of a rash act and concluded that the cost outweighed any benefit.

In contrast, Harman's *Lucifer* pursued a consistent long-term policy of baiting the law, particularly the Comstock postal obscenity law. Harman established an "open word" rule for *Lucifer* whereby no contributions would be edited because of explicit language or content.

For this policy, the staff of Lucifer were jointly and separately charged with 270 counts of obscenity; subsequently, the charges were dropped against all but Harman. Many Individualists, such as Ezra Heywood, rushed to support Harman. Tucker did not feel able to render support with enthusiasm. However, he decried the injustice of Harman's imprisonment and solicited money for the Harman Defense Fund, which originated in and was advertised by *Liberty*. Nevertheless, Tucker believed that Harman's actions imperiled the freedom of radicals to discuss Anarchism and economic reform, which were far more important issues.

An earlier incident had also created distance between Harman's and Tucker's periodicals. The non-State, non-church wedding of E. C. Walker and Lillian Harman (Moses Harman's sixteen-year-old daughter) resulted in the couple's imprisonment. Tucker firmly disagreed with the tactic, which was meant to test the law. The relationship between E. C. Walker and Tucker improved with time, perhaps because Walker also disagreed with Harman's "open word" policy. Walker resigned from *Lucifer* and used his new periodical *Fair Play*, a four-page weekly at 75 cents per year, to attack what he perceived to be *Lucifer*'s determined martyrdom. Although E. C. Walker continued contributing to *Lucifer*, it is significant that when *Fair Play* ceased (1891) he transferred the current subscriptions to *Liberty*.[25]

Individualist Periodicals Not Associated with Movements

Other periodicals that were influenced by *Liberty* were not devoted to a specific social issue, such as labor or free love, but to the tradition of Individualism in more general terms.

E. H. Fulton, mentioned previously as the editor of *The Age of Thought*, *The Ego*, and *The Egoist*, was a Tuckerite who published several Individualist-Anarchist periodicals: *The Alturian* (1895); *The 1776 American* (1920); *The New Order* (1919), which listed Steven T. Byington as a contributing editor; and *The Mutualist* (1925-1928), to which C. L. Swartz contributed. George and Emma Schumm borrowed the title of Tucker's first periodical, the *Radical Review*, publishing a short-lived version of their own from Chicago. *Radical Review* was advertised in *Liberty*, as was the Individualistic *The Whim*. Published in 1901, *The Whim* fell under the editorship of E. H. Crosby in February 1902. Its advertisement in *Liberty* described its orientation: "*The Whim* is an independent, anti-military, anti-government journal, claiming relationship to Thoreau and Tolstoy, but owning no master."[26]

Georgia and Henry Replogle's *Equity* (1886-1887), was a fortnightly journal from the experimental town of Liberal, Missouri, which had been founded by freethinkers to demonstrate the virtues of churchlessness. *Equity* stated its purpose to be the "emancipation from sex, wage, monopolistic and custom slavery, and state superstition." Tucker described it as "a tiny sheet, but a brave one."[27] Apparently, the tiny sheet was too brave. A mob formed in the community of Liberal, which had been dedicated to "universal mental liberty," and forced the Replogles to leave town.

Another Individualist paper, *The Twentieth Century* (N.Y.), elicited mixed reviews from Tucker. Under the editorship of Hugh Pentecost and T. L. M'Cready (associate editor), the *Twentieth Century* became more and more radically Individualist. Its advertisement in *Liberty* stated: "This Journal advo-

cates Personal Sovereignty in place of State Sovereignty, Voluntary Cooperation as opposed to Compulsory Co-operation."[28] Although Tucker's opinion of M'Cready was high, he grew increasingly critical of Pentecost, eventually
questioning his integrity. Pentecost responded in kind, aiming subtle insults at
Liberty in the pages of the *Twentieth Century*. Tucker reported on one such incident: "This meant, I could not help perceiving, a condemnation of the personnel
of *Liberty*'s office. We are fighters, and therefore savages, according to Mr.
Pentecost, and this fact stands to our dishonor."[29]

Tucker also had a mixed response to the periodical *Alarm*, with his ambiguity basically revolving about questions about the proper use of force. Originated
by Albert R. Parsons, one of the Haymarket martyrs, the paper's editorship was
assumed by Dyer D. Lum (1887) upon Parsons' arrest and subsequent execution; with Lum, the paper acquired Individualistic tendencies. Lum was on cordial terms with *Liberty*, having contributed a series entitled "Eighteen Christian
Centuries: or, the Evolution of the Gospel of Anarchy," but he became severely
critical of Tucker's stand on the Haymarket incident.

Tucker's attitude toward the use of force polarized the general Anarchist
movement. The Individualist Anarchists, who generally opposed all but defensive force, were labeled "Boston Anarchists" because *Liberty* was issued from
Boston. The Communist Anarchists, who often accepted the use of force as a
strategy, were labeled "Chicago Anarchists" because Chicago was a hotbed of
activity and the site of the violent Haymarket affair in 1886. Burnette G.
Haskell, editor of the San Francisco *Truth*, first applied these polarizing labels.

Another periodical that became radically Individualist by virtue of a change
in editors was the *American Idea*. When C. M. Overton left the paper, M. D.
Leahy (a head of the Freethought University in Liberal, Missouri) and W. S.
Allison assumed the editorship. In Tucker's words, it became "a stanch and
straight advocate of Anarchism," which he requested subscribers to "encourage
. . . by generous subscription to his paper."[30]

Many contributors to *Liberty* were involved in Individualist publishing efforts of their own. Clara Dixon Davidson, whose brilliant article on children's
rights illuminated that debate, published *L'Enfant Terrible* (1891) from San
Francisco. *The Progressive Age* was edited by Voltairine de Cleyre from Grand
Rapids, Michigan.

C. L. Swartz, and, later, J. Wm. Lloyd, edited *The Free Comrade* (1900-
1902, 1910-1912). The *Galveston Daily News* achieved prominence in *Liberty*
through the work of its chief editorial writer, James L. Walker, whose articles
Tucker frequently reprinted. For a short time, the *Chicago Evening Post* was
coedited by Victor Yarros, who became an associate editor of *Liberty*. An unusually high percentage of those who contributed to Liberty were professional
journalists or experienced "amateurs" who, true to the definition of that word,
pursued publishing for the love of it.

Spencerian Periodicals

Victor S. Yarros was virtually the only Spencerian to remain with *Liberty* after the egoism debate: indeed, for a brief three-year period following the 1887 debate, he too converted to egoism.[31] Yarros defended the radical Spencerian tradition exemplified by Herbert Spencer's most politically extreme work *The Right to Ignore the State* (1844, chapter in *Social Statics*).

In advancing the most radical Spencerian position, Yarros incurred the displeasure of more conservative Individualist papers, which considered themselves to be the true Spencerians. Indeed, many papers thought Anarchism was a stumbling block for Individualism. The *Denver Individualist*, formerly the *Arbitrator* (1889-1890), attacked Tucker on this point. In an article published in the *Individualist* entitled "Why I am an Individualist," its editor, Frank Stuart, challenged Anarchism and Tucker. The *Spencerian Today* (formerly *Waterman's Journal*), edited by J. Morrison-Fuller, called upon *Liberty* to produce evidence supporting Anarchism. On this exchange, Yarros commented: "*Today* occupies considerable space with an attempt to answer a recent *Liberty* paragraph." He continued by criticizing *Today*'s rejection of Anarchism without which, he declared, it will "remain a voice crying in the wilderness."[32]

E. L. Youmans's *Popular Science Monthly* was the most prominent vehicle of Spencerian thought in America. Although it did not openly respond to *Liberty*, Tucker reprinted several articles from its pages.

British Individualists[33]

In terms of contributing articles and engaging in debate, the British Individualists were the most active foreign presence in the pages of *Liberty*.[34] British periodicals, such as *Commonweal* (1885-1892)—the monthly publication of the Socialist League—were also followed closely by both Tucker and Yarros.

The British Individualists who engaged their American counterparts in debate differed from most of *Liberty*'s other contributors in several ways. For the most part, they advocated limited government and, like their mentor Herbert Spencer, they shied away from Anarchism. The labor theory of value, so integral to *Liberty*'s philosophy, was not widely accepted among the British Individualists.

One of *Liberty*'s lengthiest and most intriguing debates pitted the American Hugo Bilgram against the British J. Greevz Fisher on the justice of interest. Another major debate involving Fisher, children's rights, pointed up a third difference between the two groups. This exchange was, at bottom, the fundamental conflict of egoism versus natural rights. The egoists claimed that rights derived from contract and, thus, were unhappily led to conclude that young children had no rights because they were unable to contract for them. The British, however, had not participated in the earlier egoism controversy in *Liberty* and they still took a straight natural rights stand. To them, children had all the rights that any human being could claim.

In sum, the British differed from the Americans in their rejection of Anarchism, of the labor theory of value, and of egoism.

Auberon Herbert's *Free Life* (1890-1901), quoted nineteen times in *Liberty*, was perhaps the most prominent British Individualist periodical. Its prospectus, as it appeared in *Liberty*, read: "We shall oppose all hereditary privilege, all religious establishments, all artificial regulations tending to monopoly in land; and we shall equally oppose all attacks upon property of every kind."[35] Of *Free Life* and Herbert, Tucker wrote: "In a letter to me, written when he was contemplating the establishment of *The Free Life*, Mr. Herbert proposed that, in case of any friendly discussion between his journal and mine, each should reprint all that the other might say. Mr. Herbert will observe that I have been prompt to act upon his suggestion, and I have no doubt that he will reciprocate."[36] The "friendly discussion" referred to involved Anarchism, which Herbert rejected.

Wordsworth Donisthorpe, the British correspondent of *Liberty* and its most frequent British contributor, edited *Jus: A Weekly Organ of Individualism* (1885-1888). *Jus* originated as an organ of the Liberty and Property Defense League; it ceased when Donisthorpe resigned from the League in protest over its marked tendency to defend privilege rather than liberty. On the demise of *Jus*, Tucker wrote: "There are no more than two papers on Liberty's exchange list which the cause of Liberty could not have better spared . . . it is comforting to think that, as this good ship went down . . . it nailed to its mast-head colors more unmistakable than ever, and thus made its death more glorious than its life."[37] This referred to Donisthorpe's explicit embrace of Anarchism in *Jus*'s final issue. Donisthorpe's association with Tucker undoubtedly moved him in that direction.

Another sympathetic British periodical was the *Personal Rights Journal*, the organ of the English National Association for the Defense of Personal Rights, which was edited by J. H. Levy for over thirty years. Much of *Liberty*'s discussion of the *Personal Rights Journal* revolved around that publication's defense of government. "On the whole," Victor Yarros observed, "we find plenty of evidence that these are times that try English Individualists' souls. That the most thoughtful of them will finally frankly accept the anarchist position is a foregone conclusion. Let us watch them now."[38] Unfortunately, one of the things Yarros watched the *Personal Rights Journal* subsequently do was to review unfavorably his pamphlet "Anarchism: Its Aims and Methods"; the *Personal Rights Journal* remained an adherent of limited government.

Albert Tarn's *The Herald of Anarchy* (1890-1892), a London monthly, was an exception to the British Individualists' rejection of Anarchism. In its advertisement in *Liberty*, *The Herald of Anarchy* declared that it "seeks to destroy the authority and prestige of national government as well as to combat all other forms of tyranny; advocates free access to land, the abolition of national monetary laws and restrictions on credit, free contract and free love."[39] The debate between Tarn and Herbert on Anarchism was followed carefully by *Liberty*.

Henry Seymour was another of the English Anarchists, a founder of the neo-Proudhonian English Anarchist Circle, and an admirer of Tucker. In his periodical, *The Anarchist* (1885-1888), a four-page monthly beginning in March 1885,[40] he published George Bernard Shaw and Henry Appleton, both of whom also contributed to *Liberty*. "It is gratifying," Tucker wrote of *The Anarchist*, "to observe that it is to wage uncompromising war on lines precisely parallel to those of *Liberty*."[41] Later, however, Tucker indicated that *The Anarchist* was leaning toward Communist Anarchism. Seymour disputed the charge, writing, "*Liberty* says I have abandoned liberty in embracing Communism. This is un-true. I have embraced Communistic-Anarchism, but by no means Communism. I am Anarchist at least as entirely as ever. I simply embrace *voluntary* Commu-nism on ethical and economical grounds."[42] After this periodical, Seymour ed-ited the London *The Revolutionary Review* (1889), a monthly which lasted less than a year.[43]

The Eagle and the Serpent, a bimonthly from London (1898-1902), was an exception to the British insistence upon natural rights as the basis for Individu-alism. Edited by John Basil Barnhill under the pseudonym of Erwin McCall, this periodical presented the egoist ideas of Stirner, Nietzsche, and Ibsen, deriving its title from a passage from Nietzsche—"The proudest animal under the sun [the Eagle] and the wisest animal under the sun [the Serpent] have set out to recon-noiter."[44] Welcomed by *Liberty*, *The Eagle and the Serpent* was the London agent for Georgia and Henry Replogle's American periodical *Egoism*.

John Morley's *Pall Mall Gazette* from London was among those British periodicals that received lukewarm attention from Tucker. He considered the *Pall Mall Gazette* to be "a moderately liberal journal, but prone to eschew that intensity of utterance to which men engaged in vigorous battle for great ideas generally give vent."[45] The London monthly *Freedom* (1886-1927) received initial attention from *Liberty*, probably because its editor Pierre Kropotkin was a man whom Tucker admired.[46] The prospectus of the Individualistic *The Whirl-wind* (1890), edited by Herbert Vivian and Stuart Erskine, was reprinted in *Lib-erty* under the heading "Welcome the *Whirlwind*"; the prospectus read: "In poli-tics we shall be individualists, instantly protesting against the encroaching tyranny of our grandmother, the state."[47] Although it was generally well re-ceived, Yarros criticized *The Whirlwind*'s anti-Semitism.[48]

Liberty also maintained ties with British freethought and free love groups. It reprinted articles from G. W. Foote's *Freethinker* and reported the activities of Charles Bradlaugh and Annie Besant. George Bedborough's free love periodi-cal, *The Adult: A Journal for the Advancement of freedom in Sexual Relation-ships*, received some mention as the organ of the Legitimation League. *Liberty*, however, had little enthusiasm for this League, critically reviewing a pamphlet entitled "Legitimacy" by J. Greevz Fisher, a vice president of the League. The *Adult* and the Legitimation League were more closely associated with the free love interests of *Lucifer, the Light Bearer* and Moses Harman.[49]

Appendix 1

French Periodicals

Given the immense influence Proudhon had upon Tucker, *Liberty* naturally felt strong ties to radical movements in France. These ties manifested themselves in two ways: translations and reprints. Tucker, along with several of *Liberty*'s associates, was a bilingual Francophile and translated many works from French to English. Some of these were reprinted within *Liberty* itself; others were offered for sale independently, and were advertised within *Liberty*.[50] The shorter translated pieces were generally articles rendered directly from French periodicals. "The State: Its Nature, Object and Destiny" by Proudhon, for example, was translated by Tucker directly from Proudhon's popular periodical *La Voix du Peuple*, which followed on the heels of the suppression of *Le Peuple*. Because Tucker was an ardent fan and collector of Proudhon's periodicals, one of *Liberty*'s greatest expressions of pleasure came as the result of a particular gift from John Henry Mackay. Tucker exclaimed:

> Through the thoughtful kindness of my friend, John Henry Mackay, of Germany, I experienced a few days ago one of the pleasantest surprises of my life. For many years it has been my wish to obtain possession of a file of the newspapers which Proudhon edited in Paris during the years 1848, 1849, and 1850. Mackay has gratified this desire. . . . I now have on my desk a complete file of "Le Peuple," and a file of "Le Representant du Peuple," which lacks only the half-dozen numbers that the French government confiscated."[51]

The periodical from which articles were most frequently translated and reprinted in *Liberty* was Henri Rochefort's *L'Intransigeant*. Next in importance was George Clemenceau's *L'Aurore*. *Le Revolte* (subsequently *La Revolte*) edited by Pierre Kropotkin received praise from Tucker as "our ardent and admirable contemporary."[52] Tucker was especially pleased by *Le Revolte*'s condemnation of those American Socialists who refused to protest laws against Chinese immigration into America. *Le Temps* and *L'Audace* were also quoted briefly.[53]

Australian Periodicals

David Andrade, *Liberty*'s Australian correspondent, contributed several excellent articles on the progress of radical Individualism in Australia. Part of this progress was Andrade's *Honesty* (1887-1889), an Anarchist periodical from Melbourne. This twelve-page monthly was published by the Cooperative Publishing Company at 85 cents per year. *Liberty* was its role model; *Honesty*'s advertisement proclaimed: "It is sufficient description of *Honesty*'s principles to say that they are substantially the same as those championed by *Liberty* in America."[54] *Honesty* listed Tucker's name and address for American subscriptions.

W. R. Winspear's *Australian Radical* from Hamilton was also associated with *Liberty*. According to Tucker, the *Australian Radical* changed its format in 1888 from State Socialism to Anarchism. This weekly reprinted articles from *Liberty*.

Other Foreign Connections

Although the German egoist Max Stirner had immense impact upon *Liberty*, German periodicals were not followed with the same interest as British or French ones. Tucker's inability to read German fluently may have accounted for this oversight. Much of his knowledge of Stirner and other matters requiring translation came from George Schumm, who was bilingual in German. Adolf Brand's *Der Eigene* and Johann Otten's *Zeitschrift fur den Individualistischen Anarchismus* were commented upon by Tucker. German-American papers monitored by *Liberty* included: Heinzen's *Pionier*, Reitzel's *Arme Teufel, Der Wecker*, and *Der Freidenker*.

It is difficult to assess *Liberty*'s connection with Spanish periodicals. *Revista Social* and *La Revolución Social* were mentioned briefly, and *Liberty* contributor Steven T. Byington—considered one of the three or four brightest Tuckerites—engaged in debate over Individualist Anarchism with the editor of *A Vida*. *A Vida* had printed a Spanish translation of an article that Byington had submitted to Tucker.[55] *A Vida*'s source for the article was a French paper that had translated Byington's piece directly from *Liberty*. Whether other foreign periodicals were in the habit of translating and reprinting *Liberty* is speculation.

Although Tucker exhibited great interest in Russian nihilism and in the assassination of the Czar (1881), few Russian periodicals were mentioned in *Liberty*. Victor Yarros, who had fled Russia to avoid arrest, was probably the only associate of *Liberty* with enough background in that language and culture to appreciate and translate the various periodicals. There is, however, no evidence that he did so. *Liberty* did, nevertheless, follow the career of the Christian Anarchist Leo Tolstoi.[56]

Liberty and Literature[57]

Politics and social theory may have been the focus of *Liberty*, but Tucker was also keenly aware of the impact and importance of culture on societal attitudes.

For example, literature played a prominent role in *Liberty*'s emphasis on internationalism. Tucker kept current on the state of art and letters in France, England, and America. When Max Nordau published his antimodernist work *Degeneration* (*Entartung*), Tucker was discerning enough to solicit a critique from the one man best able to handle it—George Bernard Shaw. Shaw's subsequent essay, entitled "A Degenerate's View of Nordau," was one of the first articles by the British literary giant to appear in America. Indeed, Tucker introduced Shaw to America and later declared, "Bernard Shaw highly appreciates the fact that I was the first person to print his name in America (way back in 1885). He was hardly known in England then."[58]

Among the literary works *Liberty* translated and published were: Claude Tillier's *My Uncle Benjamin*, Zola's *Money*, Octave Mirabeau's *A Chambermaid's Diary*, Felix Pyat's *The Rag Picker of Paris*, and Sophie Kropotkin's *The Wife of Number 4,237*—an account of her experience with her husband Pierre Kropotkin at Clairvaux prison.

This fascination with cosmopolitan literature lead Tucker to publish *The Transatlantic* (1889-1890), a biweekly literary magazine. The advertisement for this publication in *Liberty* promised: "Every number has a complete translated novelette, a piece of European Music, a Portrait of a Foreign Celebrity and part of a translated European Serial." *The Transatlantic* was said to consist of the "cream of the European press translated into English. Not only from foreign periodicals, but from books as well."[59] Predictably, much of the literature that interested Tucker had political implications. When Oscar Wilde's plea for penal reform *The Ballad of Reading Gaol*,[60] was widely criticized, for example, Tucker enthusiastically endorsed the poem, urging all of his subscribers to read it. Tucker, in fact, published an American edition. From its early championing of Walt Whitman's *Leaves of Grass*[61] to a series of short stories by Francis du Bosque in its last issues, *Liberty* was a vehicle for controversial and avant garde literature.

Notes

1. Published in *Liberty* and advertised as a pamphlet for sale in its pages thereafter.
2. The exchange between Tucker and George Bernard Shaw on "Anarchism versus State Socialism" was examined in detail in Shoshana Edwards, "The Worthy Adversaries: Benjamin R. Tucker & G. Bernard Shaw," in Michael E. Coughlin, Charles H. Hamilton, and Mark A. Sullivan, eds. *Benjamin R. Tucker and The Champions of Liberty* (St. Paul, Minn.: Michael E. Coughlin, 1986), 92-100.
3. A more embracing sense of the scope of Tucker's interest in and influence upon the international press can be gleaned from chapter 1, which discussed the many books and pamphlets published by Tucker. Many were translations from the popular radical works of Europe and appeared in English for the first time when advertised in *Liberty*.
4. Benjamin R. Tucker, *The Word* (November 1872): 3.
5. Greene and Proudhon shared this stress upon banking theory, the latter seeking to validate his theory through the founding of what he called the People's Bank and through his work *Banque du Peuple*. Although the Bank was incorporated on January 31, 1849, it never opened.
6. Benjamin R. Tucker, "On Picket Duty," *Liberty* 6 (January 5, 1889): 1.
7. Benjamin R. Tucker, *The Word* (December 1876): 2.
8. Benjamin R. Tucker, *Liberty* 12 (July 11, 1896): 5.
9. Benjamin R. Tucker, "On Picket Duty," *Liberty* 8 (May 16, 1891): 1.

10. Benjamin R. Tucker, "Two Renegades Instead of One," *Liberty* 6 (January 19, 1889): 4.

11. See William Reichert, *Partisans of Freedom* (Bowling Green, Ohio: Bowling Green University Popular Press, 1976), 367-370.

12. The *Truth Seeker* was so named because Bennett believed free thought to be a prerequisite for progress in scientific thought. The paper's motto was, "Devoted to Science, Morals, Freethought and Human Happiness." Its logo included shelves of books, chemistry apparatus, and a telescope.

13. "Compliments from Liberty's Friends," *Liberty* 1 (September 3, 1881): 4.

14. Benjamin R. Tucker, "On Picket Duty," *Liberty* 1 (December 10, 1881): 1.

15. Tucker, "On Picket Duty," *Liberty* 1 (December 10, 1881): 1.

16. Benjamin R. Tucker, *Liberty* 4 (January 22, 1887): 5.

17. The current *Truth Seeker* bears little resemblance to the original periodical and should not be considered an ideological successor to it, despite the fact that it chronologically is the successor.

18. Benjamin R. Tucker, "On Picket Duty," *Liberty* 2 (November 11, 1882): 1.

19. Freethought periodicals associated with the Liberal League can be confusing to date, as they tended to use the chronology of E.M.—Era of Man—in honor of Giordano Bruno who had been burned at the stake in 1600 for scientific heresy. Harman began to use this dating system in 1883, which was 283 E.M.

Lucifer, the Light Bearer was provocatively named in order to stress that God had doomed man to ignorance in the garden of Eden, and he would have never known good from evil if not for the assistance of Lucifer, who brought knowledge.

20. Some factions within the freethought community—with which Heywood was also affiliated—decried Heywood's recklessness in publishing and blatantly circulating *Cupid's Yokes*. In the *Index*, for example, Francis Abbot proclaimed support for the obscenity laws and pleaded with fellow reformers not to tarnish their reputations.

21. The well-known freethinker D. M. Bennett, editor of the *Truth Seeker*, also served a prison term for circulating *Cupid's Yokes*. For an account of both, see Hal D. Sears, *The Sex Radicals: Free Love in High Victorian America* (Lawrence: The Regents Press of Kansas, 1977).

22. Benjamin R. Tucker, "Fiat Lux!" *Liberty* 6 (September 1, 1888): 5.

23. Ezra Heywood, "Compliments from Liberty's Friends," *Liberty* 1 (September 3, 1881): 4.

24. Benjamin R. Tucker, "On Picket Duty," *Liberty* 3 (November 22, 1884): 1.

25. James J. Martin, *Men Against the State: The Expositors of Individualist Anarchism in America, 1827-1908* (Colorado Springs, Colo.: Ralph Myles, 1970), a usually reliable source book, lists *Fair Play* as 1898-1908. *Liberty* 7 (April 4, 1891): 4, however, contains a letter from E. C. Walker and Lillian Harman announcing suspension of the periodical.

26. Advertisement, *Liberty* 14 (December 1903): 7.

27. Benjamin R. Tucker, "Fighting for Free Speech in Liberal," *Liberty* 4 (July 17, 1886): 4.

28. Advertisement, *Liberty* 6 (December 28, 1889): 8. In 1892, Pentecost's editorship ceased and the periodical leaned toward State Socialism.

29. Benjamin R. Tucker, "On Picket Duty," *Liberty* 7 (July 26, 1890): 1. M'Cready (a pseudonym for G. O. Warren) died in 1890, mourned by Tucker with the words, "Lib-

erty learns with profound sorrow the fact of the sudden death of T. L. M'Cready." Benjamin R. Tucker, "On Picket Duty," *Liberty* 7 (June 28, 1890): 1.

30. Benjamin R. Tucker, "On Picket Duty," *Liberty* 5 (March 31, 1888): 1.

31. In the 1920s, Yarros wrote an article in which he repudiated Anarchism itself, along with his past connections with *Liberty*. The article caused a bitter rift between Tucker and his former associate editor.

32. Benjamin R. Tucker, "A Recall to the Real Issue," *Liberty* 7 (July 12, 1890): 4.

33. In his book *Freedom and Authority*, William R. McKercher touches upon one reason for the high level of debate within English political circles during *Liberty*'s tenure. McKercher comments on some of the brilliant radicals who fled to England to escape persecution in their own land. "Kropotkin had come to London as an exile in 1885 . . . Errico Malatesta, an Italian . . . and Rudolph Rocker, a German emigre, arrived in the city at the age of twenty-one." William R. McKercher, *Freedom and Authority* (Montreal: Black Rose Books, 1993), 153. Chapter 3 of McKercher's book, entitled "Libertarian Propaganda and Personalities in England," provides an excellent overview.

34. In *Anarchist Portraits*, Paul Avrich remarks upon how many of the contributors to *Liberty*—quite apart from those representing British Individualism—were either British or born in Britain. In this list, he includes: William Bailie, James L. Walker, Henry Bool, Miriam Daniell, Helena Born, William A. Whittick, Alfred B. Westrup, and A. H. Simpson. Paul Avrich, *Anarchist Portraits* (Princeton, N.J.: Princeton University Press, 1988).

35. "Prospectus of Auberon Herbert's Paper," *Liberty* 6 (March 8, 1890): 2.

36. Benjamin R. Tucker, "Property Under Anarchism," *Liberty* 7 (July 12, 1890): 5.

37. Benjamin R. Tucker, "A Prophecy in Course of Fulfillment," *Liberty* 5 (April 14, 1888): 7. This appeared almost as a fulfillment of a prophecy by Yarros—"Mr. Donisthorpe cannot be long in reaching anarchy."

38. Victor Yarros, "A Crisis," *Liberty* 7 (July 26, 1890): 5.

39. The first advertisement appeared in *Liberty* 7 (November 29, 1890): 7.

40. *The Anarchist* later (January 1, 1886) became a fortnightly—at least for two months, after which it returned to its monthly format until 1887.

41. Benjamin R. Tucker, "On Picket Duty," *Liberty* 3 (April 11, 1885): 1. Foote, editor of *The Freethinker*, however, did not share Tucker's salutary opinion of *The Anarchist*, which he described as "an affliction."

42. *The Anarchist* (June 1, 1886). Despite Tucker's published statements of good will toward Seymour's periodical, Seymour behaved rather boorishly toward Tucker in an article entitled "An Arrogant Sophist" *The Anarchist* (August 1886). A few months later, however, Seymour seemed to revert more to Individualism, running articles from the brilliant Wordsworth Donisthorpe.

43. The phrase "The Revolutionary Review" had a history. It was the subtitle of Seymour's *The Anarchist* until April 1887, when the subtitle was significantly changed to "Communist and Revolutionary."

44. This was the motto of the periodical, appearing on its masthead. It did not change when the subtitle went from "A Journal of Egoistic Philosophy and Sociology" to "A Journal of Emersonian Philosophy and Sociology" (July 1900) to "A Journal of Wit, Wisdom and Wickedness" (October 1900) and finally to "A Journal for Free Spirits and for Spirits Struggling to be Free" (March 1901).

45. Benjamin R. Tucker, "On Picket Duty," *Liberty* 2 (January 20, 1883): 1.

46. Although Tucker's philosophy differed markedly from Kropotkin's own, Tucker considered him to be one of the foremost Anarchists in Europe and his periodical *Le Revolte* to be the most scholarly of all Anarchist journals. Tucker translated Kropotkin's "Order and Anarchy" and "Law and Authority," both of which appeared in *Liberty*. *Freedom: A Journal of Anarchist-Socialism* was established under the editorship of Kropotkin and Charlotte M. Wilson, an Anarchist and early member of the Fabian Society. Its subtitle changed to *A Journal of Anarchist-Communism* in 1889.

47. "Welcome the Whirlwind," *Liberty* 7 (June 28, 1890): 3.

48. Victor Yarros, "The 'Whirlwind's' Individualism," *Liberty* 7 (September 13, 1890): 6-7. The controversy revolved around the *Whirlwind*'s statement that "the proper way to deal with Jews is a rigorous boycott." Yarros was outraged, claiming that "intelligent individuals will certainly dissent."

49. For an overview of the British influence upon *Liberty*, see Carl Watner, "The English Individualists as They Appear in *Liberty*," in Coughlin, Hamilton, and Sullivan, *Benjamin R. Tucker & The Champions of Liberty*, 191-211.

50. At 225 Fourth Avenue, New York, Tucker had a large, radical bookstore. See *Liberty* 15 (June 1906): 9-10, and *Liberty* 15 (August 1906): 1-2 for an account of the establishment.

51. Benjamin R. Tucker, "On Picket Duty," *Liberty* 8 (July 11, 1891): 1. In later life, Tucker condemned Mackay due to the latter's unusual lifestyle.

52. Benjamin R. Tucker, "On Picket Duty," *Liberty* 2 (June 9, 1883): 1.

53. *Le Revolte* wrote: "And not a single socialist was found in San Francisco to say to these people that they cannot prohibit the admission to America of these poor wretches." Quoted in *Liberty* 1 (May 13, 1882): 1.

54. The first advertisement appeared in *Liberty* 4 (June 18, 1887): 8.

55. Steven T. Byington, "Four Points of Anarchism," *Liberty* 15 (August 1906): 24-34.

56. The Jewish Anarchist community was a strong radical element in America, many of whom had immigrated from Russia. Two of the English language papers favored by the Jewish Anarchists were *Liberty* and Dyer Lum's *The Alarm*.

57. Again, the ensuing description provides only a flavor of Tucker's impact upon the literary awareness of American Individualism. Please see chapter 1 for a deeper sense of his influence.

58. Joseph Ishill, ed., *Free Vistas* 2 (Berkley Heights, N.J.: Oriole Press, 1937), 278.

59. *The Transatlantic*, subtitled *A Mirror of European Life and Letters*, was first advertised in *Liberty* 6 (October 5, 1889): 8, as being issued on the 1st and 15th of the month. Herbert Gutman, in the introduction to the Greenwood reprint of *Liberty*, mentions another literary periodical, *Five Stories a Week*.

60. Tucker published both a cloth and paper edition of this over-600-page poem, which was first advertised in *Liberty* 13 (May 1899): 8.

61. First advertised in *Liberty* 1 (July 22, 1882): 4, Tucker appended a challenge to various officials responsible for the suppression of *Leaves of Grass*. He advised them of his intention to sell the work and offered to deliver a copy of it to them at their place of choice to be used in evidence against him. There were no takers.

Appendix 2

Liberty's Library

Over the course of Benjamin Tucker's periodical *Liberty* (1881-1908), the subscribers were often regaled with "recommended readings"—in essence, the "must" titles for individualists to have on their bookshelves.

The descriptions are *Liberty*'s own, usually rendered on the last page of the issue where books were offered for sale through the *Liberty* office (Boston) and then Tucker's own bookstore (New York).

Liberty's Library

Anarchism—A Concise Statement. By FAC. To be had of the publisher. Address all orders to the publisher. Ge. Gillen, Irvington, N.J.

Anarchism: Its Aims and Methods. By Victor Yarros. An address delivered at the first public meeting of the Boston Anarchists' Club and adopted by that organization in its authorized exposition of its principles. With an appendix giving the Constitution of the Anarchists' Club and explanatory notes regarding it. 30 pages.

Anarchism or Anarchy? A Discussion between William H. Tillinghast and Benj. R. Tucker. Prefaced by an Open Letter to Rev. William J. Potter.

An Anarchist on Anarchy. An eloquent exposition of the beliefs of Anarchists by a man as eminent in science as in reform. By Elisee Reclus. Followed by a sketch of the criminal record of the author by E. Vaughan.

The Anarchists. A Picture of Civilization at the Close of the Nineteenth Century. By John Henry Mackay. Translated from the German by George Schumm. A poet's prose contribution to the literature of philosophic and egoistic Anarchism. The author traces his own mental development in London amid the exciting events of 1887,—the manifestations of the unemployed, the rioting at Trafalgar Square, and the executions at Chicago. The antagonism between

173

Communism and Anarchism sharply brought out. One of the world's great artists places his pen at the service of Anarchism. 315 pages.

Anarchists' March. Tune: Bjorneborganes Marsch (Finnish War Song). Words by J. Wm. Lloyd.

The Ballad of Reading Gaol. By C.3.3.—Oscar Wilde. A poem of more than 600 lines, dedicated to the memory of a trooper of the Horse Guard who was hanged in Reading Gaol during the poet's confinement there. An English classic. Cloth and paper.

The Ballot. By William Walstein Gordak. A short poem illustrating the absurdity of majority rule. Printed as a leaflet, with an effective advertisement of *Liberty* on the back. Excellent for propagandism.

A Blow at Trial by Jury. By Benj. R. Tucker. An examination of the special jury law passed by the New York legislators in 1895. A speech delivered by the editor of *Liberty* at a mass meeting held at Cooper Union, New York, June 25, 1897, under the auspices of the Central Labor Union, Typographical Union No. 6, and other labor organizations. Distribution of this pamphlet among lawyers and legislators will tend indirectly to interest them in Anarchism.

Bombs: The Poetry and Philosophy of Anarchism. By William A. Whittick. 187 pages. Cloth and paper.

Captain Roland's Purse: How it is Filled and How Emptied. By John Ruskin. The first of a projected series of Labor Tracts.

Causes of the Conflict Between Capital and Labor. By D. H. Hendershott. A 92-page pamphlet showing that all the wealth in the world consists of unconsumed wages earned by somebody, but that most of it is withheld from the earners through Interest, Rent, Profit, and Taxes.

Church and State, and Other Essays. By Count Leo Tolstoi. "Church and State" is translated by authorization from Tolstoi's own manuscript. It was written several years ago, but it being the author's boldest work, severely denunciatory of the powers that be, he has kept it in manuscript in consequence of the arbitrary *regime* in Russia. Now he has determined to publish it in the United States. It is an uncompromising assault upon both Church and State from the standpoint of Christ's teachings. Cloth and paper.

Citizen's Money. A critical analysis in the light of free trade in banking. By Alfred B. Westrup. 27 pages.

Co-Operation: Its Laws and Principles. An Essay showing Liberty and Equity as the only conditions of true co-operation, and exposing the violations of these conditions by Rent, Interest, Profit, and Majority Rule. By C. T. Fowler. Containing a portrait of Herbert Spencer.

Co-Operative Homes. An Essay showing how the kitchen may be abolished and the independence of woman secured by severing the State from the Home, thereby introducing the voluntary principle into the Family and all its relationships. By C. T. Fowler. Containing a portrait of Louise Michel.

Corporations. An essay showing how the monopoly of railroads, telegraphs, etc. may be abolished without the intervention of the State. By C. T. Fowler. Containing a portrait of Wendell Phillips.

The Dawning. A Novel. "Oh Heaven! Apollo is once more among the herdsmen of Admetus, and the herdsmen know not it is the Sun-God!" An octavo volume of nearly four hundred pages, bound in cloth.

Everybody's Law Book. Is the title of this 768 page work prepared by J. Alexander Koones, L.L.B. member of the New York Bar. It enables every man and woman to be their own lawyer. It teaches what are your rights and how to maintain them. When to begin a law suit and when to shun one. It contains the useful information every businessman needs in every State in the Union. It contains business forms of every variety useful to the lawyer as well as to all who have legal business to transact.

The Fallacies in "Progress and Poverty." A bold attack on the position of Henry George. Written for the people, and as revolutionary in sentiment, and even more radical than "Progress and Poverty" itself. By William Hanson. 191 pages. Cloth.

A Female Nihilist. A thrilling sketch of the character and adventures of a typical Nihilistic heroine. By Stepniak, by "Underground Russia."

The Financial Problem: Its Relation to Labor Reform and Prosperity. Demonstrating the abolition of interest to be unavoidable. By Alfred B. Westrup. 30 pages.

Free Political Institutions: Their Nature, Essence, and Maintenance. An abridgment and rearrangement of Lysander Spooner's "Trial by Jury." Edited by Victor Yarros. Chapters: I. Legitimate Government and Majority Rule, II. Trial by Jury as a Palladium of Liberty, III. Trial by Jury as Defined by Magna Carta, IV. Objections Answered, V. The Criminal Intent, VI. Moral Considerations for Jurors, VII. Free Administration of Justice, VIII. Juries of the Present Day Illegal.

The Fruits of Culture. A Comedy in Four Acts. By Count Leo Tolstoi, translated by George Schumm. Its first publication in English.

God and the State. One of the most eloquent pleas for liberty ever written. Paine's "Age of Reason" and "Rights of Man" consolidated and improved. It stirs the pulse like a trumpet call. By Michael Bakounine. Founder of Nihilism and Apostle of Anarchy. Translated from the French by Benj. R. Tucker. 52 pages.

Henry George, Traitor. By Benj. R. Tucker. Proving that the leader of the Single-Taxers was a hypocrite and a coward in his sanctioning of the hanging of the Chicago Communists.

The Herald of Anarchy. English Organ of Anarchism. Seeks to destroy the authority and prestige of National Government as well as to combat all other forms of tyranny: advocates free access to the land, the abolition of national monetary laws and restrictions on credit, free contract, and free love. Published monthly at the Labor Press, 57 Chancery Lane, London, W.C., England.

Heroes of the Revolution of '71. A souvenir picture of the Paris Commune, presenting Fifty-One Portraits of the men whose names are most prominently connected with that great uprising of the people, and adorned with mottoes from Danton, Blanqui, Pyat, Proudhon, J. Wm. Lloyd, Tridon, and August Spies. Of all the Commune souvenirs that have ever been issued this picture stands easily first. It is executed by the phototype process from a very rare collection of photographs, measures 15 inches by 24, and is printed on heavy paper for framing.

Ideo-Kleptomania: The Case of Henry George. By J. W. Sullivan. The author offers evidence to show—That Henry George took his doctrine bodily from Patrick Edward Dove. That academic authority has pronounced Henry George's arguments against Malthus simply those of William Godwin and Herbert Spencer, without a new thought added. That his attack on the wages-fund theory Henry George but reemployed ideas already well-used in economic disputes, without giving credit to the thinkers with whom they originated. That Henry George entertains the peculiar belief that a writer may put ideas into print as his own, no matter how he comes by them. With Henry George's denial of plagiarism. One Hundred Pages.

Instead of a Book, By a Man Too Busy to Write One. A Fragmentary Exposition of Philosophical Anarchism. Culled from the writings of Benj. R. Tucker. A large, well-printed, and excessively cheap volume of 524 pages, consisting of articles selected from *Liberty* and classified under the following headings: (1) State Socialism and Anarchism: How Far They Agree, and wherein They Differ; (2) The Individual, Society, and the State; (3) Money and Interest; (4) Land and Rent; (5) Socialism; (6) Communism; (7) Methods; (8) Miscellaneous. The whole elaborately indexed.

International Address. An elaborate, comprehensive, and very entertaining Exposition of the principles of the Working-People's International Association. By William T.[sic] Greene.

Involuntary Idleness. By Hugo Bilgram. An exposition of the causes of the discrepancy existing between the supply of and the demand for labor and its products. 119 pages. Cloth.

The Iron Law of Wages. By Hugo Bilgram. This pamphlet demonstrates that wages could not be kept down to the cost of the laborer's subsistence were it not for the monopoly by a privileged class of the right to represent wealth by money.

The Kreutzer Sonata. By Leo Tolstoi. Suppressed by the Czar. Translated by Benjamin R. Tucker. This novel is the boldest work yet written by the famous Russian author. Dealing with the questions of love and marriage, it urges a morality that is more than puritanical in its severity, while handling the delicate subject with all the frankness of the realistic school. In St. Petersburg and Moscow manuscript copies pass from hand to hand and are read aloud in literary circles.

This book, so far as the central lesson to be drawn from it is concerned, is of a reactionary character, and should not be regarded as a part of *Liberty*'s propaganda. Yet it is a work of interest, almost a masterpiece of art, a romance not without sociological importance. No lover of independent thought can fail to admire its rare unconventionality, the fearless way in which the author addresses polite circles upon a subject which they generally taboo [sic]. Cloth and paper.

The Labor Dollar. By Stephen Pearl Andrews.

Labor Library. 30 standard works by 21 authors,—Marx, Darwin, Spencer, Huxley, Hyndman, Gronlund, Bebel, Annie Besant, Kropotkin, Reclus, Lasale, Bradlaugh, George, etc. Bound in 3 vol. Cloth. Modern Press 250 1/2 Bowery, New York.

Land Tenure. An essay showing the governmental basis of land monopoly, the futility of governmental remedies, and a natural and peaceful way of starving out the landlords. By C. T. Fowler. Containing a portrait of Robert Owen.

Love, Marriage, and Divorce, and the Sovereignty of the Individual. A Discussion between Henry James, Horace Greeley, and Stephen Pearl Andrews. Including the replies of Mr. Andrews, rejected by the New York Tribune, and a subsequent discussion, occurring twenty years later, between Mr. James and Mr. Andrews.

Lucifer. Devoted to the Earnest, Candid, and Fearless Discussion of Methods Looking Toward the Elimination or Total Abolition of all Invasive Laws and Customs. Special attention is now being given in its columns to the marriage and divorce laws, for an alleged violation of which two members of the LUCIFER corps, Edwin C. Walker and Lillian Harman, are now in prison, and for months have been subjected to privations and indignities unprecedented in English-speaking countries. Published every Friday. Address: M. Harman & Son, Valley Falls, Kansas.

[This advertisement was later changed to read: "Special attention is now being given in its columns to the marriage and divorce laws and also to the 'Comstock Postal Statutes' from an alleged violation of which three of the LUCIFER staff,—M. Harman, E. C. Walker, and G. Harman—are now under bonds for appearance at trial."]

Modern Marriage. By Emil Zola. Translated from the French by Benj. R. Tucker. In this, his latest story, Zola takes four typical marriages,—one from the nobility, one from the bourgeoisie, one from the petty bourgeoisie, and one from the working people,—and describes, with all the power of his wonderous art, how each originates, by what motive each is inspired, how each is consummated, and how each results.

Money. By Emile Zola. Translated by Benj. R. Tucker. This novel, the latest from Zola's pen, represents the author apparently at the very zenith of his career. Having pictured in his previous novels the religious world, the political world, the art world, the industrial world, the commercial world, the mining world, the agricultural world, the railroad world, and the half-world (demi-monde), he now focuses his camera upon the world of finance.

The scene is laid in Paris, and centres in the Stock Exchange. Woven into a romance of absorbing interest, the reader meets every type of speculator pictured to the life. Black Fridays are described as only Zola can describe, and their woful [sic] results are traced into every sphere of existence. In short, the power of money for good and for evil, the virtues and vices attendant upon its accumulation, are set forth with a skill that astonishes.

Love and Socialism also figure largely in this book, which is one of the severest blows ever dealt at plutocracy in the form of fiction.

The book has a specially designed cover as startling as beautiful, is printed in large type on good paper , and contains a fine half-tone portrait of the author.

Money and Currency. By A. H. Stephenson and G. F. Stephens. The invention of money—the standard of value—government issues of money—the best currency—solution of the money question.

Mutual Banking. Showing the Radical Deficiency of the existing Circulating Medium, and how Interest on Money can be Abolished. By William B. Greene.

My Uncle Benjamin. A Humorous, Satirical, and Philosophical Novel. By Claude Tillier. Translated from the French by Benjamin R. Tucker. With a sketch of the author's life and works by Ludwig Pfau. This novel, though it has enjoyed the honor of three translations into German, has never before been translated into English. It is one of the most delightfully witty works ever written. Almost every sentence excites a laugh. It is thoroughly realistic, but not at all repulsive. Its satirical treatment of humanity's foibles and its jovial but profound philosophy have won its author the title of "the modern Rabelais." My Uncle Benjamin riddles with the shafts of his good-natured ridicule the shams of theology, law, medicine, commerce, war, marriage, and society generally. 312 pages. Cloth and paper.

The Outcome of Individualism. By J. H. Levy. Late lecturer on Logic and Economics at the British Institution and the City of London College, Honorary Secretary of the National Liberal Club Political Economy Circle. Personal Rights Assocation.

A Politician in Sight of Haven Being a Protest against the Government of Man by Man. By Auberon Herbert.

Prohibition. An essay on the relation of government to temperance, showing that prohibition cannot prohibit, and would be unnecessary if it could. By C. T. Fowler.

Prostitution and the International Woman's League. By Henry Edger.

Proudhon and His 'Bank of the People.' By Charles A. Dana. Being a defense of the Great French Anarchist, showing the evils of a specie currency, and that interest on capital can and ought to be abolished by a system of free and mutual banking. Cloth and leatherette.

The Quintessence of Ibsenism. By G. Bernard Shaw. Pronounced by the London "Saturday Review" a "most diverting book," and by the author "the most complete assertion of the human will as against all laws, institutions, 'isms,' and the like, now procurable for a quarter." Ibsen's works have been read very widely in America, and there have been almost as many interpretations as readers. This conflict of opinion will cause the liveliest curiosity to know what view is taken by Mr. Bernard Shaw, who is not only one of the keenest students of Ibsen, but one of the wittiest writers in England. He takes up the plays verbatim, subjects each to searching analysis, and extracts the quintessence of the whole. Nearly 200 pages.

The Radical Review. Vol. I., handsomely bound in cloth, and containing over sixty Essays, Poems, Translations, and Reviews, by the most prominent radical writers, on industrial, financial, social, literary, scientific, philosophical, ethical, and religious subjects. 828 pages octavo. Single copies offered.

The Rag-Picker of Paris. By Felix Pyat. Translated from the French by Benjamin R. Tucker. Four Thousand Copies Sold the First Week. Third Edition now in Press. A novel unequaled in its combination of dramatic power, picturesque intensity, crisp dialogue, panoramic effect, radical tendency, and bold handling of social questions. Originally written as a play, this masterpiece achieved the greatest success known to the French stage. Recently, and just before his death, the author elaborated his play into a novel, in which form it presents a complete panorama of the prison of the present century.

The Reorganization of Business. An Essay showing how the principles of cooperation may be realized in the Store, the Bank, and the Factory. By C. T. Fowler. A portrait of Ralph Waldo Emerson.

The Rights of Women and the Sexual Relations. An Address to an Unknown Lady Reader. By Karl Heinzen. Translated from the German by Emma Heller Schumm. "[T]he most cogent argument yet written infavor of a larger personal liberty for the sex. It is made accessible to English readers tardily yet in time, when the whole civilized world is blinking at the mockery of many if not most marriages."—Editorial in *Philadelphia Press.* Cloth and paper.

The Science of Society. By Stephen Pearl Andrews. This work, long out of print, is now republished to meet a demand which for a few years past has been rapidly growing. First published about forty years ago, and yet in its teachings still far in advance of the times, it comes to the present generation practically as a new book. Josiah Warren, whose social philosophy it was written to expound, was in the habit of referring to it as the most lucid and complete presentation of his ideas that ever had been written or ever could be written. It will undoubtedly take rank in the future among the famous books of the nineteenth century.

It consists of two parts, as follows:

Part I—The True Constitution of Government in the Sovereignty of the Individual as the Final Development of Protestantism, Democracy, and Socialism.

Part II—Cost the Limit of Price: A Scientific Measure of Honesty in Trade, as one of the Fundamental Principles in the Solution of the Social Problem.

[First advertised as being published by Sarah E. Holmes, then later published by Benj. R. Tucker.]

Slaves to Duty. By John Badcock, Jr. A unique addition to the pamphlet literature of Anarchism. It assails the morality of superstition as the foundation of the various schemes for the exploitation of mankind. Max Stirner himself does not expound the doctrine of Egoism in bolder fashion. 30 pages.

So the Railway Kings Itch for an Empire, Do They? By a "Red Hot Striker," of Scranton, Pa. A reply to an article by William M. Grosvenor in the *International Review.*

Social Wealth: The Sole Factors and Exact Ratios in Its Acquirement and Apportionment. This handsome octavo volume of 320 pages treats of the usurpations of Capitalism, showing that Land and Labor are the only natural capital, or source of wealth; exposing the trick of treating variable and invariable values as one; and explaining the true mean [sic] of Value in Exchange; showing that in the production of wealth cooperation always exists, and exposing the fraudulent methods by which equitable division is defeated; exploding the "Taxation" and other "Remedies" for the wrongs done Industry proposed by George, Wallace, and Clark, and demonstrating that the scientific is the only safe method of investigation for the employer or the employed who seeks salutary reform.

Socialistic, Communistic, Mutualistic, and Financial Fragments. By William B. Greene.

The Sociological Index. The Sociological Index is a classified weekly catalogue of the most important articles relating to sociology, as well as to other subjects in which students of sociology are usually interested, that appear in the periodical press of the world.

The catalogue is compiled in the interest of no sector party, the choice of articles being governed solely by their importance and interest.

The articles thus catalogued are clipped from the periodicals and filed, and *these clippings are for sale* . . .

Spooner v. McConnell, et al. An argument presented to the United States Circuit court, in support of a petition for an injunction to restrain Alexander McConnell and others from placing dams in Ohio. 1839. 80 pages.

The State: Its Origin, Its Nature, and Its Abolition. By Albert Tarn, an English Anarchist. 19 pages.

The Story of an African Farm. A Novel. By Ralph Iron (Olive Schreiner) A romance, not of adventure, but of the intellectual life and growth of young English and German people living among the Boers and Kaffirs, picturing the mental struggles through which they passed in their evolution from orthodoxy to rationalism; and representing advanced ideas on religious and social questions. A work of remarkable power, beauty, and originality. 375 pages.

A Strike of Millionaires Against Miners: Or, The Story of Spring Valley. By Henry D. Lloyd. A book to be read by everyone who wants to learn the methods by which, in this free and glorious Republic, the people are being robbed of their labors and liberties. It takes the coal business as the most representative of the tendency to monopoly, so rapidly converting all the great industries of the country into private estates for the Lords of Industry, and it tells the story of Spring Valley, Illinois made famous by the cruel lock out there to starve the men into giving up their union and taking lower wages—as a typical "modern instance" of this tendency. It uses this story as an illustration of the wicked drift of our entire business system towards exaggerated wealth for the few, and extreme poverty for the multitude.

Sturm. To German Readers. By John Henry Mackay. A Collection of Egoistic and Anarchistic poems in the German language. Second edition, with dedicatory poem to Max Stirner. 115 pages. Cloth.

System of Economical Contradictions: Or, the Philosophy of Misery. By P. J. Proudhon. Translated from the French by Benj. R. Tucker. This work, one of the most celebrated written by Proudhon, constitutes the fourth volume of the Complete Works, and is published in a style uniform with that of "What Is

Property?" It discusses, in a style as novel as profound, the problems of Value, Division of Labor, Machinery, Competition, Monopoly, Taxation, and Providence, showing that economic progress is achieved by the appearance of a succession of economic forces, each of which counteracts the evils developed by its predecessor, and then, by developing evils of its own, necessitates its successor, the process to continue until a final force, corrective of the whole, shall establish a stable economic equilibrium. 460 pages, octavo, in the highest style of the typographic art. Cloth and full calf, blue, gilt edges.

Taxation or Free Trade? A Criticism upon Henry George's "Protection of Free Trade." By John F. Kelly. 16 pages.

The Thirty-Six Trades of the State. By Arsene Alexandre. Translated from the French by Benj. R. Tucker. Showing the state as a jack-at-all-trades and good at none.

Three Dreams in a Desert. By Olive Schreiner. An allegorical prose-poem beautifully picturing the emancipation of woman and foreshadowing the results thereof.

The Transatlantic: A Mirror of European Life and Letters. (Issued on the 1st and 15th of the month.) Made up of the cream of the European press. Translated into English. Not only from foreign periodicals, but from books as well. The Transatlantic brings within the realm of all Europe's newest discoveries in Science, proudest achievements in Art, latest productions in Literature, freshest society and fashion gossip. Every number has a complete translated Novelette, a piece of European music, a portrait of a foreign celebrity, and part of a translated European serial. Transatlantic Publishing Co. 328 Washington Street, P.O. Box 210, Boston.

True Civilization: A Subject of Vital and Serious Interest to All People, but Most Immediately to the Men and Women of Labor and Sorrow. By Josiah Warren. A Pamphlet of 117 pages, now passing through its fifth edition, explaining the basic principles of Labor Reform,—Liberty and Equity.

The Twentieth Century. Hugh O. Pentecost, Editor, T. L. M'Cready, Associate Editor. Each number contains the Address of the preceding Sunday, delivered by the Editor in Newark, Brooklyn, and New York. Our Motto: "Hear the other side." This journal advocates Personal Sovereignty in place of State Sovereignty. Voluntary Cooperation as opposed to Compulsory Cooperation, the Liberation of the human mind from Superstition, and the application of the principles of Ethics toward Social Regeneration. But it is meant also to be a broad-minded, unsectarian meeting place for the representatives of all schools of Religious and economic thought, Orthodox and Liberal Christians, Spiritualism, Hebrews, Agnostics, Liberals, Infidels, Atheists, Freethinkers, and Secularism of every shade of opinion; Anarchists, Protectionists, free-traders, Single Taxers, Nationalists and Socialists, advocates of peaceful measures of social regeneration, and revolution, will all be welcomed to the columns with equal cordiality, fairness, and respect. Twentieth Century, No. 4 Warren St., New York City.

Unity. To Those who "Do not Care for a Religious Paper." Would it make any difference to you if you knew of one that does not advocate the doctrines of everlasting punishment, vicarious atonement, miracles, and an infallible Bible?—

One that does stand for common sense in religion, "truth for authority," believes that religion should be friendly to science, and advocates a religious fellowship that will welcome all of every belief who are willing to work for truth, righteousness, and love in the world?—

One that does not fill its space with learned or ignorant discussions of scripture texts, but does give every week 32 columns of fresh and rational reading, including a sermon on some living topic, editorials and contributions on current events; and news of the progress of liberal religious thought?

A Vindication of Natural Society. By Edmund Burke. Showing the Inherent Evils of all State Governments. "In vain you tell me that artificial government is good . . . The thing—the thing itself is the abuse."—Burke. 36 pages.

Voluntary Socialism. By F. D. Tandy. A complete and systematic outline of Anarchistic philosophy and economics, written in a clear, concise, and simple style. It is followed by a suggestive bibliography of books of service to those who wish to study the subject more deeply, and contains also a complete index.

Voluntary Taxation. An essay showing that the public revenues should be considered as insurance premiums, not to be exacted by compulsion. By J. Greevz Fisher. 31 pages.

What Is Freedom, and When Am I Free? Being an attempt to put Liberty on a rational basis, and wrest its keeping from irresponsible pretenders in Church and State. By Henry Appleton. 27 pages.

What Is Property? Or an Inquiry into the Principle of Right and of Government. By P. J. Proudhon. Prefaced by a Sketch of Proudhon's Life and Works, and containing as a Frontispiece a fine steel Engraving of the Author. Translated from the French by Benj. R. Tucker. A systematic, thorough, and radical discussion of the institution of property,—the basis, its history, its present status, and its destiny,—together with a detailed and startling exposé of the crimes which it commits, and the evils which it engenders. 500 pages octavo. Cloth and full calf, blue, gilt edges.

What's Bred in the Bone. By Grant Allen. This novel was awarded the prize of $5,000 offered by the London "Tidbits" for the best work of fiction. "One of the best written, original, and interesting stories printed during the decade." Stephen Fiske, in the *Spirit of the Times*.

"The author has displayed a great deal of skill in the construction of his story, not alone in the plot, but in the way in which it is worked out, and his use of language as a delightful contrast to much of the slip-shod English so often found in current fiction."—*San Francisco Chronicle*.

"An ingenious story, admirably written. Mr. Tucker, who seems to have a genius for getting hold of exceptionally good manuscript, has given it to American readers in a neat, cheap, and attractive edition."—*Denver News*.

What's to Be Done? A Nihilistic Romance. Written in prison. Suppressed by the Czar. By N. G. Tchernychewsky. With a portrait of the author. Translated by Benj. R. Tucker. Cloth and paper.

Wheelbarrow. Just published by the Open Court Publishing Company. Articles and discussion by Wheelbarrow (Gen. M. M. Trumbull) on the Labor
Question, the controversy with Mr. Lyman J. Gage, of Chicago, on the Ethics of
the Board of Trade, the Controversy with Mr. Hugh O. Pentecost and others on
the Single Tax Question. With Autobiography. Cloth, 303 pp.
    The Wind and the Whirlwind. A poem worthy of a place in every man's
library, and especially interesting to all victims of British tyranny and misrule. A
redline edition, printed beautifully in large type, on fine paper, and bound in
parchment covers. Elegant and cheap. 32 pages.
    Wind-Harp Songs. By J. Wm. Lloyd. Poems of life, love, nature, liberty,
and death. An appropriate gift book. Nicely bound.
    Work and Wealth. By J. K. Ingalls. 13 pages.

Special Categories Advertised

Lysander Spooner's Pamphlets

Sold for the Benefit of the Spooner Publication Fund.
    The undersigned [Benj. R. Tucker] has purchased from the heirs of the late
Lysander Spooner all of his printed pamphlets and unpublished manuscripts, and
proposes to sell the former to obtain means for the publication of the latter. The
list given below indicates all of Mr. Spooner's works with the exception of five
or six which are entirely out of print. Of some there are but three or four copies
left, and there are stereotype plates of but few. Some may never be reprinted.
Those persons who apply first will be served first. The pamphlets are catalogued
below in an order corresponding closely to that of the order of publication.
    *The Deist's Immortality, and an Essay on Man's Accountability for His
Belief.* 1834. 14 pages.
    A Question for the Clergy. A four-page tract.
    The Unconstitutionality of the Laws of Congress Prohibiting Private Mails.
Printed for the American Letter Mail Company. 1844. 24 pages.
    Who Caused the Reduction of Postage? Ought He to Be Paid? Showing that
Mr. Spooner was the father of cheap postage in America. This pamphlet em-
bodies the one mentioned immediately before it in this list. 1850. 71 pages.
Soiled copies and copies minus the first 16 pages, which consist of a preface and
a letter from Mr. Spooner to M. D. Phillips, offered at a discount.
    Illegality of the Trial of John W. Webster. Containing the substance of the
author's larger work, 'Trial by Jury', now out of print. 1850. 16 pages.
    *The Law of Intellectual Property; or, an Essay on the Right of Authors and
Inventors to a Perpetual Property in Their Ideas.* Stitched in parts, but unbound.
1855. 240 pages. Part I of the same, containing 166 pages offered separately.

Address of the Free Constitutionalists to the People of the United States. A refutation of the Republican Party's doctrine of the non-extension of slavery. 1860. 54 pages.

A New System of Paper Currency. Showing its outline, its advantages, security, practicability, and legality, and embodying the articles of association of a mortgage stock banking company. 1861. 122 pages.

Considerations for Bankers and Holders of United States Bonds. Showing that the author's system of paper currency cannot be legally prohibited or taxed, and that the legal tender acts and the national banking act are unconstitutional. 1864. 96 pages.

No Treason No. II. 1867. 16 pages.

No Treason No. VI. Showing that the constitution is of no authority. 1870. 59 pages.

A New Banking System. Showing the capacity of the country for furnishing an enormous amount of loanable capital, and how this capacity may be made operative. 1873. 77 pages.

The Law of Prices: A Demonstration for the Necessity of an Indefinite Increase of Money. 1877. 14 pages.

Our Financiers: Their Ignorance, Usurpations, and Frauds. Exposing the fallacy of the Inter-convertible bond scheme, and contrasting therewith some rational conclusions in finance. 1877.

Revolution: The Only Remedy for the Oppressed Classes of Ireland, England, and Other Parts of the British Empire. No. 1. A reply to Dunraven. This is the pamphlet of which the Irish revolutionary party distributed 100,000 among the British aristocracy and bureaucracy. 1880. 11 pages.

Natural Law; Or, the Science of Justice. A treatise on natural law, natural justice, natural rights, natural liberty, and natural society; showing that all legislation whatsoever is an absurdity, a usurpation, and a crime. Part First. 1882. 21 pages.

A Letter to Thomas F. Bayard. Challenging his right—and that of all the other so-called senators and representatives in congress—to exercise any legislative power whatever over the people of the United States.

A Letter to Scientists and Inventors on the Science of Justice and Their Right of Perpetual Property in Their Discoveries and Inventions. 1884. 22 pages.

A Letter to Grover Cleveland on His False Inaugural Address, the Usurpations and Crimes of Lawmakers and Judges, and the Consequent Poverty, Ignorance, and Servitude of the People. 1886. 110 pages.

Latest Socialist and Anarchist Periodicals

Karl Marx: *Capital.* First and only authorized English translation by Sam. Moore and edited by Fred. Engels. Demy 8vo. in 2 vols., cloth.

H. Belfort Bax: *The Religion of Socialism.* Cown 8vo., cloth gilt.

H. M. Hyndman: *The Bankruptcy of India.* The Chicago Riots and the Class War in the United States. Socialism and Slavery.

August Bebel: *Women in the Past, Present, and Future.*

J. E. Thorold Rogers: *Six Centuries of Work and Wages.* Abridged. Cloth.

E. Aveling. *The Student's Darwin. Woman Question. Curse of Capital.*

R. Heber Newton: *Social Studies.* Cloth. Present Aspect of the Labor Movement.

Annie Besant: *Modern Socialism. Evolution of Society.*

William Morris: *Art and Socialism.*

Elisee Reclus: *Evolution and Revolution.*

Zacher: *The Red International.* The American Agent of the *London Anarchist, Freedom, Justice. Commonweal,* and *To-day.* Bodollo's Labor News Agency. 104 & 106 E. 4th Street, New York.

Liberty's Portrait Gallery:

Michael Bakounine: Russian Revolutionist, founder of Nihilism, and apostle of Anarchy. A fine, large photo-lithograph printed on heavy paper.

P. J. Proudhon: The profoundest political philosopher and economist that has ever lived. A steel plate engraving, suitable to frame and hang.

Selected Bibliography

Andrews, Stephen Pearl. *The Science of Society.* Vol. 1, *The True Constitution of Government in the Sovereignty of the Individual as the Final Development of Protestantism, Democracy, and Socialism.* New York: Fowler & Wells, 1852.

———. *The Science of Society.* Vol. 2, *Cost the Limit of Price: Scientific Measure of Honesty in Trade as One of the Fundamental Principles of the Solutions of the Social Problem.* New York: Fowler & Wells, 1852.

Avrich, Paul. *The Haymarket Tragedy.* Princeton, N.J.: Princeton University Press, 1984.

———. *Anarchist Portraits.* Princeton, N.J.: Princeton University Press, 1988.

———. *An American Anarchist: The Life of Voltairine de Cleyre.* Princeton, N.J.: Princeton University Press, 1978.

Berkman, Alexander. *Now and After: The ABC of Communist Anarchism.* New York: Vanguard, 1929.

Coughlin, Michael E., Charles H. Hamilton, and Mark A. Sullivan, eds. *Benjamin R. Tucker and The Champions of Liberty.* St. Paul, Minn.: Michael E. Coughlin, 1986.

David, Henry. *History of the Haymarket Affair.* New York: Farrar & Rinehart, 1936.

De Leon, David. *The American as Anarchist. Reflections on Indigenous Radicalism.* Baltimore: Johns Hopkins University Press, 1978.

Eltzbacher, Paul. *Anarchism: Exponents of Anarchist Philosophy.* Translated by Steven T. Byington, edited by James J. Martin. Plainview, N.Y.: Libertarian Book Club, 1960.

Foner, Philip. *The Haymarket Autobiographies.* New York: Humanities Press, 1969.

Greene, William Bradford. *Mutual Banking.* West Brookfield, Mass.: n.p., 1850.

———. *Equality.* West Brookfield, Mass.: n.p., 1849.

Goldman, Emma. *Living My Life.* New York: Dover, 1970.

Hall, Bowman Newton II, "A History and Critique of American Individualist Anarchists' Economic Theories." Ph.D. diss., Duke University, 1971.

Hillquit, Morris. *History of Socialism in the United States.* New York: Funk & Wagnalls, 1903.

Ishill, Joseph, ed. *Free Vistas* 2. Berkley Heights, N.J.: Oriole Press, 1937.

Joll, James. *The Anarchists.* Cambridge, Mass.: Harvard University Press, 1980.

Kline, William Gary. *The Individualist Anarchists: A Critique of Liberalism.* New York: University Press of America, 1987.

Krimerman, Leonard I., and Lewis Perry, eds. *Patterns of Anarchy.* New York: Doubleday-Anchor Books, 1966.

187

La Boetie, Etienne de. *The Politics of Obedience: The Discourse of Voluntary Servitude.* Original ca. 1550; reprint, New York: Free Life Editions, 1975.

Malone, Dumas. *Jefferson and the Rights of Man.* New York: Little, Brown, 1951.

Marsh, Margaret S. *Anarchist Women 1870-1920.* Philadelphia: Temple University Press, 1981.

Marshall, Peter. *Demanding the Impossible: A History of Anarchism.* London: Harper Collins, 1992.

Martin, James J. *Men Against the State: The Expositors of Individualist Anarchism in America, 1827-1908.* Colorado Springs, Colo.: Ralph Myles, 1970.

McElroy, Wendy. "Benjamin Tucker, *Liberty,* and Individualist Anarchism." *The Independent Review* II, no. 3 (winter 1998): 421-34.

McKercher, William R. *Freedom and Authority.* Montreal: Black Rose Books, 1993.

Mises, Ludwig von. *Human Action.* New Haven, Conn.: Yale University Press, 1949.

Perry, Lewis. *Radical Abolitionism: Anarchy and the Government of God in Antislavery Thought.* Ithaca, N.Y.: Cornell University Press, 1973.

Proudhon, Pierre Joseph. *What Is Property? An Inquiry into the Principle of Right and of Government.* New York: Fertig, 1968.

Pyat, Felix. *The Rag-Picker of Paris.* New York: B. R. Tucker, 1890.

Reichert, William. *Partisans of Freedom.* Bowling Green, Ohio: Bowling Green University Popular Press, 1976.

Sears, Hal D. *The Sex Radicals: Free Love in High Victorian America.* Lawrence: The Regents Press of Kansas, 1977.

Schuster, Eunice Minette. *Native American Anarchism: A Study of Left-Wing American Individualism.* New York: AMS Press, 1970.

Spooner, Lysander. *The Lysander Spooner Reader.* San Francisco: Fox & Wilkes, 1992.

———. "No Treason No. I, The Suppression of the Rebellion Finally Disposes of the Pretence That the United States Government Rests on Consent." Boston, 1867; reprint, chap. in *The Lysander Spooner Reader.* San Francisco: Fox & Wilkes, 1992.

———. "No Treason No. II, The Constitution." Boston, 1867; reprint, chap. in *The Lysander Spooner Reader.* San Francisco: Fox & Wilkes, 1992.

———. "No Treason No. VI, The Constitution of No Authority." Boston, 1870; reprint, chap. in *The Lysander Spooner Reader.* San Francisco: Fox & Wilkes, 1992.

———. "A Letter to Thomas F. Bayard: Challenging His Right and the Right of All Other So-called Senators and Representatives in Congress—to Exercise any Legislative Power Whatever over the People of the United States." Boston, 1882; reprint, chap. in *The Lysander Spooner Reader.* San Francisco: Fox & Wilkes, 1992.

———. "Natural Law; or the Science of Justice; a Treatise on Natural Law, Natural Justice, Natural Rights, Natural Liberty, and Natural Society, Showing All Legislation Whatsoever Is an Absurdity, A Usurpation and a Crime." Boston, 1882; reprint, chap. in *The Lysander Spooner Reader.* San Francisco: Fox & Wilkes, 1992.

———. "A Letter to Grover Cleveland, On His False Inaugural Address, the Usurpations and Crimes of Lawmakers and Judges, and the Consequent Poverty, Ignorance and Servitude of the People." Boston: n.p., 1886.

———. *Law of Intellectual Property or an Essay on the Right of Authors and Inventors to a Perpetual Property in Their Ideas.* Boston: Bela Marsh, 1855; reprint, Weston, Mass.: M&S Press, 1971.

———. *An Essay on Trial by Jury.* Boston: n.p., 1852.

———. *A Defence of Fugitive Slaves, against the Acts of Congress of February 2, 1793, and September 18, 1850.* Boston: n.p., 1850.

———. *A New System of Paper Currency.* Boston: n.p., 1861.

———. *Constitutional Law Relative to Credit, Currency and Banking.* Worcester, Mass.: n.p., 1843.

———. *A New Banking System: The Needful Capital for Rebuilding the Burnt District.* Boston: n.p., 1873.

———. *Poverty: Its Illegal Causes and Legal Cure.* Boston: n.p., 1850.

Stirner, Max. *The Ego and His Own.* Translated by Steven Byington. New York: B. R. Tucker, 1907.

Tillier, Claude. *My Uncle Benjamin.* Boston: B. R. Tucker, 1890.

Tucker, Benjamin R. *Instead of a Book, by a Man Too Busy to Write One; A Fragmentary Exposition of Philosophical Anarchism.* New York: B. R. Tucker, 1893.

———. *Individual Liberty.* Edited by Clarence Lee Swartz. New York: Vanguard Press, 1926. http://flag.blackened.net/daver/anarchism/tucker/tucker.html [18 May 2002].

———. *Liberty; Not the Daughter but the Mother of Order.* Reprint, New York: Greenwood, 1970.

Walker, James L. *The Philosophy of Egoism.* Denver: n.p., 1905.

Warren, Josiah. *True Civilization an Immediate Necessity and the Last Ground of Hope for Mankind. Being the Results and Conclusions of Thirty-nine Years' Laborious Study and Experiments in Civilization as It Is, and in Different Enterprises for Reconstruction.* Boston: n.p., 1863.

———. *True Civilization: A Subject of Vital and Serious Interest to All People but Most Immediately to Men and Women of Labor and Sorrow.* Cliftondale, Mass.: n.p., 1869.

———. *Equitable Commerce. A New Development of Principles as Substitutes for Laws and Governments, For the Harmonious Adjustment and Regulation of the Pecuniary, Intellectual, and Moral Intercourse of Mankind Proposed as Elements of New Society.* New Harmony, Ind.: n.p., 1846; reprint, New York: Burt Franklin, n.d.

———. *Practical Details in Equitable Commerce, Showing the Workings in Actual Experiment, During a Series of Years, of the Social Principles Expounded in the Works Called "Equitable Commerce," by the Author of This, and "The Science of Society," by Stephen Pearl Andrews.* New York: n.p., 1852.

Watner, Carl, George H. Smith, and Wendy McElroy. *Neither Bullets Nor Ballots: Essays on Voluntaryism.* Orange, Calif.: Pine Tree Press, 1983.

Wilde, Oscar. *The Ballad of Reading Gaol.* New York: B. R. Tucker, 1899.

Woodcock, George. *Anarchism: A History of Libertarian Ideas and Movements.* Cleveland: Meridian Books, 1962.

Zola, Emil. *Money.* Boston: B. R. Tucker, 1890.

Index

194   *Index*

About the Author

Wendy McElroy's other books include the anthology *Freedom, Feminism, and the State*; plus *Sexual Correctness*; *The Reasonable Woman: A Guide to Intellectual Survival*; *Dissenting Electorate: Those Who Refuse to Vote and the Legitimacy of Their Opposition*; *Individualist Feminism of the Nineteenth Century: Collected Writings and Biographical Profiles*; *XXX: A Woman's Right to Pornography*; *Queen Silver: The Godless Girl*; and *Liberty 1881-1908: A Comprehensive Index*.

Ms. McElroy was Series Editor for Knowledge Products' popular audiotape series, *The World of Philosophy*, *The World's Political Hot Spots*, *The United States at War*, and *The United States Constitution*, and she authored the scripts for *Vindication of the Rights of Woman*, *The Liberator*, *Civil Disobedience*, and *Discourse on Voluntary Servitude* in the Audio Classics Series. A weekly columnist for FoxNews.com, she is a contributing editor to several periodicals, the author of numerous articles in various magazines and scholarly journals, and the editor of the popular feminism site, www.ifeminists.com. She is a Research Fellow at The Independent Institute, which co-published her most recent work, an anthology entitled *Liberty for Women*. Her personal Web site is www.wendymcelroy.com.